Paul Scott's Raj

By the same author

Paul Scott's Raj

ROBIN MOORE

HEINEMANN : LONDON

William Heinemann Ltd
Michelin House, 81 Fulham Road, London SW3 6RB
LONDON   MELBOURNE   AUCKLAND

First published by William Heinemann 1990
Copyright © Robin Moore 1990
All Paul Scott material first published in this volume,
copyright © N.E. Avery Scott 1990

A CIP catalogue record for this book
is available from the British Library
ISBN 0 434 47588 2

Printed and bound in Great Britain
by Clays Ltd, St Ives plc

The exercise of a veracious imagination in historical picturing seems to be capable of a development that might help the judgment greatly with regard to present and future events. By veracious imagination, I mean the working out in detail of the various steps by which a political or social change was reached, using all extant evidence and supplying deficiencies by careful analogical creation. . . . I want something different from the abstract treatment which belongs to grave history from a doctrinal point of view, and something different from the schemed picturesqueness of ordinary historical fiction.

George Eliot

Contents

Acknowledgements

I am indebted to the holder of copyright for Paul Scott's unpublished materials, N.E. Avery Scott, for permission to include substantial quotations from them in this volume. That such permission was granted while the official biography is in progress is largely due to the liberal co-operation of Mr Bruce Hunter and Ms Hilary Spurling. I am profoundly grateful for their assistance. The materials to which I have had access are deposited in the Department of Special Collections, McFarlin Library, The University of Tulsa, Oklahoma, and the Harry Ransom Humanities Research Center, The University of Texas at Austin. During my residence at Tulsa Mr Sidney F. Huttner and his staff were unstinting of their time and attention. At the Humanities Research Center Ms Cathy Henderson cheerfully co-operated with some quite unreasonable requests from this short-term visitor. I owed the opportunity to spend a semester at Tulsa as a Fulbright Senior Scholar and Visiting Professor to the Australian–American Educational Foundation and Dr Thomas F. Staley (then Provost of Tulsa).

At the beginning of my inquiry, Mr Andrew Robinson of Granada Television contributed to my awareness of responses to *The Jewel in the Crown*, while Sir Denis Forman and Mr Christopher Morahan gave me the benefit of their reflections on the serial. The study was assisted by an interview with Mr J. Enoch Powell and by his various writings and comments on the Raj. It is my privilege that Scott's own publishers are also the publishers of this book. Mr Tom Weldon has contributed to the substantial improvement of two sections of my original manuscript.

A special debt is owed Mrs Joan Stephenson for converting scrawl and dictation into clean copy.

Flinders University of South Australia
March 1990

Prologue

When Paul Scott died in 1978 he had published thirteen novels. None of them had brought him the fame that he deserved, or even riches. The climax of his literary career was the award of the Booker Prize for his comic masterpiece, *Staying On*, in November 1977. He was recovering from surgery in Tulsa, Oklahoma, and was too ill to return to London to receive it in person. In his active years as a full-time author, the high-inflation period 1960–75, his taxable earnings only once fell below £2000 but only exceeded £3000 on one occasion. His total taxable income from royalties in 1975–6 was £1800. *The Raj Quartet* attracted a loyal but small readership. Neither the British nor American edition of any of the four novels sold 10,000 hardback copies in his lifetime.

When Granada screened the television serial adaptation of the *Quartet*, from 3 January to 3 April 1984, Scott's admirers increased a thousandfold. *The Jewel in the Crown* attracted eight million viewers on Tuesday evenings and a further million for Sunday repeats. For fourteen weeks Tuesday was a stay-at-home evening. It was said that the streets of London were as quiet as they had been during the Blitz. In December Alistair Cooke introduced the series reverentially on Masterpiece Theater to enraptured audiences in the USA. Repeats in both countries and screenings by networks throughout the world have consolidated the belated recognition of Scott's genius, though scholars have yet to endorse it.

Media comment on the serial was vast, often uninformed, sometimes *parti pris* (for it aroused strong passions). The controversy was not about the serial's fidelity to Scott's text but concerned its authenticity as a representation of the last years of the British Raj, 1942–7. The dominant line of criticism was that *The Jewel in the Crown* was not about the real India at all, nor even recognisably about the British as they actually were in India. Curiously this argument came from opposite ends of the political spectrum, from Indian littérateurs as well as conservative Britons. The critic Gita Mehta, best known perhaps for her popular book on 'Marketing the mystic East', *Karma Cola* (1980), struck this note on 11 February in the *Spectator*: 'the issue is not imperialism versus nationalism but class. Despite the news footage, the frequent references to the Quit India Movement, the Indian National Army, the Burma Front, the Defence of India Rules, what is on offer is soap opera about the British middle class (which could as easily have been set in Bournemouth as in India) in which status performs the function provided by wealth in soap operas like *Dallas* and *Dynasty*.' In *The Times* Ferdinand Mount was 'taken aback by how far the ITV series . . . falls short of the claims made for it'. [1] Here was 'barley water rather than a chota peg'. The puzzle was the 'huge enthusiasm among people of the better sort' for this soap opera. The answer must be its accommodation to 'the present nostalgia for the Raj'. Co-director Jim O'Brien was stung into writing a letter to *The Times*:

> Why, I ask myself, does he savage so thoroughly? Perhaps what he resents most about the book (and the series) is Scott's compassion and Liberalism. There is no mindless nostalgia for the Empire in Scott's world. He saw quite clearly the love for India felt by many of the British who lived there, but he also saw the anguish and disappointments that affected the last years of The Raj. That, I suspect, is what makes Mr Mount angry. He believes that writing about the Empire critically is a bad show, and a television company that broadcasts it to a post-colonial Britain is just not playing cricket. . . . [2]

The usual medium for soap opera for 'people of the better sort', the BBC, set up *Did You See . . . ?* panels, with Ludovic Kennedy, to discuss the series on 12 February and 18 March. On the first occasion M.M. Kaye, author of *The Far Pavilions* and whose agent Scott had once been, was especially critical of the credibility of Ronald Merrick. On the second the experts were Enoch Powell, who served in India during the war; Kailash Budhwar, who lived through Scott's India; the Rajkumari Amar Kaur of the former princely state of Kapurthala; Joan Brander, who was in the Women's Voluntary Service during the war

and came from an Anglo-Indian family; John Morton, who
spent seventeen years (1930–47) in the Indian Police Service
(Punjab); and Kenneth Ballhatchet, Professor of South Asian
History at the University of London. The *Listener* reported the
discussion.[3] Mr Powell thought that 'a story had been constructed about human passions and human qualities in interaction
which could be acted perfectly well anywhere else – in the
hot-house atmosphere of a London suburb just as much as in
the hot-house atmosphere of a hill-station in India'. India, he
thought, 'claimed one. Of course it was a mirage. The British
and the Indians saw a mirage, they lived a mirage and they both
loved that mirage. They clung to it, and were shattered to discover that, after all, like so much in India and its history, it was
just a mirage, but had the intensity, fascination and gripping
character of a mirage.' The Rajkumari criticised the shallow-
ness of Sarah Layton's comments on India and Mrs Brander
questioned the authenticity of the older spokeswomen for the
Raj and their clothes. Mr Morton was firm: 'The portrayal of the
Indian police in the film would be as deeply offensive to Indians
in India as it is to British officers who survive in Britain.'

Christopher Morahan, producer and co-director of the Granada series, complained to the *Listener* of its selective quotations
and the biased editing of the *Did You See . . . ?* discussion itself.
In particular, Professor Ballhatchet's views, such as the following, had not been reported: 'Attitudes to race and class have
the function of supporting vested interests and the structures of
authority, and I think this is clearly demonstrated in the film,
and indeed it's explicitly stated by Ronald Merrick himself.'[4]
Ballhatchet protested to *Private Eye*:

I was the one member of the team of 'experts' to argue for
the film's authenticity. But most of my points were edited
out of the televised version of the 'discussion'. (In fact there
was no discussion and no opportunity to correct the howl-
ers uttered by Enoch and his colleagues.) Moreover, my
comments were omitted altogether from the version of the
'discussion' in the *Listener*, while every nit was picked over
in detail. As I was also there at the time, and have recently
published a book on the subject (*Race, Sex and Class under
the Raj*) it would have been fair to give some space to the
points I made, to counterbalance the shock, horror, felt by

ex-Policeman Gussett and the Rani of Budge Budge. But Merrick is alive and well in 1984. *Vivat St Cake's!*[5]

The *Listener* gave Sir Denis Forman, the Chairman of Granada who inspired the project, space for an effective reply to the BBC's critics. He wrote that a

> strange assortment of folk with no pretensions to be critics of Paul Scott's work, or of the series, had been assembled to discuss the one point: 'Did the India of the *Jewel* chime with their own recollections of India at that time?' For the most part the answer was a resounding 'No', and this was not surprising since Paul Scott's books focus on one small arena roped off within the huge panorama of Indian life from which most of the participants had been excluded. The most beguiling remark was made by Enoch Powell, who suggested the whole of Paul Scott's saga might just as well have been set in suburbia. In the light of his past prophecies, he would, of course, be less surprised than most of us if the 6.28 from Victoria pulled into West Croydon dripping with blood from the scores of dead and dying victims of a racist massacre mounted at Clapham Junction. But the story did not quite end there. The whiff became a pong when an edited version of the programme appeared in this very journal with every favourable reference to *Jewel* . . . carefully excised.[6]

He was considerably cheered that by the time episode eight was transmitted Granada had recovered its total costs of £5.6m from British and foreign network sales. World sales would be an all-time record.

Before the final episode had appeared, two authors born on the subcontinent and resident in Britain had entered the debate about the historical authenticity of the series and Scott's text. Salman Rushdie was bitter in his condemnation of them as part of a sinister 'Raj revival'. Scott

> has an instinct for the cliché. Sadistic, bottom-flogging policeman Merrick turns out to be (surprise!) a closet homosexual. His grammar-school origins give him (what else?) a chip on the shoulder. And all around him is a galaxy of chinless wonders, regimental *grandes dames*, lushes, empty-headed blondes, silly-asses, plucky young things,

good sorts, bad eggs and Russian counts with eyepatches. The overall effect is rather like a literary version of Mulligatawny soup. It tries to taste Indian, but ends up being ultra-parochially British, only with too much pepper.

And yes, Scott is harsh in his portraits of many British characters; but I want to try and make a rather more difficult point, a point about *form*. The *Quartet's* form tells us, in effect, that the history of the end of the Raj was largely composed of the doings of the officer class and its wife. Indians get walk-ons, but remain, for the most part, bit-players in their own history. Once this form has been set, it scarcely matters that individual, fictional Brits get unsympathetic treatment from their author. The form insists that *they are the ones whose stories matter*, and that is so much less than the whole truth that it must be called a falsehood. It will not do to argue that Scott was attempting only to portray the British in India, and that such was the nature of imperialist society that the Indians *would* only have had bit parts. It is no defence to say that a work adopts, in its structure, the very ethic which, in its content and tone, it pretends to dislike. It is, in fact, the case for the prosecution. . . .

. . . it really is necessary to make a fuss about Raj fiction and the zombie-like revival of the defunct Empire. The various films and TV shows and books . . . propagate a number of notions about history which must be quarrelled with, as loudly and as embarrassingly as possible.

These include: . . . the view (which underlies many of these works) that the British and Indians actually understood each other jolly well, and that the end of the Empire was a sort of gentlemen's agreement between old pals at the club; the revisionist theory . . . that *we, the British, weren't as bad as people make out*; the calumny, to which the use of rape-plots lends credence, that frail English roses were in constant sexual danger from lust-crazed wogs (just such a fear lay behind General Dyer's Amritsar massacre); and, above all, the fantasy that the British Empire represented something 'noble' or 'great' about Britain. . . .[7]

Tariq Ali takes issue and emphasises Scott's historical purpose:

Scott was attempting an ambitious project: to dissect in every possible way and inspect the insides of the ruling class (or, to be more precise, the ruling race) of British India. The reason their lives matter is precisely because they governed and ruled India for nearly two centuries. How could they do so?[8]

And, he might have added, what were the consequences of their manner of doing so?

The world, to a large extent, learns its history of the Raj from the works of Paul Scott. It is necessary to discover his sources and examine the conclusions that he drew from them.

1

An Obsession with India

1

In 1960, at the age of forty, Paul Scott became a full-time author. Just before Christmas he wrote euphorically to John Willey, his editor at William Morrow and Co. Inc., New York, to whom he owed his freedom: 'I couldn't be happier, basically. I'm free, doing what I want to do, my publishers' accountants aren't pulling long faces at too many red figures, it's been a good year, and I'm feeling fitter than I have for years and years.'[1] This mood had much to do with a recent windfall. Willey had sold the reprint rights of Scott's *Chinese Love Pavilion* (1960). Scott's share of the sale was $8750, 'more money than I've ever had my hands near all at one time'.[2] He had also obtained his first driver's licence since 1946 and bought a new Ford Anglia, 'Little Bentley'. That year, too, he enjoyed inventing a fictive persona for himself; but the creation soon brought him to a crisis that ended his exuberance.

In his first novel as a full-time author Scott invented an Indian birth and childhood for his first-person narrator. He was striving to represent the career of an English political agent in a princely state. He found the book difficult to write. The reality of British India escaped him and the final impression was so 'dreamlike' that he realised that he could not write of India again without going back there. He had left in 1946 and it was mid-1961 as he finished *Birds of Paradise*.

To celebrate a difficult work completed, and perhaps to escape a sense of disappointment, he spent a night on the town. He went on from the Mandrake Club near Leicester Square to the Gargoyle Club off Dean Street, Soho, and, missing the last bus, cavalierly set off to walk home to Hampstead Garden Suburb. Reaching the Pond at Hampstead in drizzling rain, he sought an unlocked parked car in which to take a little rest. A kindly police patrol car picked him up and drove him home. In the aftermath he felt ashamed of his bender: after all, 'no-one told me I'd got cancer'.[3]

That autumn Scott was working on a short comic novel set in London during a forty-eight-hour crisis in the life of gin-sodden George Spence, who has to raise a sum of money for a niece. George is slightly older than Scott, divorced, and lives on a small legacy. In a confessional letter to Muriel Spark Scott confides that he didn't want to write the book and hated having to do so to work off his publisher's advance.[4] He spent most of a week in October a bit drunk and most of another in early November very drunk. News that John Braine had sold the film rights to *Life at the Top* for £30,000 made him feel envious and then ashamed and depressed. He writes of feeling poor and resenting it, and of a rather absurd suicide attempt. He finished *The Bender* in 1962. It was not very successful financially though the BBC adapted it for television. He abandoned a sequel to it after eighty pages as 'just dull'.

In 1963, Scott was confronting a crisis of creativity. He wrote to Peter Green, who had sometimes put work his way in the literary world, of his 'few real friends in this bloody racket'.[5] He went on, 'this – to put it crudely – is my shit-or-bust year (or maybe eighteen months)'. He was nearing the end of four years of freedom and *Bender* would not float him forward. He was on 'a tight money string, and a tighter time string'. He wrote to an old friend that he felt 'like an eternal examination candidate'.[6] He had failed to become a fashionable writer, and editors gave his books to 'the new boy critics'. The mandarins of the Sunday press never noticed him.

Ill health compounded his problems as he worked on the last of his pre-*Quartet* novels, *The Corrida at San Feliu*. Roland Gant, his oldest friend in publishing and now his publisher at Secker and Warburg, was interested in tropical diseases and believed Scott displayed the signs and symptoms of amoebiasis. These were incorporated in the character of the middle-aged author–hero of *Corrida*. Edward Thornhill's stop–start work methods and erosion of will left him incapable of completing a manuscript. Scott was on a starvation diet and believed he had ulcers.

This was the situation of Paul Scott as he planned a return visit to India for which his publishers had agreed to pay. It would recharge his batteries, he would say, or show that there were no batteries to recharge. He was in his early forties, married with two daughters, aged fifteen and sixteen, and living in a mortgaged semi-detached house, 78 Addison Way, Hampstead Garden Suburb, insured value £6500. He worked in a first-floor room that looked to the front over a road busy with buses and trucks and to the back over a garden and Little Wood beyond. Its bookshelves contained a growing collection of works on the Raj. On the walls were hung an oil sketch of him in 1943, and a 1961 portrait, both by Robert Mason, whom he met when they were on the same cadet draft to India in 1943. On his desk were notebooks and exercise books in which he entered his neat holograph drafts, a typewriter, a packet of Bachelor cigarettes. He seldom left the house, though in 1963 he sailed to the USA for the launching of *The Bender*, and from 1960 to 1963 the family took summer holidays on the Costa Brava at Tamaris, the setting of his novel about the burnt-out writer. From this time and place the *Raj Quartet* would soon begin.

2

Scott acknowledged that he was 'one of those people who hate biographical details of any sort, especially these days when rather more attention seems to be paid to what a writer does, is, was and says than to what he writes'.[7] Biographical aspects 'never seem to me to get anywhere near the actual fiction'.[8] He was not forthcoming to those who expressed interest in writing biographical studies of him. Only three years before his death he wrote to such a correspondent: 'There isn't much biographical stuff on record at the moment. I've always kept it at a minimum, since it has generally seemed to me to be irrelevant to the work itself. On top of which there's this inclination every novelist must have to nurse his autobiography, knowing it might be the last novel he ever writes'.[9] Here was a whimsical warning to posterity that any autobiographical remains might contain fictional embellishments. It is a truism that when Scott wrote or spoke of himself and his past he disclosed only what he thought the world should know at the time. Yet he lived on the page and he left so many pages for deposit in archives that he must be considered a willing subject. A brief account of the man must preface an historian's study of his major fiction.

Scott had no family connection with India, except that an aunt had been married to an engineer who once worked in Bombay. She probably told him of the Towers of Silence where the Parsis exposed their dead to the vultures. Nor were any of his family writers, though his mother, to whom he ascribed a powerful imagination, claimed to have written novels in a cupboard by candlelight before she married Thomas Scott in 1916. He did inherit a talent for drawing. His father was a commercial artist. He remembered his mother posing in sables and minks during summer, one hand on hip and the other indicating a vista, as his father, 'a dab hand at furs', sketched for Blundell Brothers' catalogue.[10] Thomas Scott was in partnership with his sister Florence, who concentrated on hands, legs, faces, feet and other parts while he excelled at intricate patterns on silk and cotton dresses (and corsets). Their staple work was for the Manchester mail-order clothing firm, Nobles – 'low-class stuff'. Their cousins, Louise, George and Gilbert Wright, were also commercial artists, whose prized client was Harrods of Knightsbridge. Both enjoyed success as painters, George with horses and Gilbert with hunting scenes. The Scott – Wright relations were 'vaguely incestuous', with instances of brother and sister marrying sister and brother. The family traced its descent from the eighteenth century engraver and naturalist, Thomas Bewick. Paul's only sibling, his elder brother, was christened Peter Bewick Scott.

Paul Mark Scott was born on 25 March 1920, an Aries, he observed, 'impulsive, impatient, but a hard worker'.[11] His father was born in Leeds in 1871, his mother Frances Mark in 1886 in London. Thomas Scott settled in north London in the first decade of the century but remained a Yorkshireman in spirit, insisting that when his county lost at cricket it was robbed rather than beaten. Paul felt himself to be both a Victorian and a Yorkshireman, rejoicing at winning the *Yorkshire Post* prize for fiction in 1971, and proud to send his younger daughter to York University in 1966. The age gap of half a century, and the fact that Thomas's own father, George Bewick Scott, a wine merchant, was born in 1830, gave Paul an unusually long reach into mid- and late-Victorian and Edwardian England and the dominant liberal political philosophy. It might be said that he was born with a sense of the past: 'One acquires in bone, flesh and mind, certain resonances that are nothing to do with what you have personally seen, heard or experienced.'[12] Scott was born in an upstairs bedroom at 130 Fox Lane, Palmers Green, a rented semi-detached house in a middle- to lower-middle-class suburb settled by commuters as late Victorian London sprawled. He lived there with his parents and brother until 1933. But he felt that more important to his life was the house about a mile away that his father rented for his two spinster sisters, Florence and Laura, who lived there amidst the family furniture they had brought down from Headingly. Its name was Wyphurst, in High Street, Old Southgate. At 9 a.m. Thomas set off for his day's work there, sometimes not returning until 9 at night. This was 'the studio' and from the age of four or five it was a high point in Paul's week when he and Peter visited it on Saturday mornings. It was a larger, more elegant house, and as such an object of his mother's jealousy. As an economy measure Thomas brought the whole family together in Wyphurst during the depression. Maternal envy now became outright hostility in a house truly divided, with the women on the two sides observing fraught silences for weeks on end. Paul loved both sides and felt that his lasting inability to express emotion, except in writing, stemmed from the experience. In 1936 Thomas could again afford a second house and moved his wife and children to 15 Cannon Road.

When he was six Scott was sent to The College, the preparatory part of Winchmore Hill Collegiate School, to which he progressed. It was a school for the Sons of Gentlemen, which his father could ill afford. For Thomas, a true gentleman who seldom raised his voice, it accorded with the same sense of the fitness of things that caused him to insist that Paul wear white gloves at his first dance in 1937. The other pupils mostly came from grander houses. In north London Scott imbibed an early sense of social distinctions, partly from the school experience, from which he was wrenched and sent to work at fifteen, partly from the disdain that the Scott side of the family felt for the Mark side, who all lived in south London. As distinct from the Scotts, too, the Wrights lived in fashionable Richmond. 'Weekends in Richmond (a Rolls, a chauffeur, manservants and a nanny) were set off against years in Southgate (Shanks's pony, the bus, and making do).'[13]

In the same year that Scott went to school he read his first book, Elinor Glyn's *Three Weeks*, a somewhat unsuitable tale of adultery for a six-year-old. (Twenty years before, the romantic novelist had appeared scantily dressed on a tiger skin in the stage version of it, been seen and courted by the recently displaced Viceroy of India, Lord Curzon, and for a decade remained his mistress.) Then, too, he saw his first film and became for a decade a 'fanatical film fan'.

And within three years, that's to say by 1929, my brother and I had set up in the film business as producers, directors, designers and photographers. . . .

The films we produced were drawn in Indian ink, with mapping pens, on long narrow strips of greaseproof or tracing paper, which were gummed together and passed through a projector made out of a cigar box, a 60-watt bulb, and the lens from an old pair of binoculars. The images we drew were free-hand. Frames of dialogue were interspersed to help the stories along. When it came to close-ups of the leading characters we traced these from photographs of popular stars. The whole was projected on to a screen painted silver and authentically edged in black.

The business of making films absorbed me for about four years. When my elder brother grew out of this exacting occupation, he contributed technical assistance. The projector became infinitely more sophisticated. The screen was only revealed to the audience after a velvet curtain had been raised by invisible wires and had disappeared mysteriously behind an immense gilded proscenium arch made of painted plywood. By this time too my films were running for sixty minutes and had also become more sophisticated with some sequences in colour. Romance, drama, comedy, costume, and modern – one film would take me an entire autumn to complete, to be ready for its Christmas Gala release. I suppose we never gave more than two shows a year. The *creation* of the film was the main thing. The stories were all more or less original, but the stars were real, sub-contracted from Paramount, Fox, RKO and Metro-Goldwyn Mayer. My last epic was a sophisticated comedy called *The Girl in the Porch*, and starred Miriam Hopkins, Alice White (making a come-back) and Fredric March. Coming across it years later and riffling it through my fingers, I noted that scenically it was distinctly avant-garde. And script-wise, just a little naughty. Unconsciously so, I think. But at last I understood a remark by my headmaster that while this boy's English essays showed promise, he lacked discrimination.[14]

None of these masterpieces survives.

The experiences of the studio 'as a sort of basic childhood country' and of precocious film-making were 'curious sources of creative imagination'.[15] After he finished the *Quartet* Scott wanted to celebrate his suburban 1920s and 1930s 'and leave them crystallised in some kind of permanent form'. He rejoiced to recall them: 'Perhaps it was the early lesson about the flatness of life and the rotundity of art that lies at the bottom of my attitude to things around me.'[16] The practice of film-making led on to an awareness of 'the power of words' and he overheard his English teacher telling another schoolmaster that 'he could be an author if he wanted to be'.[17] He might have become an artist, for Gilbert Wright offered to take him on. His father, sobered by long years of unrewarding work, instead hired him out at fifteen to a Regent Street firm of accountants, C.T. Payne.

Scott enjoyed his years as a trainee accountant, learning more about the way of the world as a junior audit clerk going from office to office in the City than he would have by staying at school. At first he attended evening classes in bookkeeping, English and mathematics, and then took a correspondence course to matriculate. In 1937 he won the Royal Society of Accountants' silver medal for advanced accounts and next year came fifth at the preliminary accounts examination. He was reading widely and writing poems, plays and a novel. He remembered elevenpenny lunches at teashops and social evenings at the pub, learning to dance (a life-long enjoyment) and taking out girls, going to the Proms and to the opera at Sadlers Wells. He attributed his success at accounting to his photographic memory, for his heart was already in writing. He was discovering the modern literary giants. T.S. Eliot was the strongest abiding influence on him and his favourite poem was 'East Coker'. But before the war he also read Ibsen and Chekhov, Auden and Isherwood. His first published works were letters on film criticism in the *Picturegoer*. In June 1939 he moved with his family to his last pre-war home, 63 Bourne Hill.

With encouragement from a neighbouring literary couple,

Ruth and Clive Sansom, he suspended his accountancy studies and wrote poems that were published. He was also wres-
tling with his sexual inclinations. He wrote to the Sansoms
in 1940 confessing homosexual experiences, which he thought
expressed his nature.

In 1940 Wyphurst was bombed and his aunts were killed. From
vacillation over whether to join the Territorial Army or the
Peace Pledge Union he emerged on 17 July 1940 as a volunteer
private soldier in the Royal East Kent Regiment (the Buffs) at
Slough. He advanced to become a brigade intelligence sergeant
but was turned down for a commission when he revealed his
literary aspirations. On 23 October 1941 he married Nancy Edith
Avery, a nurse, in a little church at Torquay, Devonshire. In
late 1942 he volunteered for India and became an officer cadet
at Wrotham.

3

Scott sailed for Bombay in February 1943 with about one hundred other cadets and spent several weeks of encampment in
Cape Province. In June he arrived at Officers' Training School,
Belgaum, in western India, just north of Goa.[18] The train from
Bombay stopped at Poona, which looked to the officer cadets
like Clapham Junction with palms. At the end of a further
journey on the metre-gauge line they were met at Belgaum by
trucks and promptly delivered to OTS. The landscape seemed
odd and Scott had to readjust his mental image of a school white
and ornamental outside, dark and cool within, framed by very
green foliage against intense sunlight, its parade ground a lawn.
The day was grey and the sun was hidden. The wet monsoon had
set in and 'everything looked dull and felt damp'. The trees were
sparsely leafed. The cadets debussed in a tarmac-lined square
and entered a low L-shaped building with a verandah on its
longest side. This was the mess, bar and ante-room. At four
o'clock they ate a meal, also grey but coloured by hunger,
and served by Indians in white cotton and bare feet in the
high-roofed, white distempered mess. 'The word went round,'
Scott recalled in an early novel that recorded the experience,
'We're Sahibs now.'[19]

The cadets straggled down a hill to the long huts that would
house them. Each hut was divided into twelve suites and the

cadets paired off to share a suite and a bearer. The bearer was Scott's 'first Indian', Abdul, who proved to be trustworthy but not bright. He spoke no English. Scott's second Indian was his *munshi*, who taught him enough Urdu to pass his elementary examination. The only sentence that he remembered by the 1960s was '*Kheton se, mandir (al) tak, auraten chale gae hain*' (The women walked through the fields towards the temple).[20]

Scott shared his quarters with his painter friend, Robert Mason, and they were both full of the pride of ownership:

> In the sitting-room on which the glass-paned door opened directly there were two desks, two upright chairs, two easy chairs, a table, a spotted mirror. The walls were distempered cream. The inner door led to the bedroom. The beds were made. Mosquito nets bunched from the ceiling. Between the beds was a wicker table and a wicker chair for each man. The door led into the bath-house. The floor of this was concrete and sloped to a hole in the outer wall. Two galvanized iron baths were half-filled with warm water. In one corner stood a washstand with a marble top, two china hand-basins, two aluminium soap-racks. The door led out to the back of the hut and, to the left, was the latrine.[21]

They would spend six months there.

At Belgaum Scott consolidated his friendship with James Leasor, a journalist and novelist with whom he had shared a cold Nissen hut at Wrotham. Leasor recalls their urinating to put out wood fires in the stove because of the smoke during the night.[22] On the troopship out they both responded to a call for anyone with journalistic or writing experience to help with the ship's daily paper. At Belgaum they produced with others a weekly wall newspaper. Both were writing novels in spare moments. Leasor remembered Scott as 'much more serious-minded than many of us', 'unusually grave, composed, almost introverted'. In a photograph taken of him in shorts at Belgaum, with a knapsack and a shooting-stick, he looks anxious. But Leasor acknowledged a lighter and livelier side to his character. They would visit the local cinema on a Saturday night, have a Chinese meal, and ride back to camp in a gharry – or sometimes engage in gharry races back, with promises of huge tips to the winning driver. They sometimes breakfasted together at Green's Hotel. They collaborated in personation to complete their courses:

> When the time came to pass out I still could not make any sense of Morse code, which was apparently essential, although I never used it thereafter. Scott couldn't understand the intricacies of the internal combustion engine. Since we wore a piece of cardboard with our number on our bush jackets and the examiners did not know us by name, it was easy for us to change places for the Morse code and MT tests. As a result, we both passed.

It must have been risky. For a serious breach of discipline, even for venturing beyond the cantonment to the out-of-bounds native town, a cadet might be 'returned to unit' and remain a 'British Other Rank'.

Scott hated Belgaum: 'When I first went to India, I didn't like it at all. I was just an urban young man, and I looked at this place, and I said, my God, what a mess it is. . . . My stomach was upset, you know; I couldn't eat anything. I was sick all the time, almost jaundiced.'[23] He had 'a mild but persistent jaundice – not bad enough to take myself off to hospital, bad enough to turn my bathwater yellow'.[24] He could eat only cauliflower cheese, and a little Indian servant in the mess made sure he had a plateful even when it wasn't on the menu. Had he reported sick he would have been hospitalised for three weeks and then put on another course full of strangers. He felt that his friends were his lifeline to security in an alien country. From the beginning he felt the antagonism of the local people, which the stern repression of Gandhi's 1942 'Quit India' revolt had generated. 'We weren't allowed to stray far from the School in case the locals chucked stones at us.'

Scott was commissioned into the Royal Indian Army Service Corps and spent a further six months at its OTS, three at Kakul (now the Sandhurst of Pakistan) in the North West Frontier Province, and three in the Punjab divided between the Mechanical Transport School at Lahore and the Air Supply School at Chaklala, near Rawalpindi. He felt that he was never going to get a real job, but that he was experiencing some of the Raj's best-known cantonments and 'living the old pre-war Indian military and civilian life'. While there had been very few

Indian cadets at Belgaum, Scott met many Indians with one pip up at Kakul.

> I don't recall ever feeling that they were different or that they thought of me as a member of the insufferable raj. You messed, worked, played together. I remember a Sikh up at Kakul. The Bengal famine had left a shortage of rice, and the order had gone out that no young British officer should eat curry. We had to have stew. This Sikh and I sat together – it was one of those huge messes with tables for four. He saw me eyeing his curry and rice, and I saw him eyeing my awful stew. Beef stew at that. One day we just glanced at one another and silently exchanged plates.[25]

From Kakul Scott visited Abbottabad, the pretty hill station nearby, where Mason made his oil sketch of him. He was within easy reach of Nathiagali, once the summer capital of the NWFP, with a former Governor's House. From Chaklala he might readily visit the summer resort of Murree, where fine houses command 'magnificent views over forest-clad hills into deep valleys, studded with villages'.[26] Here was the Lawrence School for the sons of British soldiers. Scott's mind was receiving impressions from which the imagination might in due course create the hill station of Pankot and its Rifles. At the same time his lighter side was indulged, drinking, dining and dancing at Lahore's famous Faletti's Hotel.

From Chaklala Scott was posted to command a section of the Fourteenth Army's Number One Air Supply Company in Bengal, 120 men, Hindus, Muslims, Sikhs, Chindits and Nepalese. On the day of the Normandy landing (6 June 1944) he was in Delhi en route to Comilla. Air Supply's operations involved dropping and landing men, rations, equipment, armaments, and so on. In April Japanese troops had crossed the Indian border to threaten Kohima in Assam and lay siege to Imphal in the princely state of Manipur. Air Supply was vital to the campaigns to drive them out of India and then recapture Burma. By 1945 RIASC accounted for a third of the entire Indian Army. 'The focal point of the war had become the airfields of Bengal,' wrote Scott.[27] He put up his third pip in October, when his section advanced to Imphal, where it remained until the fall of Rangoon in May 1945. He was engaged in supplying 19th Division as it

moved forward and in drops to other parts of Burma and to the
Chindits. For Scott it was mainly desk work, supervising stocks
and loadings. Occasionally he would go on a drop, always when
there had been a crash on an airstrip, to encourage the ejection
crews.

From Comilla, headquarters of the Tippera District and a
trading centre in peacetime, Scott visited Agartala in the neighbouring princely state of Tripura. W.J. Reader, a Cambridge
historian who was a wartime officer attached to the Indian Signal
Corps, recalls that there 'the ruler had a palace – the Shishmahal
– rising sheer from a lake, and it shone silver in moonlight'.[28] J.B.
Harrison of the Baluch Regiment, a 'wartimer' who became an
academic historian of India, writes similarly of Imphal, 'with its
cluster of villages round the Maharaja's palace and reedy lake
very Shangri-la'.[29]

Scott's exercise of command over an Air Supply Section
brought relationships with two Indians that were important for
his fiction, N.K.D. Purkayastha ('Nimu') and B.V.V. Narayana
Dass. He arrived to find Comilla damp under heavy clouds and
the officers and sepoys almost out on their feet after working
night and day. Nimu, a havildar (sergeant) clerk, felt affection
for Scott, writing after Scott's demobilisation that he had lost an
officer and a friend he would never forget.[30] Scott promoted Dass
from naik (corporal) to havildar in charge of stock control. In
1946 Dass wrote, recalling loading bombers with huge ammuni-
tion boxes, 'I cannot forget you and your pleasant administration
in my life.'[31] Nimu and Dass would appear by name in Scott's
first published novel. His relationships with them were the
key to his understanding of the emotional interdependence of
British officers and Indian NCOs and jawans. An Indian officer
who joined the army in 1938, Major-General D.K. Palit, asserts
that 'it was with the jawans (the other ranks) and the servants
that the British felt most intimate'.[32] In his first novel Scott has
the central character, a paternalistic young officer, reflect that
the men of his section 'were part of him and belonged to him in
a way nothing in his life had ever belonged'.[33] They worshipped
him. 'It was . . . his standing up for you against the least threat of
outside interference that made the back-breaking routine sparkle.'[34] W.J. Reader recalls that 'as a junior officer one was firmly
impressed with one's total responsibility for the troops' welfare',

and believes that 'it is necessary to insist on this paternalist out-look'.[35] Such insistence is a prominent characteristic of Indian military memoirs, which encapsulate the officer–NCO/jawan relationship in the term *man bap* (mother–father). 'The British Officer took into himself all the problems and troubles of his men,' asserts Lieutenant-General T. Henderson Brooks.[36] Scott had been inducted into a part of the mystique of the Raj.

In summer 1945 Scott's division was posted to Malaya. They were part of Operation Zipper, so called it is said because nothing was buttoned up. They embarked on a troopship at Bombay in August just before the Japanese surrender, landed at Port Swettenham, and arrived at Singapore just after it. In a 1976 interview Scott spoke of Malaya as beautiful, marvellous, clean and prosperous – 'any moment you expected Dorothy Lamour and Bob Hope to emerge from the bushes'.[37] But, though he would use it as a setting for fiction, Malaya was a 'non-situation' for him:

> And then I started thinking of India. It was at that moment that I realized that I had fallen in love with India. In other words . . . my eyes were filled with the image of India, and all I wanted to do was get back and gaze at those barren, arid plains. Which I don't understand to this day, except that I know that every time I see them again, the heart gives a little beep. . . . When I was in Singapore, just before Christmas, I was posted to the staff of Allied Land Forces, which would have meant that I would have had to stay in Singapore for the rest of my military career, which was then at least six months until I was released. And, I thought, *I must go back to India*. I had fallen in love with the place and the people.

He was 'homesick' for India. He had 'loved' Kakul and Chaklala and 'adored' Bengal and Imphal, but only when he left India did he realise that it had entered his bloodstream.

He pulled strings to rejoin Number One Air Supply Company in India. His section had been the only one to reach Malaya; the others, cut off by the peace, were encamped in Bihar. One friend helped him to fly from Kallang to Rangoon on 28-29 December, another to fly on to Calcutta on New Year's Eve. With ten rupees in his pocket and the field cashier's office closed for three days, he entered the Grand Hotel, walked down the long corridor from Chowringhee, and tested the theory that if you sat in the lounge someone would soon turn up who knew you well enough to lend you money. Someone did, and he rejoined Air Supply at Chas, and neighbouring Lohardaga, in the Ranchi District of Bihar. He remained there under canvas until his number came up in June. He was demobilised at Deolali.

Scott's six months in Bihar were an idle time spent 'doing little but absorbing India'.[38] Harrison has described Lohardaga as 'then a village set among terraced rice fields carved out of dense sal jungle like some giant Greek amphitheatre'.[39] It was forty-six miles by rail or seventy-five minutes by jeep from Ranchi, a small cantonment town and summer capital of the Government of Bihar, with a population of some 100,000. Harrison remembers Ranchi as rather dusty and ramshackle, its main street half bazaar. On a twenty-four hour leave Scott and a friend, Captain Jim Corben RIASC, would visit Ranchi. The club barman there mixed a powerful cocktail, and a good curry and a comfortable bed were available at a little white but rather tatty bungalow called the Grand Hotel. On a forty-eight hour leave Scott would drive to Dhanbad, and catch the 8.00 a.m. train to Calcutta (Howrah) via Asansol, where Carew's gin, which he confessed to soaking up with the atmosphere, was distilled. He recalled the Bihar months as 'blissfully happy', remembered towns like Dhanbad and Asansol with 'some pleasure'. He wrote later of 'my deep affection for the filthiest city in the world', Calcutta.[40]

4

Scott volunteered for India without knowing anything substantial about it. He had not read Forster's *Passage to India*. He did not enjoy the talking animals in Kipling's *Jungle Book* and liked only the vigorous vulgarity of his *Barrack-Room Ballads*. He mistrusted Macaulay's essays on Clive and Hastings as founders of empire. He knew 'that there had been a Mutiny, a Black Hole, and that sometimes the chaps had to have a scrap with the Pathans and settle the Khyber'.[41] He had heard of atrocities at Cawnpore in 1857 and that something called a residency had been besieged at Lucknow. In his youth Gandhi appeared as a name and a face in the newspapers and in a song sung by Gracie

Fields called 'Granny's Little Old Skin Rug'.⁴² He arrived in India with no particular wish to know more about it and without any sense of it as 'the splendid and glittering heart of the British Empire'.⁴³ The officer cadets were not encouraged to embark upon any serious reading about the country, its history and culture.

Scott once wrote of India as 'the place where I was born a second time. . . . After just three years this country was in my bones. I am always happy to be back there. Parts of it are terrible. Parts beautiful. Topographically, visually, it enlarges me. No wonder. What could be more different than [Palmers Green].'⁴⁴ Yet he distinguishes his attachment to India from that of a fellow officer:

> On the boat, in the same cadet group, there was a man called Clayton. It turned out he lived . . . within a stone's throw of where I was born. We obviously lived in different climates. I'd never met him. . . . He was about my age. By then a paratrooper. He was at the same OTS in Belgaum. He was commissioned into the Gurkhas. He adored India. He stayed on in Assam, to plant tea. I last saw him in 1955 it must have been. He came home to visit his ageing parents. . . . Then went back to his Indian wife and their children. The East had called him in a way it has never quite called me.

He once told an Indian audience:

> When I first came here, one did not, as an English soldier, easily meet many of the indigenous population or become what would be described as intimate. On the other hand I believe that the topography and physical actuality of a country impose something of their character upon the people to whom it belongs – and perhaps eventually upon those who visit it. So you may say, if you like, that I approached you first through the lie of your land and the way the light falls on it.⁴⁵

His wartime in India

> began as a period of dislike, and straightforward homesickness for an honest neon-sign and a handsome pylon, for the

purely English light that fell, as Eliot described it in 'East Coker':

> Across the open field, leaving the deep lane
> Shuttered with branches, dark in the afternoon.[46]

It ended with the realisation that he was 'homesick in quite a different way – for the sight and smell of an arid Indian plain'.

Scott's visual delight in India was shared by an artist wartimer who reached India in 1942. Sergeant Clive Branson was a Communist who refused to be commissioned. He was killed on the Arakan front in 1944. He was born in India but brought up in England, attending Bedford Grammar School and the Slade School of Art. He achieved considerable success as an artist, including the exhibition of two paintings at the Royal Academy in summer 1930. The Indian landscape made him long for a paint box. Weeks before his death, while he was on night guard, he writes a poem that ends with the light of dawn:

> When from the hills, not seen till touching the trees,
> Morning, like a flock of flamingoes, wings
> To settle in the branches and spread across the fields.[47]

In many other ways, too, Branson's letters home anticipate Scott's reflections. He was then far more politically committed and historically concerned than Scott, but the development of his attitudes was similar. He was struck at once by his own ignorance and that of his colleagues:

> We went by train from Bombay to a camp outside Poona. Everyone was filled with amazement at the appalling conditions in which people live – this has been the subject of many very lively discussions since; . . . without the slightest divergence of opinion on the basic fact that, after 175 years of Imperialism in India, the conditions are a howling disgrace. For this reason, and its reactions on our own immediate future (and present), the slogan among the British Other Ranks of 'India for the Indians' is universally popular.

They did not assimilate the established attitudes, feeling sympathy for the people of the country and aversion from 'the disgusting snobbishness of the Anglo-Indians both to the Indians and to the newly arrived British soldiers'. The regular army treats Indians 'in a way which not only makes one tremble for the future but which makes one ashamed of being one of them'. They often came to India 'to get away from family trouble in blighty', and became alienated from both people at home and Indians. Their movements severely circumscribed, British troops were 'prisoners all right out here'. He deplored 'the continued arrogance, extravagance and domination of the white Raj'. He reflected on the British tendency to insularity: 'One thing I have learnt out here more than anything else is that life in England, and therefore one's outlook towards people and the world, is hopelessly divorced from the rest of humanity.' The effect of India was to make him want 'to see and learn more, much, much more'. After the war 'I know I shall want to come back to India, where I can feel I am with humanity and not just one of a stuck-up little part of it'. Returning to camp from leave in Bombay, he felt 'back again now with racial hatred, anti-nigger sahibs, etc'. He meets an 'old sweat' (regular soldier) who tells of 'trouble at . . . .' When asked to explain, he replies, 'Women raped'. Branson comments: 'It would have made me laugh outright – fancy Congress students demonstrating for the release of Nehru by raping women – had it not been such excellent Fascist propaganda.' He writes of 'the shouting, bawling, threatening which invariably signifies that a white sahib is talking to a wog'. He was excited by opportunities to talk with Indian students as 'human beings' and that his army companions 'lost quite a lot of the feeling of exiles' as they too entered such discussions. His abiding message was: 'never will any of us who have come to India for this war forget the unbelievable, indescribable poverty in which we have found people living *wherever* we went, and in millions. We are all agreed that if the people back home knew of their conditions there would be a hell of a row – because this state of affairs is maintained in the name of the British.' His letters rehearse the themes Scott was to make his own: racism; imprisonment; exile; ignorance and indifference; insularity.

Scott's recollections of wartime India do not suggest that he was appalled by racism at that time. He arrived without preconceived notions about sahibs and memsahibs: 'They didn't strike me as my kind of people – and there were things about them that struck us all as rather funny – but I only met one or two who struck me as monsters of arrogance and prejudice.'[48] They seemed 'funny' because they were out of phase with contemporary Britain. Their anachronistic mores were symbolised for Scott in their persistence with the now quaint custom of 'calling'. In a review of a regular officer's autobiography he would write:

> The remarkable thing is that this account of the sahibs and memsahibs of the very early 1920s will at once be recognizable to men who were simply out there with emergency commissions in the last war. Nothing had fundamentally changed. The greatest crime the wartime officer cadet could commit was still a social one – forgetting to call on the colonel and his lady by signing the book outside the gate of Flagstaff House.[49]

Palit recalls 'cycling around the cantonments dropping visiting cards into numerous "Not-at-Home" boxes hanging on the outer gates of spacious houses – I never once was invited to a British home'.[50] Reader regarded the custom as 'fossilised nonsense' in 1941: 'You signed your name in a book at the great man's gate and smoked one of his cigarettes if so inclined. Then a week or two later, in the letter rack at the Mess, you would find a visiting card – "Major-General Roland Dening IA".'[51] In time Scott met some Anglo-Indians, almost exclusively military rather than civilian, and felt that some of them were his kind of people, English people in exile. Commander-in-Chief Auchinleck admitted:

> The British regular officer of the Indian Army, with comparatively few exceptions, has made the Indian Army his life's career, joining it at a very early age . . . remaining with it until he retired. . . . This long continued residence in India with no experience of service in the United Kingdom tended to make the Indian Army officer parochial in his outlook and behind the times generally in his knowledge of his profession.[52]

After three years of war the racial exclusiveness of British

toward Indian officers had been eroded. General Palit insists
that before the war there had been 'hardly any friendships
between Indian and British officers and virtually no social or
cultural interaction'.[53] A 'rigid apartness . . . was enforced on
the officer cadre in Peshawar and northern Indian cantonments'. After a year or two of war the arrival of newly commissioned British officers changed the atmosphere and 'easy,
relaxed friendships' began to develop.

The sense of imprisonment in the cantonment that Scott and
Branson felt was shared by other young officers. Encamped at
OTC at Bangalore, Hugh Tinker 'made tiny, tentative efforts to
catch a glimpse of India', through visits to Indian cinemas and
to the native city to see a classical dancer, and leave visits to
Seringapatam and Cochin.[54] He recalls the long middle years of
the war, weary and depressing, when for a young Indian Army
officer between twenty-one and twenty-three years of age life
was moving from one dreary cantonment to another. Harrison
writes of spending nearly four-and-a-half years in India, mostly
near its borders:

> And everywhere on that round tour of frontiers the army
> provided a transparent box in which to live, a world of
> its own. My own temperament played a part doubtless
> but I don't think my experience of isolation within India
> was very different from that of the other British war-time
> officers in the battalion. I certainly do not remember any of
> them forming friendships with Indians and Indian families
> which led them out of our world. . . . Having joined the army
> I did see the world of India – but how eccentrically.[55]

He had but twenty days in Bombay and Calcutta, and thus
saw virtually nothing of expatriate professional or non-official
middle-class life.

Scott was to become ashamed at his own, and his country-
men's, ignorance of India: 'India and Britain have been connected historically, politically, economically, for a very long
time. It angers me a little that we should know so little about
one another. We know less than they. Our ignorance of the
country we ruled or influenced for over 200 years – my ignorance of it, which I've tried to correct – is almost morally

unforgivable. . . !' [56] He, too, felt responsible for India's condition under British rule:

> India was also my home. It is difficult to describe but I think in a curious way India in those days was every English person's home, even if it had not been visited. Because we ruled it and benefited from it, it contributed to our well-being and upbringing. It was mysteriously in our blood and perhaps still is. In any case, that is what I felt, and gradually I became appalled at the thought of how little I knew of our history there. [57]

Besides his visual and emotional attraction to the landscape, India's centrality to British history and politics was a source of Scott's growing fascination with the country.

There is another strand to Scott's sense of rebirth in India: India's intensification of his awareness of elements in the human condition. This appears clearly in his attachment to Calcutta, for 'the miseries and vitality of the entire subcontinent are brought to the boiling point in this explosive city'. [58] The urban disaster that is Calcutta was 'the open running sore on the body of the smiling image of the civilised world's enterprise to date; the obscene side of the glittering coin struck by Kenneth Clark; . . . the place where life is – here humiliated almost beyond endurance but stubborn and defiant. Which explains my affection for the city . . . .' In Calcutta, once a British city of palaces, history was 'rendered down to a colonnaded front, an architectural perfection of form and balance', juxtaposed with concrete monstrosities and tinpot roofs. [59] The vanished age of reason was here perversely illustrated, a decline 'rooted in mercantile rapacity, imperial indifference, political chicanery, industrial dishonesty, the imponderable power of nature itself'. [60]

In three years Scott had seen much of India. He had served for months at a time in distinct parts of the provinces of western India (Bombay), the north-west (Punjab and the Frontier) and the east (Bengal and Bihar). Of British India he had seen the capital, New Delhi, the large commercial cities of Calcutta and Bombay, seats of central and provincial government, cantonment towns large and small, such clubs (Nirvanas for which Indians might pine in vain) as the Bombay Gymkhana, the Poona Turf and the Ranchi, the grand and less than grand

hotels, the officers' messes. M.M. Kaye asserts that 'he saw
little or nothing of the "Raj"', that 'the India he saw was not
the true "Raj", for by that time the lines had become blurred
by war' and the knowledge that Indian freedom must follow
it.[61] Certainly he saw the Raj in its civilian form as an out-
sider, and from the inside an army undergoing transformation.
But he shared some of its mysteries. He exercised command
over Indians and established paternalistic relations with Indian
NCOs, though he did not get to know middle-class professional or
politically committed Indians. He saw something of the hill stations, though not the most celebrated – Simla and Darjeeling. He
also glimpsed the Indian princely states (Tripura, Manipur and
Kashmir – or at least its capital, Srinagar), but met no Political
Agents or Residents. He saw nothing of the south and little of the
United Provinces (certainly nothing of Agra, Benares, Kanpur
or Lucknow) or Rajasthan. He felt that he knew quite a lot about
India visually, that it 'obviously made the kind of impression
that turns into an obsession'.[62] Had he not been married he might
well have accepted the offer extended to those of his rank to stay
on for two years' further service.

Scott's range of Indian experience was typical of that of
wartime officers and he sailed home knowing nothing more
about the country than thousands of others. His fascination
led him on to a lifetime's reading and reflection that would
give meaning and extension to his experience. His acquaintance
with India and Anglo-India had been far too limited a basis
for the portrayal of the declining edifice of the Raj. What
made him different was that he was a creative artist whose
imagination had been engaged by India. Lord Radcliffe, the
King's Counsel who in a few hectic weeks devised the lines of
partition to demarcate India and Pakistan in August 1947, once
wondered that India had so little inspired the artistic and literary imagination of the British.[63] Scott was unique, the wartimer
who became the novelist of the Raj *in extremis*. But several
wartime British officers became scholars for whom Indian
history and politics would be a life-long preoccupation. They
included Kenneth Ballhatchet and John Harrison, Professor
and Reader in South Asian History at the University of London;
W.H. Morris-Jones, Director of the Institute of Commonwealth
Studies at London; Eric Stokes, Smuts Professor of the History

of the British Commonwealth in the University of Cambridge; Hugh Tinker, Professor of Asian Politics at London and Director of the Institute of Race Relations. Some of them would have stayed on in India in the civil administration or journalism had there been opportunities to do so. Instead, like Scott but in other ways, they created an informed British interest in India, previously a monopoly of the servants of the Raj.

5

On 18 June 1946 the Permanent Under Secretary of State for India wrote to Scott to thank him for his services to his country and to grant him release with the honorary rank of captain. He arrived home with a cheque for £98 5s: gratuities for £28 for forty months' service as sergeant, £52 10s for thirty months as a commissioned officer, and other ranks' post-war credit of £17 15s. The inadequacy of such riches for a life of literary leisure was soon exposed by his wife's pregnancy. He turned down a job at £6 a week with the merchant bankers, Brown Shipley, and another in the accounts department of the RAF Malcolm Club in Belgravia. He was hired as a bookkeeper by an officer who had published his poems in a wartime broadsheet, Captain Peter Baker, founder and chairman of a London publishing firm, Falcon Press. He resumed studies in accounting though he never qualified. He became secretary of Baker's four associated publishing companies while Roland Gant, the closest friend he ever made in publishing, handled the advertising. For four years they worked together at offices located at 6 Crown Passage, Pall Mall. They both resigned in 1950 in alarm at growing indications of their chairman's financial irresponsibility. Scott left with three months' pay in hand in lieu of notice.

Until summer 1950, Scott recalled, 'my own writing had more or less failed'.[64] He had been writing plays and a novel, achieving only rejections. The first, never published, novel then going the rounds was declined by seventeen publishers. Between jobs, he now drew on his Air Supply Company experience to write in three days a ninety-minute radio play, *Lines of Communication*, whose British officers and Indian NCOs were versions of colleagues at Comilla. At this stage the senior partner in a firm of literary agents, Pearn, Pollinger and Higham, offered him a job, with a partnership in prospect. His literary abilities and

his publishing experience were well suited to the career of an
agent that he began in October 1950. Scott's play was accepted
by the BBC and was performed in February 1951. There began a
decade of dual employment: as a full-time agent, handling such
authors as M.M. Kaye, Muriel Spark, Elizabeth Cadell and John
Braine, and as a professional author. He became a partner in
David Higham Associates, the side of the firm with which he
stayed when it split.

6

Within months of his return to England in June 1946 Scott had
begun to dream of India. After a letter or two he lost touch
with Jim Corben, who was still waiting to be demobilised late
in 1946. He sometimes attended reunions in the late 1940s and
the 1950s (last in 1963) and occasionally exchanged letters with
RIASC officers. He kept up a correspondence with Nimu, who
remained in the army, and Dass. In April 1951, when he heard
that the *Daily Express* had sent James Leasor to India for a
month, he wrote to Nimu, 'How I wish I were there.'[65] In 1956,
when Leasor published an account of the siege of Delhi during
the Mutiny, *The Red Fort*, Scott rang him up and for some years
they met monthly for lunch at a Chinese restaurant in Soho.
Dass wanted to be a stenographer but in 1948 settled as a cloth
merchant and dress manufacturer in a village of 3000 people in
Madras Presidency. Gifts were exchanged – a Parker pen on
Scott's side, a lace tablecloth and bed sheets, tea and bangles
for Scott's daughters on Dass's. Scott repeatedly assured Dass
that he would visit him one day. In 1964, just before he fulfilled
the promise with remarkable consequences for his fiction, he
wrote, 'I have dreamed of being there for so many years.'[66]
   Scott recalled that in the eighteen years after his post-war
return to England he spent much of his time 'browsing among
. . . dull, wise books' on the 'India that had fascinated me'.[67]
On occasion he spoke of repairing his ignorance of India by
a close, if amateur and unsystematic study of the history of
the British connection. In 1947 he read Forster's *A Passage to
India* (1924) for the first time, with a feeling that he had never
actually met anyone like its British characters, 'the Turtons and
the Burtons'. The same year he read his first novel by an Indian,
R.K. Narayan's *The Dark Room* (1938). He also began collecting

books on British India and borrowed others. However, there is reason to doubt that he undertook any serious research for the five books that he wrote on a part-time basis in his decade as a literary agent. Throughout the 1950s, with one exception, his novels were not really about the British connection with India, though all made some use of his Indian military experience as background.

The novels of the 1950s, all published by Eyre and Spottiswoode, were *Johnnie Sahib*, *The Alien Sky*, *A Male Child*, *The Mark of the Warrior* and *The Chinese Love Pavilion*. He summarised their themes in a lecture:

> The first was about the difficulty one officer had in India during the war taking over another officer's job. The second was about an Englishman to whom Indian independence meant losing a job he loved. The third was about a man back home in London from the war in the East, too ill from tropical infection to do a proper job and feel he had a stake in the future. The fourth was about an officer in India obsessed with the idea that men had died because he hadn't done his job properly and that his job now was to bring out in a young cadet those qualities he lacked himself but which he thought important. The fifth was a bit of a hybrid, but the job motif recurs . . . [in] a theme of madness brought on by obsession with occupations for their own sake – occupations disrupted or invented by war.[68]

In his mature years he expressed dissatisfaction with the first three and was not proud of the fifth.

Scott commented on *Johnnie Sahib* (1952), 'that first frightful little novel was . . . autobiographical'.[69] Eyre and Spottiswoode gave it a prize for their best novel of the year. It concerned the effect of increasing bureaucratisation upon the command of a section (platoon) of Air Supply in Comitarla (near Comilla) and Burma from June 1944. Captain Johnnie Brown was a leader who secured remarkable loyalty from his men and maintained a liaison with a Eurasian nurse. The situation replicated Scott's experience of being 'organized by the sort of people who had scoffed at the whole conception of supply by air – so a lot of the originating fun went out of it'. Brown was posted away as unsuited to the new regime and was replaced by an officer unequal to the task.

The title of *The Alien Sky* (1953) recalls Maud Diver's reference to the British in India as 'members of one great family, aliens under one sky' *(The Englishwoman in India*, 1909). It was set in June 1947, immediately after the announcement of Mountbatten's plan to partition the subcontinent between India and Pakistan, with the princes acceding to one or the other. The locations are imaginary, primarily a small cantonment town (Marapore) in close connection with a princely state (Kalipur) and a village (Ooni). For scenes in the hotel and the club and descriptions of the cantonment Scott drew on his experience of Ranchi. Harsh judgement is delivered on Britain for the fate of Indians caught up in the imperial withdrawal and the Partition, not by the British themselves but by a visiting American who was following the trail of his dead brother's relationship with a Eurasian woman. M.M. Kaye enjoyed the novel enormously. Compton Mackenzie admired it and encouraged Scott to pursue the Eurasian theme. However, while there are anticipations of the *Quartet*, the book is insubstantial, revealing only a flimsy grasp of the complexities of the British connection.

A Male Child (1956) opens with the first person narrator bound for India as a cadet officer in 1942. He is soon repatriated with an apparently incurable tropical disease and the novel follows his casting about for a basis of life in post-war Britain. *The Mark of the Warrior* (1958) is set in Belgaum and concerns training for facility in jungle warfare. In a lecture that he gave in India in 1972 Scott referred to its expression of his own first response to India:

> about fourteen years ago I wrote the following passage describing a young soldier's reaction to his first Indian billet and I don't think I could have written it, after the event, in just this way, if I had not, however subconsciously, felt it at the time.

> Behind the hut was a stretch of rough, uncut grass. Bushes formed a hedge. The hill sloped away from the hedge, and its trough could not be seen. But, beyond, the land lay in folds covered in grass of a green which Ramsay now knew was a green he did not know because a fiercer rain, a stronger sun, a drier dust, had stained its pigment. He stood in the doorway of his and Lawson's hut and saw that the sky had no colour he recognized

and that the shape of the land was not a shape which
he understood in his bones. He became aware of a scent
in which there was mixed the smoke from fires he had
not seen and the tang of earth he had not touched; and
when the breeze moved there was in it the breath of men
he had not met; and his blood stirred.

Like Ramsay, I had not wanted to come out here, I was sent;
like Ramsay, my ignorance was immense, as great as my
disappointment at finding it, when I arrived, raining.[70]

While that novel contained a writing out of his recognition of
ignorance of the British connection with India, *The Chinese
Love Pavilion* (1960) begins with a contrary first-person affirmation in India before the war: 'India was of my bone.' The
narrator's family had a tradition of service in India that had
died with his grandfather before he was born. He had dreamt
of renewing the connection by joining the Indian Army but
instead joined the office of a shipping company in Bombay. The
escapade was a failure for he could not feel 'self-identification
with the under-privileged' or ever become mother–father to
grown men and women. His 'inheritance was an illusion'. The
main action of the novel takes place in Malaya and concerns a
Eurasian woman.

7

During his decade as a literary agent Scott was unable to locate
themes for major fiction. The demands of full-time employment, of close attention to the writing of other authors, cramped
his imagination. Though India continued to fascinate him and he
pursued a study of its history, he had little time for reading. By
the end of the 1950s he had acquired no more than some twenty-
five books on British India, three or four on India generally, and
a few on the war in Burma. They concerned the whole two centuries of British rule: studies of such proconsuls and generals
as Warren Hastings, Elijah Impey, Philip Francis, Eyre Coote,
Roberts of Kandahar, and Lord Mountbatten; accounts of early
Calcutta and Madras; of British social life, the Penal Code, the
Indian Civil Service; recollections of political officers, civilians,
and military men; histories of the making of British India and
analyses of the constitutional problem in the twentieth century.

The impression is of an unsystematic study over the long post-war period, which would contrast with the post-1960 intensive study of the later Raj and the accumulation of a further 120-odd volumes.

By the late 1950s Scott was feeling tired, unwell and disillusioned with contemporary Britain. Like many wartime servicemen he had rejoiced at Labour's electoral triumph in 1945. The 'old anti-progressive guard was swept out of power' and now 'the road would lead to the elimination of social injustice, poverty, class-consciousness, and Imperial domination abroad'.[71] But the dawning age of affluence of the 1950s brought back 'the illiberal world of dog eat dog'.[72] 'Tory manipulated post-war-post-socialist plenty' introduced 'the extraordinary new world of purchasable artefacts', a new age of insularity, self-interest and cultural narrowness: 'The hunger to be, rather than not to be, to have and to hold and never to lose, never to give away again and yet not become, ever, less than cynical about one's possessions, is perhaps the whole point about the English today.'[73] Scott was losing his sense of moral commitment to his work. His self-image of 'the Fat Boy of Dean Street', carrying two extra stone of agent's fat, sums up his prevailing mood of discontent.[74] If he were to develop as a novelist he needed to step outside the publishing world and into some new deep stream of experience.

Scott's opportunity came in October 1959, when his American publisher, William Morrow, guaranteed him a livable income, £1800 per annum for three years. The payments would be advances against novels and would be reduced by the sum of his actual literary earnings during the period. In March 1960 the agreement took effect and he resigned his partnership in David Higham Associates.

2

Return to India

1

Scott wrote *The Birds of Paradise* (1962) between September 1959 and June 1961. It was the first novel that he set in a civilian Indian background. As first-person narrator he gave himself a fictive rebirth as the son of a member of the Indian Political Service in an Indian States Agency. The imaginative leap beyond his personal experience of wartime India required a study of historical sources.

The narrator, William Conway, a forty-one-year-old partner in a London merchant banking firm, seeks refuge from the values of the consumer society by taking a year's sabbatical leave in April 1960. Through him Scott projects his own disillusionment with contemporary Britain:

> We were Consumers. This was my obsession. . . . there was no longer anything you could contribute as an ordinary man [and] . . . the out-of-the-ordinary man was up against it too. There wasn't a square inch of earth that hadn't been discovered, trampled on, littered with cigarette ends and Kwikkaffy tins; not a square mile of ocean that hadn't seen the passage of a million balsa-wood rafts; not a social or political concept that hadn't been tried, tested and discredited, not an idea that hadn't been had before and been applied and then disowned; not an instinct that hadn't been written up by Freud or Jung, not a microbe that hadn't been bottled by Pasteur or Fleming; not an act of mercy left unperpetrated by UNRRA or Schweitzer.
>
> It had all been done. The moulds were cast. They only had to be serviced, filled with the molten sub-standard iron of inherited good intentions and upended to produce little tombstones of inferior, repeat performances.[1]

Scott dedicated the book to Wil Morrow 'with gratitude and thanks for my own sabbatical year'.

Scott described the origins of *Birds of Paradise* in a 1961 lecture, 'Imagination in the Novel': 'You begin with an image, a dumb charade, for instance a woman appearing in a doorway. She seems to be acting out a phrase: The end of things. . . .'[2] After trying several abortive non-Indian settings for the image, he found 'the idea of fine feathers' becoming attached to it, and 'it was the idea of birds of paradise that glittered'.[3] He associated it with the princes of India. It was the case that the feathers of birds of paradise were still treasured like crown jewels at the court of Nepal. The natives of the Pacific islands where the birds were found always cut off their feet in the process of removing their skins for sale. For Scott that emphasised their celestial origins; if they had no feet they could not perch. The princes, too, claimed celestial origins but had been divested of power by the British: 'Their feet, you could say, have been cut off. . . . While the British ruled, the Princes were kept going in all their feudal magnificence. . . . But when the British went and all their lands were merged with the lands of the new dominion they appeared, you might say, in their true light – they had been dead all the time. . . .'[4]

Scott peppered his image with his knowledge of British India until the theme of a novel emerged:

The Princes were advised by Englishmen. The big states had what were called Residents. The smaller states, sometimes grouped together for these purposes, were advised by what were called political agents. These men, agents and Residents, represented the British Crown which had certain powers over the states but would not otherwise much meddle in a state's internal affairs. The States were separated politically from what was called British India. They were self-governing. The Indian politicians of British India had no particular love for them. Few were run on anything like democratic lines. The lasting monument to the perfidy of Albion is, to me, the way we pointed British India towards democracy but preserved through thick and thin the autocracy of the Princes as if for all the world oceans separated them. But they were feudal islands in a democratic, socialist sea. And when we gave the Indians back their sea we left the feudal islands to their fate and right up to the last few weeks assured the rulers of those islands that no arrangement would be reached with

British India for independence without there being princely consultation. This is something history will forget, if only because betrayal of undemocratic institutions like feudal kingdoms is never called betrayal. India has made progress. It is all free and democratic now. It is right that the feudal kingdoms should no longer exist. But to the novelist the smell of betrayal can never smell like roses. He is interested in people, and uncommitted to policies. How did it seem to the people concerned, those men of the Political Department, whose careers had been spent advising native rulers, encouraging them to rule their kingdoms well and be a credit to the British Crown which protected them? Might it not have seemed to some of them that their careers had been ill-spent that ended in betrayal from above? And read between the lines of recorded history and you find that the Political Department did not have much love for Lord Louis Mountbatten's political bulldozer. Why? Because at least some of them knew that a way of life they had dedicated themselves to had come to an end. They, too, perhaps, appeared at doorways, to survey the ruins of their public lives, unable to meet the eyes of the Maharajah they had encouraged, frustrated, loved perhaps, stood by, stood out against. Was there amongst them no man who felt dishonoured? For a dozen who said, 'Well, old boy, times change, you've got to be realistic,' wasn't there one who was silent, packed his bags, folded his tent, and barely had the nerve to say goodbye?[5]

Bill Conway was the son of one who had been conscience-stricken by the betrayal of the princes: Sir Robert Conway, Resident at Gopalakand, who was responsible for relations with six small states combined in an Agency. Bill probes the mystery of his father's disgrace at the end of his career. He had been born in the Agency State of Tradura and sent home when he was ten for an English upbringing by his uncle Walter. From 1929 to 1939 they lived in a vaguely Tudor Surrey house and Bill's books (like Scott's) included such items as *The Making of British India* (1923) by Ramsey Muir; Henry Dodwell's *The Nabobs of Madras* (1926); *Echoes from Old Calcutta* (4th edn 1908) by H.E. Busteed; *The Letters of Warren Hastings to Sir John Macpherson* (1927); and *A Passage to India*. At school he was known as 'Rajah'. He cherished an ambition to enter the Indian Civil Service. However, during a visit home in 1936

Sir Robert decreed that he should go into Walter's merchant banking firm, essentially because Britain's promise of Indian independence would abort an Indian career.

Bill did not see his father again until 1945. He was interned as a prisoner-of-war in Malaya and visited Gopalakand after his release. There he realised that the fate of the princes would be absorption into independent India. British policy had been to advance the princes towards integration with British-governed India 'so slowly that it was difficult not to see the laggardly pace as deliberate, as part and parcel of a bloody-minded game of divide and rule'.[6] Two years later he followed the end of the Raj in the British press:

> And reading the accounts of this new decline and fall, I was lost sometimes in admiration of the way we English could twist an essential retreat until it looked like a voluntary advance, could seem to shrug our shoulders in paternal amusement at the antics the jackals got up to and tap our feet in the background as if we had been waiting for thirty years and not three months for them to decide what to do about their freedom, could lop the chain of paramountcy and take the attitude that only the badly ruled states would suffer.[7]

Sir Robert lived on in India until his death in 1950. Oddly, *The Times* carried only a short, formal obituary. He had written to Bill of his intention to make a record of his career, and cryptically of his attempt, at independence, to ward off his prince's capitulation. But no record came to light.

Bill Conway searched the shelves of his public library for a reference to the accession of Gopalakand to India. He consults V.P. Menon's *The Story of the Integration of the Indian States* (1956) and such titles as *The Last Viceroy*, *India Since Partition*, *Betrayal in Delhi*, *The New Dominion* and *Farewell to the Princes*:

> Here was the historical perspective of events that intermittent reading of *The Times* reports from Delhi in 1947 had only confirmed my preconceived notions of, because I had anticipated the general drift of them.
>
> What the British Crown had taken from these princes – supreme authority in the three matters of external affairs, defence and communication – they were now asked to give

to one of the new self-governing dominions. This sounded
reasonable enough but it was the thin end of the wedge
. . . . How could a Congress-dominated government leave
matters there? It could never have been part of their
policy to preserve the internal autocratic authority of the
men who were descended from the great Moghuls and
the fierce Rajput warrior kings. The British might lock a
politician up without trial but a criminal always got a fair
hearing. The princes had dungeons where men languished
unsentenced for stealing bread. Now the writing was on the
wall, but it seemed that so many of the princes had failed to
see it. They actually welcomed the British announcement
that paramountcy over the states would come to an end
automatically with the end of British rule. The old musty
curtain was flung aside and revealed a freedom and power
almost greater than they had dreamt of. But not for
long. The winds of crisis changed quarter and blew from
colder regions. The Maharajahs ate crow. With nearly
six hundred of them they ate it in different ways, a few
eagerly, most reluctantly, some by forcible feeding. Some
threatened to accede to Pakistan even if geographically
such an accession would have been nonsensical; others
were as much coerced into accession by their own people
as diplomatically persuaded by the politicians of the new
India. They had riots in their own capitals, riots they
described as raised by Congress-inspired rabble but which
Congress described as the struggle of their enslaved subjects for democratic freedom. Sometimes there were shows
of arms by India, as in the case of Hyderabad, the most
powerful of all the states. The Maharajahs twisted and
turned and the old Political Department burnt records
like an embassy preparing to evacuate. And in the end
there were only the details to work out, the quid pro quo
for the surrender of ruling powers and internal autocratic
authority. One by one the states were formed into provinces
or merged with provinces of what in our own day had been
called British India. The quid pro quo was the retention
of title and prince's privileges for the ruler and his heirs,
whose successions to the in-name-only *gaddis* would be
subject to the approval of the President of the Republic
instead of the Crown Representative. There were to be
payments, as well, an annual privy purse for the upkeep
of palace, family, servants and pensioners. In this way the
work of men like my father was taken out of their hands to
be brought to its logical end.[8]

Bill quotes from the only paragraph on Gopalakand that he could find:

> Gopalakand provided a good example of the obstruction sometimes encountered when the rulers were still being influenced by retiring British Residents. The Resident in Gopalakand, Sir Robert Conway, persuaded Sir Pandir-akkar on more than one occasion to go back on promises given verbally to the States Department; and actually interrupted a private conference between the Maharajah and the representatives of the department and threatened to tear up the draft documents which he described as instruments of a blackguardly policy of intended seizure and forfeiture, masquerading as agreements between free parties.[9]

Bill recognised the element of truth in his father's judgement, but: 'There was nothing logical in the continued existence of places like Gopalakand, and nothing could have saved them once the illusion of stately togetherness was destroyed. That illusion had been created by their preservation and protection under the single head of the British Crown. The illusion vanished with the Crown. . . .'[10] He wondered whether, in 1936, his father had 'foreseen something else, as well? The day, for instance, when, if I followed in his footsteps, I would finally admit that it was all *maya*, that nothing a man could do with his life would really satisfy him, unless he were a slug and content with the sight of his own slimy wake?'[11]

'Illusion', as Scott later noted for his lecture, 'is the thing that has come to an end.'[12] Bill 'understood how vulnerable is the illusion that a man has of his own importance, not of his importance to others, but of his importance to himself, and how to speak of what drives him to sustain the illusion, of the means he finds to drive himself, of the dark that falls on him when the illusion is gone, is virtually impossible'.[13] But what of the opening image, the woman in the doorway? At the end of the novel Bill sees her in middle age in the doorway of the cage that contained the birds of paradise in Tradura. She was his childhood sweetheart. Leaving the cage their bodies touched. Her skin was 'as hard as flint' because, Scott explained, of her sadness at the sight of the birds and all that they used to represent to her. 'But she has a long experience now of living with reality.'[14]

The serious historical point of *Birds of Paradise* is that the Raj's ostensible dedication to serving India masked imperial self-interest. The rhetoric of the Raj belonged to a world of self-deception or illusion. Had Britain been serious about unifying the two Indias she would have followed a policy of bringing them together, rather than upholding princely apartness. The Political Department was playing divide-and-rule. Bill Conway was left uncertain whether this realisation caused his father to commit his future to the real world of making money in Britain rather than the illusory world of bearing the white man's burden.

The idea of the Raj as illusion, and Scott's beginning his novel with the end of the illusion, prepare his reader for the *Quartet*. In the first novel of the sequence the setting is Mayapore, which means place of illusion. Throughout the *Quartet* Scott proposes his locations as those where 'the British came to the end of themselves as they were'. The ideas are tentative in *Birds*, demanding Scott's renewal of his Indian experience to give them substance.

2

Birds of Paradise is the first of Scott's novels to be grounded on thorough research. For zoological details he sought help from the Natural History Museum in Kensington. In the central hall he came upon a glass case of stuffed birds of paradise. A kindly and efficient Mrs Joyce Pope gave him lists of books and articles. At Hatchards he buys a second-hand two-volume book, Alfred Russel Wallace's *The Malay Archipelago: The Land of the Orang-utan and the Birds of Paradise* (1869). He finds a live specimen at the zoo.

For information about the princes and their relations with the Political Department he borrows Menon's *Integration of the Indian States*, which he was to find 'invaluable as a political guide to some of the facts' for his fiction.[15] His notes from it survive, together with a list of books consulted, which he probably borrowed from the Golders Green Road branch of the Hendon Public Library. It includes E.M. Forster, *The Hill of Devi* (1953); Sir K. Fitze, *Twilight of the Maharajas* (1956);

S. Gopal, *The Viceroyalty of Lord Irwin 1926–31* (1957); E.W.R. Lumby, *The Transfer of Power in India 1945–7* (1954); Sir P. Griffiths, *Modern India* (1957); and Jim Corbett, *Man-Eaters of Kumaon* (1946).

To corroborate his sense of the precariousness of an Indian career after about 1935 Scott wrote to the India Office Library. Philip Mason (pseud. Woodruff), *The Guardians: The Men Who Ruled India* (1954), suggested that recruitment to the ICS ceased in 1939. Was that, asked Scott, because of the war or from a policy of Indianisation? Was there a falling off in competition of Englishmen after the passing of the India Act in 1935? Would a member of the Political Service have reason to dissuade his son from entering the ICS after 1935? The Library's reply offered no answers but enclosed a pamphlet regarding recruitment up to 1945. It showed that competition in England had indeed diminished from the mid-1930s. Sir Robert Conway might truly have believed that independence would terminate an ICS career begun in the late 1930s. Scott wrote to Maurice Temple-Smith at Eyre and Spottiswoode, 'Conway Senior's "You think it all eyewash" acquires, in this light, the subtlety it was meant to have.'[16]

Here was a matter of historical judgement where Scott's imagination served him well. A recent study of the ICS reveals that in 1935 only five Europeans could be secured for the service. Of those who sat the examinations, held jointly for the Indian and Home Services, none of the top twenty would go to India. To keep up the desired European complement in the ICS it was necessary to resort to selective appointment rather than competitive examination for half the total European entry between 1936 and 1939. The Secretary of State believed that 'uncertainty as to the future of the Service' was the primary reason for the difficulty in finding European recruits.[17]

Scott consulted his author friend Gerald Hanley, who wrote the original screenplay for Attenborough's *Gandhi* about the choice of names for his Indian characters. Hanley emphasised that Indian names had meanings and urged him to use actual names: 'the ex-sahib colonels, pandits and Bombay wallahs are all waiting to find your mistakes'.[18] He recommended James Tod's *Annals and Antiquities of Rajasthan* (1829–32) for Rajput details and urged Scott to beware of 'the Indian devil who waits for that slip about a Parsi wearing the wrong bracelet on Tuesday'. One such critic was Susan Gillespie, who felt that one of the scenes in *Birds*, where Conway has his son beaten by a syce, was implausible.[19]

3

Scott was aware that his long absence from India made the setting of *Birds* seem 'dreamlike. When I wrote that book I'd not been in India for fourteen years, and after I'd written it I knew I'd never write another book about India until I'd been back there to substitute the reality for the dream.'[20] He agreed with his agent, David Higham: 'I've scraped the bottom of my barrel on India.'[21] The insubstantial nature of *Birds* might be explained as true to its theme, the remembrance in early middle age of childhood experience and a brief visit at the end of the war. Peter Green indeed praised this aspect of the book: '"In the end is my beginning" – with such contrapuntal skill is the novel constructed, so delicately managed the time sequence . . . .'[22] M.M. Kaye admired the book's haunting quality. But John Willey regretted its 'lack of immediacy': 'Everything of yours that I have read is told in the mood of remembrance of things past.'[23] There was 'a membrane between the reader and the novel'. He advised Scott to adjust his technique: 'This would be a matter of letting present actions really take over in your novels – of putting your characters into a setting, letting them look up and down, forward and back, and get involved before our eyes, rather than meditating on how they came to be where they are as if their lives were over.'[24] With *The Bender* Scott was writing of the here and now, but he faced another problem. He felt that he wrote best when he was seriously engaged with his subject, and: 'I can't take anything that happens in London seriously! At least not at the moment, or in that way.'

The resolution of Scott's dilemma must be a return visit to India. By December 1961 he had set himself 'the very real objective of going to the Far East again very soon. . . . I want, very badly, to go to India next year. . . . To breathe fresh air east of Suez might unbung all kinds of barrels.'[25] Scott's transition from part-time to full-time writing had been backed by his American publisher. Now his return to India was to be financed by a British publisher. He had been with Eyre and Spottiswoode since 1950 but did not get on well with the young men who gradually took over from its old regime. He declined Muriel Spark's suggestion that he move to Macmillan but in June 1962 transferred to Secker and Warburg, where Roland Gant had recently become a director. Secker's offered to pay £400 towards a trip abroad when the time was right. They published *Bender* in 1963 and *Corrida* the next year. In 1964, when Gant moved to the parent company, William Heinemann, Scott followed him.

4

As he was completing *Birds* Scott felt that he was laying the foundations for three or four further novels on British India. There seemed 'so damn much to all the people', he wrote to John Willey: 'The compulsion to engage in a really big novel about India – a kind of decline and fall if ever there was one, an Anglo-Indian war and peace – bubbles away under the surface.'[26] He was moving beyond his own memory as a source: 'In *Birds* I was beginning to skim off some of that compulsive interest that goes beyond personal experience.'[27] From 1960 experience was substantially extended by reading. He would later write to Freya Stark that his reading was 'the basis for whatever now passes as knowledgeability about the place'.[28]

Between 1960 and 1977 Scott reviewed over a hundred books – novels and non-fiction – concerned with India. The number is small in relation to the 800-odd books that he reviewed in all, but many of the Indian pieces were of substantial length. Most were published in the *Times Literary Supplement*, anonymously as was its practice until late 1974. They have, for the most part, not previously been attributed to him. Scott's reviews are a crucial source for tracing the development of his understanding of the history of the Raj, and thus for revealing the interpretative backdrop to the themes of the *Quartet*.

Working on *Birds* had caused Scott to question the principles and purposes that the Raj had claimed as its justification. His subsequent reading confirmed his conclusion that between the wars the moral basis for the Raj had become an illusion, with dividing and ruling supplanting uniting and liberating as imperial orthodoxies. Among his sparse planning notes for his 1964 return to India is the following quotation from Nehru's *The Discovery of India* (1946): 'The future historians of England will have to consider how far England's decline from her proud eminence was due to her imperialism and racialism, which corrupted her public life and made her forget the lessons of her own history and literature.'[29]

Scott's concern for imperial ends and means in India emerges in his reviews for the *TLS* in the early 1960s. He praised R.P. Masani, author of *Britain in India* (1960), for his recognition of important distinctions:

> He . . . has an instinct for separating a good intention from a disagreeable effect – a first requirement when the subject under consideration is the British Raj – and a feeling for the differences which must always exist between the men who formulate a policy and the men who try to interpret it or tend to ignore it in the provinces, districts, courts and clubs, of an oriental empire.[30]

Consistent with the theme of *Birds of Paradise*, Scott complains that in Masani's book, 'Almost no mention is made of the autocratic Princely States which the British preserved through thick and thin with one hand while pointing the rest of India to democracy with the other.' In a review of a study of centrally planned development of rural India, Kusum Nair's *Blossoms in the Dust* (1961), he indicated another contradiction of British policy:

> there are two Indias. The British Raj helped to keep them separate. There was always a dichotomy of principle in its rule, perhaps because its representatives fell into two main categories: the Educator whose vision of a better future was bound up from a practical point of view with the idea of matriculation, and the Romantic Feudalist who felt that the Indian paradise would be found under the village peepul tree directly the inhabitants had learnt to use dung as manure and not burn it as fuel. The visiting card marked 'Failed B.A.' and the thumb-print on a deposition in a rural dispute are as much the marks left on India by the British as are the English language and the forms of civil administration.[31]

The threads of Scott's thought on the contradictions of British rule are drawn tightly together when he relates the Raj's preservation of divisions in India to the ultimate tragedies of

the bloody partition of India in 1947. This occurs in his review
of Penderel Moon's *Divide and Quit* (1961), an authoritative
account of the consequences of partition as viewed from the vantage point of the Muslim-majority Punjab state of Bahawalpur:

Mr Moon opens his account of the partition of India with
a short survey of the extremely complicated events which
led up to it, goes on to describe in some detail the slaughter,
arson, rape and abduction that accompanied the movements of Hindus, Muslims and Sikhs in the princely state
of Bahawalpur where he was Revenue and Public Works
Minister; and then, in a brief summary, discusses the
following questions: Were the happenings in Bahawalpur
typical of the disorders elsewhere? Could the massacres
and migrations have been prevented? Could Pakistan
have been avoided? Could the Sikhs have been peacefully
accommodated in some other way? In other words, who, if
anyone, was to blame for (a) partition and (b) the bloodshed
that marked it?
  One day, it is to be hoped, someone – preferably an
Englishman – will examine the whole situation in the light
of our own failure to unify a country we were always eager
to describe, publicly anyway, as a sacred trust. Even in
Mr Moon's liberal and fastidiously argued investigation
this fundamental aspect of a modern but classically pro-
portioned tragedy is implied rather than dealt with; and
one of the implications – that our responsibility for what
finally happened partly lay in our belief in the virtues of
parliamentary democracy – is startling, not to say controversial. Paternalism under the peepul tree may have
appealed to the men on the spot, but it has a lot to answer
for in our colonial history. . . . In the end the principal
actors in this drama were powerless. That is one measure
of its tragedy. Another measure is that no one, even now,
is exactly sure how many people lost their lives. It seems to
have become fashionable to see the approximate figure of
200,000 as a gratifying alternative to the millions who might
have died in the civil war that might have raged if we had
resisted Pakistan or hung on to India a bit longer; but are
not those 200,000 a measure, too – a measure of our failure
as rulers and civilizers?[32]

The next year he reinforces the point in a review of Taya
Zinkin's *Reporting India*:

The only excuse for the partition of India was the promise it seemed to hold out of peace between Hindu and
Muslim. Looking now not only back upon the massacres
of 1947 but also (over Mrs Zinkin's shoulder) at . . . more
recent pictures of riot and bloodshed, partition emerges
even more clearly as the supreme failure of the British
in wielding their power and exercising their influence. It
established a precedent for the immediate division of spoils
men threatened to quarrel over.[33]

Almost on the eve of his 1964 return to India, Scott reviewed,
under the *TLS* byline 'The End of the Raj', Michael Edwardes's
The Last Years of British India (1963) and K.K. Aziz's *Britain
and Muslim India* (1963). Both authors were 'interested in the
part that sympathisers of the British left played over the years
in the development of the Indian Congress into a body that
claimed to be constitutionally representative of all India, and
in the corresponding but less direct part the right played in
the growth of the Muslim League into a minority opposition
strong enough to force partition as the price of emancipation'.[34]
Scott followed Aziz's arguments with particular interest but was
unconvinced that Muslim ideals, needs and aspirations required
separate Muslim nationhood:

Perhaps the crux of the matter is that communal sentiments were never subjected by the British occupying
power to serious analysis, and no attempt was ever made
to remove or minimize this particular source of danger to
the professed ideal of Indian unity and eventual freedom.
To the men who never visualized such freedom coming
in their lifetimes this religious enmity (if it *was* religious
more than political and economic) was comforting proof
that the subject people were not yet ready for self-rule, and
the men who were determined to give them their freedom
within a foreseeable future were unfortunately mostly to be
found in England, and from that distance the danger looked
minimal.

Seen in the light of a failure to examine with a view
to trying to remove a major community problem while
there was still time (say from 1857 onwards) the partition
of India must remain as a burden on the British liberal
conscience.

5

By early 1964 Scott's interest had thus been awakened in the
relation between the mechanics of Empire and the tragedy
of partition. His earlier concentration on reassessing his own
personal experience and examining the betrayal of princes and
the fate of Eurasians had, by historical inquiry, been extended to
embrace the workings of the Raj and their fateful consequences.
Further intimations of his preoccupations at the time are given
by his reader's reports on manuscripts submitted to several
publishers.

In 1960 Scott read the military reminiscences of a retired
lieutenant-colonel who had served in India and Malaya from
1930 to 1945. His wife had died of fever in a prisoner-of-war
camp. Scott was contemptuous of the author as 'the kind of
man we should all be so much better off without. He is a
parody of himself, his type. And they are all dead from the
neck up and from the navel down.'[35] They bulldozed their way
through life, had lumps in their throats when the bugle played
taps, conformed communally to a code of honour and self-
sacrifice, and prided themselves on speaking ill of no man
save the enemy. Their expression groaned with such clichés as
'rare qualities', 'zest for life', 'quiet humour' and 'stimulating
company'. In 1962 he read another representation of the genre,
inter-war Anglo-Indian military reminiscences. It was similarly
cliché-ridden with 'good chaps', 'enchanting girls' and everyone
was 'happy, healthy and sporting'.[36] Scott wondered what happened to the 'right bastards' (elsewhere described as 'flaming
arseholes' of the mess) and 'ripe bitches'. It caused him to
reflect, too, on the lack of published details of Anglo-Indian
life, on the punkah (which he believed the unknowing thought
was a drink), bungalows, syces, servants, Residents and Political Agents. Beyond the myths of military reminiscences there
awaited to be revealed the working lives of *The Civil*, of com-
missioners, judges and district officers, of the medical, public
works and forestry services.

Scott was enraged by a 1962 manuscript by an Englishwoman,
the wife of an engineer on the site of a new steel works close
to the Bihar–West Bengal border. Scott knew the terrain well
and remembered it with pleasure. He condemned the book as

the epitome of the memsahib mentality, to which the whole countryside was uninteresting and the towns 'indescribably filthy': 'Not once, throughout the entire book, does she consider the possibility that 250 years of British influence and 100 years of direct colonial rule might have some charges to answer for producing an Indian middle class so unlike her own.'[37] He believed that the Bengalis whom she maligned in print would see her as a symbol of the forces that had starved and exploited them for centuries.

6

The extension of Scott's interest in India may be seen in the shift from an itinerary that he planned in December 1960 to the one that he booked in 1964. On the earlier occasion he talked with Donald McLachlan, editor of the *Sunday Telegraph*, who was thinking of commissioning some articles on India. Scott proposed visiting East and West Pakistan as well as India. He would fly to Rawalpindi, possibly stop at Lahore en route to Calcutta by rail, and visit Ranchi, Comilla and Chittagong, and then Dass in his South Indian village. It would be very much a return to wartime haunts. He would follow up his interest in Eurasians, explore middle-class social life and the post-partition refugee camps. Nothing came of this.

As he began planning the 1964 visit he told Gant that he would 'be much more interested in the European and American people now living in India, and in the Anglo-Indians'.[38] The focus was shifting to the British–Indian relationship. He dropped the East and West Pakistan visits, partly from his growing distaste for military dictatorship. But: 'Apart from the principle involved there was I think also a feeling that Pakistan was so much of an English creation that to be there would burden me with guilt.'[39] He wanted to meet Indians and recover his sense of visual reality. He wrote to Godfrey Smith, who agreed to his using the magic password 'Sunday Times' if he needed it: 'After nearly eighteen years of anticipating a return to India . . . perhaps it will all turn out to be what the Indians call *maya*.'[40]

Scott planned his trip to include towns he had never seen: Benares, Lucknow, Agra and Kanpur in the UP; Jaipur in Rajasthan; Madras and Hyderabad as well as Dass's village in the south. He would revisit Bombay, Calcutta and Delhi. He

wished to stay with Indian families rather than in hotels, to
be modest in the towns and simple in the country. He sought
help with accommodation from Prem Manaktala, Managing
Director of Allied Publishers, distributors of his books in India.
Manaktala arranged for him to be the house guest of Indians in
most cities. Only for a few days in Hyderabad did he stay in
a hotel.

7

Scott landed at Santa Cruz Airport, Bombay, on Tuesday 25 February 1964. He once described the experience of such arrivals.

> It is 5 a.m., still dark; the air is warm, thick. Inside, the
> ceiling fans create draughts that flirt with the hems of
> sarees and cotton shirts. . . . The road from Santa Cruz
> into Bombay passes through a crossways settlement of
> such pestilential filth and squalor that to close the eyes is
> not enough. The mind has to be switched off too.[41]

With Mr Manaktala he reached the flat of Mrs Dorothy Ganapathy, Greenfields, Queen's Court, Queen's Road, at 8 a.m.,
encumbered by his superfluous London topcoat. At midnight
he jotted down his first impressions after the long 'magical'
flight.[42] The shock of India, once outside the airport, was
considerable, 'such an immediate impression of poverty'. In
contrast Mrs Ganapathy's flat was 'wholly delightful', with a
view across a maidan or oval (a racecourse in the nineteenth
century) to the Natural History Museum, the High Court and
the University. After dinner he discussed Indian politics with
Mrs Ganapathy and her young male guest. Mrs Ganapathy was
proudly nationalistic in outlook. His recorded thoughts recall his
review of Kusum Nair's *Blossoms in the Dust*:

> The more I think and read and talk about Indian political
> and social problems the more astonished I am at the old
> British attitude etc. It is difficult to put it into words, this
> sense I have of the British responsibility for the lack of
> education and social advancement. We grafted a layer of
> highly sophisticated political behaviour and thinking on
> to those other layers of poverty and want. The two are
> hopelessly antagonistic, I should think. That is why it will
> be so interesting to stay with Dass in his village.

For a week Scott enjoyed the metropolitan life of Bombay (which
he reminded himself was 'not India at all') with Mrs Ganapathy
and her cosmopolitan friends. The parties they attended were
intimate affairs of Hindus, Parsis and Indian Christians. They
discussed 'what everyone discusses there: politics, partition,
prohibition and Mr Morarji Desai'.[43]

Mrs Ganapathy was a Rajput, the widow of a distinguished
member of the Indian Medical Service who had been educated
at Edinburgh and Cambridge, and the daughter of an eminent
jurist, former Vice-Chancellor of Delhi University and founder
of Saugor University in Madhya Pradesh, Sir Hary Singh Gour.
She had been educated at the University of Durham and
the Sorbonne. Scott noted her 'especially endearing' habit of
speech: 'When you've finished your breakfast, we'll bash off
to the Bank.'[44] So, for a week, they bashed off to most places
of interest in Bombay: the hanging gardens on Malabar Hill
where he noticed steps into the hidden Towers of Silence, the
Elephanta Caves and Rock Temples, with 'remarkable peace on
the face of Siva'; Thacker's Bookshop, the Secretariat, the Taj
Mahal Hotel, Breach Candy Swimming Club, Juhu Beach, Milk
Colony; on Holi, the spring festival, an outdoor performance of
Uncle Vanya in English; a Hindu wedding feast at the Princess
Victoria. He was struck by the contrasts of sophisticated Indian
society, Elephanta in the morning and Chekhov at night, 'Have
the other half' in a land of prohibition, and the sights and sounds
about him, ashok trees in Queen's Road, flame of the forest trees,
coconut palms, kite-hawks and crows everywhere.

Scott's most profound reaction was of disgust at the racial
exclusiveness of British residents, 'the sad scene of modern
Anglo-Indian relations'.[45] Until his first weekend in India, Scott
recalled, he 'was cushioned from the shock of India by the
euphoria of just being back there, a state that was encouraged
by the kindness of my hostess'. When Mrs Ganapathy asked him
on the Saturday if there were anything he particularly wanted
to see, he replied:

It would be interesting for me to see some English. She
looked at her watch. It was mid-day. 'That will be rather
difficult right now,' she said. 'They'll all be in the permit
rooms' (. . . the licensed equivalent of an American speak-
easy, in the days of prohibition. All leading hotels have

permit-rooms, and depressing places they are.) However, my hostess said we would see some English next day because we were going to Juhu and it was a Sunday.

We went to Juhu and yes, there they were – the new race of sahibs and memsahibs – rather noisily segregated at one end of the hotel lounge.[46]

Of Breach Candy Swimming Club with its racial pickets, Scott wrote that Sunday night:

Let a club be as selective as its Secretary and Committee care to be, in regard to membership, but what price a club on Indian soil when members may not take an Indian guest simply because he is an Indian? Breach Candy Swimming Club. Personally, were I a member, I could not even take there as a guest H.H. The Maharajah of Bharatpur whose guest I shall probably be near Agra.[47]

An afternoon visit to an English friend of Mrs Ganapathy's who had stayed on in India was ruined by the 'studied insolence' of his two other guests, English memsahibs who 'let me know, subtly, that if I came with Indians I was on the other side of the fence'.[48] They spoke to Scott but not to the Indians, avoided being introduced to them, and feigned deafness when one of them spoke. Scott recalled:

. . . I was very angry. There were now supposed to be far more English in India than in the days of the *raj*, most of them out there on business, or as visiting experts on contract. The official picture was one of a free-mixing society, but the impression I was forming and presently formed was that apart from those whose duties were of an ambassadorial nature, the rest, as in the old days, pretty much kept themselves to themselves.[49]

He left Bombay for Madras on Thursday 3 March.

8

In Madras Scott stayed for a week with Mr Manaktala's sister, Mrs P.L. Kumar, and her husband. A meeting with an English businessman who had been in South India for forty years prompted the reflection:

Funny how the English even abroad keep up that awful skin of reserve. You can feel them judging your social background, probing for it, and being careful not to be too friendly in case they come to the wrong conclusion. And who knows – you *might* be an Anglo-Indian.[50]

He met a young Brahmin engineer, an executive with English Electric, and pressed him about how he got on with his English colleagues:

They are all right when they first come out, he said, but in six months they are spoiled, because the others have got at them.
    I stared, because what he had said came straight out of E.M. Forster. He thought my stare one of disbelief. He said, 'Lunch with me at the executive canteen tomorrow and judge for yourself.' I did so. He was right. The English executives sat at the top end of the table, the Indians at the bottom. The food was European style and quite uneatable. There was chaff, an illusion of free intercourse; but I had studied the English face in India long enough to recognize when a smile was not a smile, and a calm expression a mask to hide the feeling that one must protect oneself at all costs from being taken advantage of. And it was here that I detected another thing. Because I was with an Indian I was treated by the other English with a special kind of reserve. Their faces said, 'You've gone over. You'll be sorry.'[51]

Scott visited the Harrods of the Carnatic, Spencers, to do some shopping:

To the English, India is an enervating place: you have only to look at the young matrons in the air-conditioned coffee room of Spencers in Madras, wives of technicians from Stevenage and Luton who seem a bit lost without their prams and cardigans, to know that they wish their husbands' contracts would end soon. *They* are in a state of deep cultural shock. They do not look at the bearers when giving their orders or paying their bills; they hardly look at one another. They are glazed.
    When I first saw them I laughed, thought them pretentious little girls trying to act like memsahibs. When I saw them again two weeks later I didn't laugh. I knew that by not looking at the servants they betrayed what else it

was they were trying not to see; the poverty outside, the squalor, the filth, the whole shocking ambience of India encountered for the first time by a woman who not long ago was comfortably chatting to her friends in a new town supermarket. It was an India for which they did not feel an ounce of responsibility. The empire died almost before they were born.[52]

On his last day in Madras he met Monica Felton, who had written novels for which he had been her agent. She had been living in India for some years and had written a book on the only Indian ever to serve as Governor-General (1948–50), the nationalist leader C.R. Rajagopalachari. Scott was to be her obituarist for *The Times*.

9

Scott now took the train from Madras to Eluru, and then a bus to the village of Timmapuram, twenty-two miles away in Andhra, where he was to spend a fortnight with Dass. M.M. Kaye had warned him that that would, at a guess, be two weeks too long but Scott wanted 'a bit of rustication'.[53] He had been taken with Dass's description of his four-roomed house, with separate kitchen, eight electric lights including a large fluorescent tube, cane chairs, easy chairs and a German radio. 'There are very big trees in my village. We have table electric fans in my home. When you come to my home we will both go to the next village in a double bullock cart; when the bullock cart is going – garland of brass bells to necks of the bulls which will give sweet sound.'[54] Scott would return to his village experience for years afterwards. It was critical to his development as a novelist.

Of the many accounts that he gave of the experience two are especially poignant. First, in a 1967 lecture he emphasised the contribution of the visit to his understanding of Anglo-Indian attitudes:

I stayed for ten days in somewhat primitive conditions in a village. By primitive, I mean there was no formal arrangement for what polite people call one's morning duties, but I call going to the loo. It was a comic, fascinating, highly emotional experience, and taught me a lot about the European's fear of black countries. It was a severe strain

on my civilized liberal instincts. Towards the end of my
stay I found myself shouting. Lizards popped out of my
dressing-gown pocket. The daughter of the house washed
my feet every time I entered the compound of the hut.
The smell of breakfast cooked in clarified butter turned
my stomach. Three or four times a day I was forced to
walk, water-jug in hand because toilet paper would have
offended the sensibilities of my hosts, to that distant bourne
of an open field from which I felt this traveller one day would
certainly not return. I accompanied my host in the dark to
a village where illicit liquor was distilled, because my gin
had run out. I attended a cock-fight. I did puja to the Lord
Venkateswara – a manifestation of Vishnu the preserver
– in the local temple, and drank during the course of it
what, from its bitter taste, I suspected to be cow's urine.
I was made to eat alone. I was watched everywhere. I slept
under the stars, nudged awake by restless warm-breathed
cattle. I was shaved each morning without soap – my soap
might have been made, they thought, from the fat of a dead
animal. The barber shaved my face with a cut-throat and
water – forehead, cheeks, chin, eyelids. I smiled and was
in terror of being blinded by a slip of his hand. While I was
shaved a group of men sat and watched the extraordinary
sight of a white man getting rid of his bristles. One felt
like a cross between Sanders of the River and the King
of Siam. Sometimes a bus passed through that village and
sometimes my host took me for a ride in it. A chair would be
brought out of the house, placed by the roadside and I would
be made to sit on it. To wait at a bus-stop on a kitchen chair
gives you a curious sense of your own unlikelihood. . . .

What had happened really was that I had added to my
knowledge – not just of the customs, the manners and the
artefacts of an alien culture – *but of the terrible dependence
we have on our own familiar way of doing things if we are
to spare thought and expend kindness on people apparently
different from ourselves*. I understood better therefore the
physical and emotional impulses that had always prompted
the British in India to sequester themselves in clubs and
messes and forts, to preserve, sometimes to the point of
absurdity, their own English middle-class way of life. It
was a simple enough lesson. One could learn it from books.
It is better for a writer to learn lessons from life.[55]

Secondly, in 1969 he spoke of the experience as inflicting the sort
of cultural shock that helped to explain racialism. He described

the eyes of an observant population following him as his internal miseries required frequent visits to an ancient privy.

I made that journey many times a day, with increasing hate in my heart. The hatred sprang from fear. I was afraid of becoming desperately ill, of never getting away, of dying in this dreadful place where I was treated like an animal. The fear became irrational. *Was* I being treated like a king? Wasn't I a *prisoner*? Was the indignity I was being subjected to a payment back for some real or imaginary wrong I'd done this man when I was in a position of authority over him? Why hadn't I met his wife yet? Surely *that* was a clear sign that he didn't look upon me as a friend: I became deeply suspicious of him and of the whole set-up.

I became reluctant to go out. I wrote letters. I read old letters over and over again. I became emotionally attached to my own luggage, as though it were a fetish. Everything that reminded me I was English became precious. And gradually I felt a Sahib's face superimpose itself on my own – as I thought – mild and liberal one. I did not merely accept the chairs of honour, I expected them. When crossed in a desire I began to raise my voice, began to give him a hard time.

And yet you see, every day there was a fresh flower on the table, at every meal, every day some mark of affectionate curiosity in this extraordinary stranger. Every day six children trooped into the room to be helped with their English. I was aware of all this, but it began to mean *nothing* to me. I longed to see another white face, and to get back into my own white skin. And I thought I never would.

On the tenth day, on parting, his wife made her appearance. I thanked her for her kindness and hospitality. She said nothing, looked down at her feet, and I cursed the humility of this Indian woman, knowing that behind locked doors she ruled the roost and would probably have the whole house fumigated after I'd gone.[56]

Scott left the village early on a pretence of having lectures to give in Madras. He had an uncomfortable overnight train journey to Hyderabad:

I arrived in Hyderabad next morning, still stunned and vicious. I knocked the hand of a beggar woman off my

arm, gave the tonga wallah less than he asked for, ignored
his protests and stalked into the Ritz Palace, called for
beer and complained about the price. And then sat down in
the blessed privacy of a civilized bedroom, with bathroom
attached – blessed, blessed bathroom with all mod cons.

My relief is indescribable. But already in that relief there
was the shadow of something that appalled me – the growing
shadow of my ingratitude, my ridiculous irrational fears,
my utter dependence upon the amenities of my own kind of
civilization. But the sense of relief was enough to keep the
shadow at bay, for a while.[57]

Scott was at the Hyderabad Ritz for four days and then returned
to Madras for a further three. He stayed with an Indian called
Srinivasan, who was still adjusting to India after four years in
Liverpool.

10

Scott was met at Calcutta airport at midnight on Good Friday
(28 March) by his first Calcutta host, Neil Ghosh. M.M. Kaye,
who had arranged the hospitality, wrote of him:

Lovely bit of copy I think, poor Neil. A man without a
country if ever there was one. His family obviously never
visualised the Raj passing out in his day, and thought that
if he was turned into an imitation Englishman he would
rise to great heights in British India. Instead of which he
is left stranded, black as your hat, speaking impeccable
BBC English and rotten bad Urdu (and probably worse
Bengali!) stranded with a foot in the two countries and at
home in neither.[58]

He worked for Bird and Co., a century-old managing-agency
house with large interests in jute and coal. His rather large and
husky Australian girlfriend, Caroline Davies, became in Scott's
mind 'The Temporary Memsahib'. He told Scott his life story in
the early hours of their first meeting. A few months later he
wrote to him of being 'thoroughly browned off with conditions
here'.[59] He would leave at once if he could find a suitable job in
an overseas country that would give him citizenship, and then
return to India after a few years.

Scott was due to spend only three days in Calcutta, and then

visit Lucknow, Kanpur, Benares, Delhi and Agra and stay with
the Maharaja of Bharatpur in his palace (another of M.M.
Kaye's arrangements). However, when misinformation about
his flight time caused him to miss his plane he decided to
stay on in Calcutta. Early in his tour he had begun to miss
'headquarters' and ponder cancelling the essentially touristic
visits to the UP cities except Agra. The Maharaja had put off the
visit to Bharatpur beyond the date he found convenient. Bodily
ailments were also accumulating. He was suffering sciatic pain
in his right leg and dysentery. And in Calcutta a cyclist ran over
his foot. He was content to remain in Calcutta for a further ten
days, as the guest of Dr B.D. Nag Chaudhuri, a Nobel prize-
winning physicist, and his wife, Dipali Nag, a prominent singer
and teacher, at their house in Behala, seven miles south of the
city centre. There he spent the 'nicest' part of his tour, before
flying home a week early.

11

The 1964 visit amply served the intended purpose of recharging
Scott's batteries. After six months he reflected, 'as I look back
on it I realize just how much material I must have got stored
up'.[60] He left Calcutta 'with all I needed to begin the quartet'.[61]
He first looked for the basis of a novel in his village experience.
Even while he was in Timmapuram he began making notes for a
short novel, 'The Mango Rain'. The title was vaguely symbolic.
He had heard that in the south there was an out-of-season rain
that ripened the fruit and refreshed the spirit. He had in mind
the fruit of human love that crossed the barrier between castes,
creeds and races. But though he continued to ponder the theme
as he moved about India and in London opened a notebook on 20
April with the title 'Abstracts and Brief Chronicles: The Mango
Rain', he was too involved personally to detach himself from the
experience to give his creative imagination a fair field.[62]

Later in the year he projected a book of three or four short
stories, for two of which he had firm titles: 'The Mango Rain'
and 'A Slight Case of Cultural Shock'.[63] He first heard the
term 'cultural shock' from a Canadian woman whom he met in
Hyderabad when he was recovering from his village experience.
He was distressed by the woman's belief that friendship with
Indians was impossible because 'there was always a price

attached', an expectation of favours.[64] The plot of the 'Cultural Shock' story was to exemplify in extreme form the white person's racial exclusiveness. It was to be about

> an English woman joining her husband in Bombay where he had been settling down in a new job. Bombay appals her. We see her in relation to (a) her husband who *has* to mix (b) her old girl friend, now a memsahib of several years' standing (c) an Indian colleague of her husband whom they knew in England and (d) the Indian girl she thinks her husband has had an affair with. When she finds out that her husband really had an affair with her old girl friend she says to her, after a moment's careful consideration – 'Thank God'.[65]

The project never came to anything.

As Scott was packing to leave Madras for Timmapuram he had pinched his sciatic nerve and so hobbled about for the last few weeks of his visit, unable to walk a hundred yards. In Calcutta he was x-rayed by an Austrian doctor who diagnosed lumbarsacral diathrodal, a warping of the base of the spine, and prescribed drugs. It was now clear, too, that he suffered amoebiasis, and that it was the cause of maladies that had afflicted him occasionally since 1943. In mid-1964 it was cured by a doctor in Paris. Illness entered into his diagnosis of race relations: 'In India everyone feels slightly ill all the time. This makes them introspective and short tempered with people who obtrude upon their privacy (i.e. everyone else in sight). Things are better by evening. To begin with it is cooler. But alcohol has worked wonders by then.'[66] He asked himself, too, 'would things be better socially if there were no prohibition?'[67]

Scott had, above all, been appalled by race relations in India. He wrote to John Willey: 'What a gang of horrors the English in India still are. Only Emmerson, the literary editor of the *Statesman* (the Calcutta daily) struck me as civilized. He is married to an Indian woman.'[68] Indeed relations seemed worse than under the Raj: 'What I find so horrifying is that in India today, among the new race of Sahibs and Memsahibs (experts and advisers) the same attitude prevails, but is more explicitly grounded on colour difference.'[69] Anglo-India was 'still alive and well and living in India'.[70]

3

The Daphne Manners Case

1

The springs of *The Jewel in the Crown*, the opening novel of the *Quartet*, were Scott's wartime Indian experiences, his reading in the early 1960s, and especially the return visit of February – April 1964. His 1967 lecture to a Writers' Summer School, 'Method: The Mystery and the Mechanics', told of the book's origins. As with *Birds of Paradise* he began with an image. It came to him unexpectedly, in the dark of a restless, sleepless night in May 1964. He could trace its antecedents as the trauma of Timmapuram, 'the desire to get away, to run, the knowledge of the dangers that exist when you try to cross bridges, the whole feeling of the British in India, and the feeling of India itself – a vast, flat territory, strangely forbidding, somehow incalculable, ugly, beautiful. And there she was, my prime mystery, a girl, in the dark, running, exhausted, hurt in some way, yet strangely of good heart – tough, resilient, her face and figure a sense rather than an observed condition.'[1] He described his method as bombarding the image with knowledge, experience and imagination, hoping for a beautiful explosion.

As Scott bombarded his image of the running girl with his recent experience, Neil Ghosh's rather large Australian girlfriend came to mind. His imagination fined her down until Daphne Manners was born, tall and gangling, clumsy and shortsighted. Ghosh, a short and squat man, now grew in physical stature and attractiveness to become Hari Kumar. At their first meeting Ghosh 'talked to me in his flat till 4 a.m. about his past; and that's when Hari was born'.[2] Their relation suggested the theme of a love affair that bridged the racial divide.

The image of Daphne running became established in the context of Scott's amateur study of the later Raj. His village experience had already been translated into a symbolic confrontation between East and West:

The last great confrontation between East and West in India was in 1942. At least it was in my opinion. By that year, the Indian Congress – still motivated by the distrust of British intentions which was sown in 1919, and torn between the worldly anti-Hitler attitude of Nehru and the unworldly anti-violence attitude of Gandhi – had come out on Gandhi's side, to resist all forms of external control. Here there was an extremely interesting human and political situation. The nation that in 1940 and 1941 had stood virtually alone in its resistance to totalitarianism in Europe – depended in the East upon the stability of a country towards which it had always adopted a somewhat totalitarian attitude of its own.[3]

In 1943 Scott had, at OTS Belgaum, felt the resentment of Indians at the ruthless suppression of Gandhi's Quit India movement. His last six months in India were spent in Bihar, the province most affected by the movement.

For Scott the 1942 confrontation encapsulated themes central to the last generation of the Raj. In large measure it was a re-run of events during and after the First World War. In 1917, to maintain Indian co-operation with the war effort, Britain's Secretary of State for India had promised India eventual self-government. But with the war won the Raj extended, through the infamous Rowlatt Acts, wartime powers enjoyed under the Defence of the Realm Act. The Mahatma's first all-India satyagraha was, as those who have seen Richard Attenborough's film *Gandhi* will always remember, most brutally crushed at Amritsar in April 1919. Under the command of Brigadier Reginald Dyer, British troops fired on a peaceful gathering of protesters in Jallianwala Bagh, an enclosed open space. Some 379 Indians were killed and 1200 injured in the massacre. Dyer was cashiered but he was a hero to many in the British services who believed that he had forestalled a rebellion.

The 1942 counterpart to the 1917 promise of self-government was Sir Stafford Cripps's March mission to seek the collaboration of Gandhi's Congress and Jinnah's rival Muslim League in the war against Japan. Cripps promised post-war Dominion status but too little advance meanwhile. In Scott's view the mission was bound to fail.

The Indians said Churchill wanted it to. He had already

said in the House of Commons that the liberties envisaged in the Atlantic Charter did not apply to India. [Cripps] had nothing to offer except a plan for measures of self-government after the war. . . . The Indian Congress did not see it as for the best . . . and began to hammer out a policy – Gandhi's policy. . . . It was a declaration of war on the British – non-violent war – an ultimatum that unless self-government was granted immediately the Congress would lead the nation in a mass civil disobedience that would make India untenable as a military base. The railways would stop, the docks would close, the war factories would come to a standstill. That was the resolution. On 8 August the All-India Congress Committee adopted the resolution in Bombay.[4]

Early next morning the Congress leaders were arrested and on 10 August the Quit India movement began. Against this background of East–West confrontation there might well be a white girl running in the darkness. Scott's bombardment of his image with historical facts had consolidated the time, place and circumstance for a novel.

Scott now consciously compared Daphne and her context with that of an English mission school superintendent during the Amritsar disturbances of 1919. He had recently obtained Rupert Furneaux's book, *Massacre at Amritsar* (1963), which described the assault on Marcella Sherwood. Whilst she was bicycling to one of her schools she was intercepted by a mob in the Kucha Kurianwala, a narrow lane, and dragged to the ground. She picked herself up and ran off to a house where the door was slammed in her face. She was beaten with sticks and stones and left in the street. Dyer gave orders for a triangle to be erected where she had fallen and for six youths whom he suspected of the offence to be flogged there, though they had been neither charged nor convicted. He had known them only in connection with their recent breach of discipline while they were in custody.

Of course Daphne Manners was no missionary, and Scott now began to invent a mission teacher for his novel, investing her with qualities complementary to those that he had already ascribed to Daphne – a capacity for love, stubbornness and endurance. Scott's mission school superintendent, Edwina Crane, was a

conscious creation. She was an elderly liberal, whom he first
envisioned taking down Gandhi's portrait from her wall in 1942,
and replacing it with an old engraving of Queen Victoria receiving tribute from her subjects in India. The picture was called *The
Jewel in Her Crown*. The emergence of Miss Crane, with her good
intentions, liberal instincts, and emotional inability to cross the
East-West divide, enabled the novel to 'begin *behind* the image
of a girl who *had* crossed the bridge between East and West'.[5] The
novel does begin with Miss Crane's story, that of an essentially
Victorian governess turned school teacher who is stopped on a
lonely road by a gang. The Indian teacher accompanying her is
dragged from her car and killed. She is found holding his hand
and abstracted, dismayed at her own inability to save him. The
contrast with Daphne is laid down – the Englishwoman who,
'falling in love with an Indian, attempted to associate with him
simply as a human being'.[6] She is the measure of the limitations
of liberal principles. She is running to protect her association
with Hari against the Raj's processes of intervention.

2

At about this point in his imagining, in May 1964, Scott jotted
down: 'The use of the assumed rape of Daphne Manners to
explode pent-up fear. But is that too like the business of the
caves in Forster. And yet it happened in Jallianwala Bagh in
1920. Was this also what Forster was using? I hope not.'[7] Also:
'Daphne Manners ideal subject for rape. Friendly, unspoiled.
But rape by whom?' These were preliminary doodlings. Scott
recalled that he made 'the *first* note re the novel that I wrote'
on a postcard that he picked up in his favourite restaurant,
L'Épicure, 28 Frith Street, Soho.

> Daphne Manners was a cause célèbre. This should be built
> up into a tremendously well documented inner story, which
> can illustrate the whole of the British Indian affair. Forget
> the fact that it never happened. Imagine that it really
> shook the govt., for a second or two and was then forgot-
> ten – so that there is an illusion of authenticity, especially
> post-Dyer?[8]

Scott pinned the card to his notebook but years later noted that it 'should really be pinned to the first holograph MS book' above the heading '29 June 1964: A History as Prologue', Miss Crane's story.

The previous day he had entered in his notebook: 'Risk all. The Indian novel I ought by now to be able to write. A complex of narratives. The narratives must illustrate the theme and not be (for the sake of it) discursive. Loosely, the theme is to do with what I call the English/Indian love affair.' The form of the novel would thus be 'that of *approach*, through different eyes, through different histories, from different vantage points of time, to a central point of reference, which is exemplified in the original image' of Daphne running.[9] 'And how should the novel be narrated? By, for instance, a personification of the writer returning to India perhaps with amoebiasis.'[10] The central situation of the novel begins to appear once Miss Crane's story is told. Scott as the Stranger or the Traveller is the vestigial narrator, visiting Mayapore in 1964 to discover the truth about the alleged rape of Daphne Manners in 1942. He receives testimony from survivors who recall the events. There are two third-person narratives, Miss Crane's story and that of Hari Kumar. Three characters speak of their recollections to the narrator – Lady (Lili) Chatterjee, with whom Daphne Manners was staying; Sister Ludmila, now blind, who ran a refuge; and Robin White, Deputy Commissioner for the District. A statement or deposition is taken from a young Indian arrested for subversion. The narrator describes an evening at the club in 1964. There is a journal kept by Daphne, which tells the truth about the night of the rape. Perspective is provided by some letters that Lady Manners, Daphne's aunt, wrote to Lady Chatterjee some years later.

3

The Stranger's initial interest in the case has been aroused by an extract from the unpublished memoirs of Brigadier A.V. Reid, who was responsible for controlling the Mayapore riots once the civil authorities had appealed for military aid. Reid was consciously patterned on Dyer, with his name spelled backwards. His motivation is important: 'Never led troops in action during either war, seen a bit of fighting in NWFP but missed the great war and sees himself missing this one. At back of his mind was

probably a mistaken idea that a strong show of force on this
small scale but dangerous situation would lead the generals to
think they had misjudged his abilities.'[11] He thought the Deputy
Commissioner had been 'tarred by the brush of over familiarity
with civilian Indians'.

The character of Reid resembles that of the authors of the
military memoirs that Scott had read for publishers and exco-
riated in 1960–2. 'I loathe the type,' he confided to Roland Gant.
'But I tried to get into his skin.'[12] The reader must be able to see
'the enemy in action, if enemy isn't too strong a word'.[13] With
Reid Scott returns to the theme of illusion that he had sounded in
Birds of Paradise and implies with the name 'Mayapore', town
of illusion. Reid is 'committed to British administrative illusion
of India as somewhere curious and beautiful'.[14] He recalled
Mayapore as 'a delightful station', whereas Kumar sees its
reality and hates it.[15] The illusion blocks perception so that
Kumar's colour renders him invisible to Reid and his type.

It is clear that the main Indian bridge between East and West
in *Jewel*, the cosmopolitan Lady Chatterjee, was Scott's first
Indian hostess. 'To her a lot is owed,' Scott told John Willey,
and the novel is dedicated 'to Dorothy Ganapathy with love'.[16]
Years later he told some American students, 'I wrote a book
about her because she deserved it.'[17] He knew Mrs Ganapathy
for a Rajput and gave that identity to Lady Chatterjee, thereby
falling into the error of her Bengali Brahmin name. He borrowed the name of Lady Chatterjee's husband, Sir Nello, from
a close friend of Mrs Ganapathy's, Nello Muckerjee. In his
typescript he named Kumar's aunt and Daphne's daughter
after Mrs Ganapathy's nieces, but when he discerned her dis-
pleasure he substituted 'Shalini' and 'Parvati' for them. Of
other female characters Sister Ludmila was inspired by the
idea of Mother Theresa, though he very deliberately rebuffed
Caroline Davies's attempt to introduce him to her. He did not
want the reality of Mother Theresa to distract him from his own
creation: 'Sister Ludmila (like the Sister Theresa I heard of in
Calcutta but never met – because from my point of view she is
a character in a novel, not a real person) has seen that the *most*
the human being can do is to help others die with dignity.'[18] With
these exceptions the characters in *Jewel* are imaginary. The
knowledge and experience with which Scott began his saga in

mid-1964 must needs be supplemented by imaginative construc-
tions, as well as by further research. Robin White, the Deputy
Commissioner, represents the reforming aspect of the ICS, and
broadens the administrative context in which the rape and the
rebellion occurred. Ronald Merrick, Deputy Superintendent of
Police, was explicitly linked with Dyerism, or rule by superior
force, through his Christian name: 'Ronald means the same as
Rex or Reginald. It means someone with power who rules.'[19]

The type of White is opposed to the type of Reid, the Liberal
and the Imperialist. Scott quoted the following recollection of
Reid's to illustrate his attitude:

> When I looked out on to the *maidan* from the window of my
> room in the old artillery mess in Mayapore, or drove round
> the cantonment, I could not help but feel proud of the years
> of British rule. Even in these turbulent times the charm of
> the cantonment helped one to bear in mind the calm, wise
> and enduring things. One had only to cross the river into
> the native town to see that in our cantonments and civil
> lines we had set an example for others to follow and laid
> down a design for civilised life that the Indians would one
> day inherit. It seemed odd to think that in the battle that
> lay ahead to stop all this from falling into the hands of the
> Japanese the Indians were not on our side.[20]

He contrasted this with White's recollection of the moment he
fell in love with India, during a tour of a district with a land
settlement officer:

> My bowels were in a terrible state and I couldn't face any-
> thing, let alone toddy. I was lying on a charpoy, without a
> mosquito net, and suddenly saw this middle-aged Indian
> woman standing in the doorway watching me. When our
> eyes met she made *namaste* and then disappeared for
> a moment, and came back with a bowl of curds and a
> spoon.
> I was on my dignity at once, and waved her away, but
> she came to the bedside and spooned up a helping of the
> curds and held it out and made me eat, just as if I were
> her nephew or son and needed building up. She said nothing
> and I couldn't even look at her – only at her black hands and
> the white curds. Afterwards I fell asleep and when I woke

up I felt better and wondered whether I hadn't dreamed it all, until I saw the bowl of unfinished curds covered with a cloth, on a brass tray by the bedside and a flower on the tray next to the bowl. It was morning then, and the settlement officer was snoring in the other bed. I felt that I had been given back my humanity, by a nondescript middle-aged Indian woman. I felt that the curds and the flowers were for affection, not tribute, affection big enough to include a dash of well-meant motherly criticism, the suggestion that my indisposition could be overcome easily enough once I'd learned I had no real enemies. I remember standing in the open doorway and breathing in deeply; and getting it: the scent behind the smell. They had brass pots of hot water ready for my bathe. Before the bathe I was sat down on an old wooden chair and shaved by the *nai*, the barber, without soap, just his fingers and warm water and a cut-throat. He scraped the razor all over my face and forehead, even over the eyelids. I held my breath waiting for the cut that would blind me. But it was all gentle and efficient, a kind of early morning *puja*, and afterwards my face felt newly made and I went to the bathing enclosure and scooped water out of the brass pots of hot water that stood waiting. Brooke had the right word for it. The benison of hot water. Later I looked among the women but couldn't tell which of them had come into the hut the night before and fed me as she would have fed her own son. There was another flower on the pommel of my saddle. It embarrassed me. But I loved it too. I looked at the settlement officer. He had no flower and hadn't noticed mine. As we rode away I looked back, and waved. The people made no move in reply, but I felt it coming from them – the good wish, the challenge to do well by them and by myself. I've never forgotten that.[21]

Scott confessed to using White 'as something of a mouthpiece for my own political and historical ideas'.[22] One such idea was that practice in India, say political reform, fell far short of policy intentions in London. He wrote privately, 'My views are closer to his than to Reid's. If I had been White's age, in that year, I might have thought and spoken like this.'[23] As it was, he felt 'a certain detachment'. White was 'as much concerned with his "role" as he thought Reid was concerned with his', and felt 'a certain degree of self-conscious liberal goodness'.[24] Both were working under a moral code in 'the place where, most notably, the British came to the end of themselves as they were, the Liberals as well as the Imperialists'.[25]

4

In early June 1964 Scott began research for the novel that was to become *Jewel*. He wrote to the India Office Library in King Charles Street to inquire about materials on the Indian Civil Service, and that month studied several books on the subject there. They enabled him to draw up an organisation chart for the civil administrative structure for his District of Mayapore, of which he also drew a sketch plan.[26] He needed frequent access to one of them, Sir Edward Blunt's *The I.C.S.* (1937), and managed to borrow a copy from Charles Monteith of Faber and Faber, to whom he wrote in mid-August: 'It's the only book I've so far come across that gives a reasonably detailed picture of the organization and administration of a District of British India – and the period (late thirties) is just right for me. Philip Woodruff is good on the overall picture but not on the routine one.'[27] The same day he wrote to M.M. Kaye that he was 'having to do all kinds of research into things like Missions and civil administration and now military'.[28]

He had just inquired of the Secretary of the Church of England Zenana Missionary Society about publications on missions in India in the late 1930s and early 1940s. He was seeking 'a fairly detailed picture of the organisation and administration of mission schools', especially in a district of British India: 'their educational scope, recruitment of teachers etc, and – especially – the duties of what I think was called the district superintendent'.[29] No reply nor evidence of further inquiry is available. The name that he gave to the mission to which Miss Crane belonged was fictitious, 'Bishop Barnard'. If he was dredging his memories of wartime Ranchi he probably knew that four miles away at Namkam there were Bishop Westcott schools for boys and girls. As for other matters, Scott probably obtained relevant sources through the help of Mikes Zambakides of the Golders Green Road branch of the Hendon Public Library.

Scott's main source of information on the military was M.M. Kaye's husband, Major-General G.J. ('Goff') Hamilton. He had been an officer in the famous Queen Victoria's Own Corps of Guides but left it to command the 7/16th Punjabis in Burma.

In 1964 he was serving in Bonn/Cologne as Chief of the Joint
Services Liaison Organisation, British Army of the Rhine. M.M.
Kaye recalls:

> I think that what Paul liked about me was the fact that
> I had actually seen the real 'Raj': had lived in its hey-
> day, and belonged to a family who had served India for
> several successive generations – an 'India' family, one of
> whose members had written *A History of the Afghan War*
> (the first Afghan War) and a contemporary history of the
> Indian Mutiny. He was never tired of hearing stories about
> it: my own reminiscences as a small child, as a young
> woman, and as the wife of an officer in the famous 'Corps
> of Guides'. . . .
>   Paul used to apply to my husband, Goff, for help over
> military details, and in the copy he sent us of *The Jewel
> in the Crown* he wrote 'with grateful thanks for their help;
> and their encouragement of someone who knows India less
> intimately than they do; and in the hope that they will rec-
> ognize, affectionately, in this book, *their* India too'.[30]

In August 1964 Scott sought their help over his imaginary civil
and military cantonment, Mayapore, which was also the district headquarters. He had defined the roles of the Deputy
Commissioner, District Superintendent of Police and District
and Sessions Judge and posited the presence of a few British
and Indian units and possibly a training depot or holding battalion. Would the Station Commander be responsible for troop
administration and as the senior military officer be the man
to whom the Deputy Commissioner would apply for military
aid to the civil power? Scott wanted him to be a full colonel,
or higher, and responsible for the conduct of the troops called
out in aid. And what staff would he have? The character of his
colonel was clear but not the authenticity of his role. 'This is
only for background details but I do want to get them as right
as possible.' Drawing on his experience of Kohat and Sialkot,
Hamilton advised:

> I think the best plan is to put a Brigade into Mayapore.
> Commanded of course by a Brigadier with a Brigade Major
> and Staff Captain. He would of course also exercise com-
> mand of all other units in Mayapore in his secondary role

of Station Commander. If you had a Depot of some sort it could be commanded by a full Colonel who would of course be junior to the Brigadier.[31]

Thus Reid emerged as the Brigade Commander, responsible for security.

Scott's next problem with a novel that was taking shape as a detailed panorama of the 1942 civil disturbances in a district was 'getting right the details and drill of co-operation between the civil and the military'.[32] Hamilton tried without success to get him a copy of the Indian Army Training Pamphlet, *Duties in Aid of the Civil Power*, which described the stages to be taken by magistrates and the military at times of civil disturbances, though he was probably the general who gave him 'a private look at some up-to-date stuff on similar lines'. That had to suffice. The India Office Library advised Scott that the pamphlet was closed until the 1990s under the 'fifty-year rule' and other military connections failed to turn up a copy. The modern version refreshed his memory 'sufficiently to be able to dispense with the original pamphlet'.[33]

Scott searched in vain for studies of the Quit India movement. Luzac and Co., the Oriental booksellers opposite the British Museum, could offer him nothing but told him of a slim volume by Amba Prasad, *The Indian Revolt of 1942* (1958). As he needed an Indian account of the events this sounded like 'a godsend' and at his request Mrs Ganapathy sent him a copy by airmail. It is a careful work, for which Dr Prasad, a Reader in History at Delhi University, was awarded an MA by Stanford University. It gives accounts of the Cripps Mission and its failure; the origins and nature of the revolt; and the extent of violence on both sides. It provided a firm historical framework within which Scott might set his imagination to work. Though the details of crowd behaviour and official response are scant, they are sufficient to identify the main targets of local agitation (railways, post offices, police stations), some faces in the crowd (students and peasants), and the pattern of stern repression. However, there is nothing in the book to suggest to Scott the *éminence grise* of the Mayapore revolt, Pandit Baba. Scott created this mysterious figure to represent the more extreme Hindu nationalist element in the freedom movement. Studies written after *Jewel* validate his historical plausibility. Such a figure was a professor of chemistry at Benares Hindu University, Radhe Shyam Sharma, who roused students on the campus, escaped arrest, walked the seventy miles to Allahabad with the shaven head and saffron robes of a sadhu, and proceeded to his native Gwalior, a princely state.[34] The parallel with Baba's seeking refuge at Mirat is striking.

A further authority to whom Scott turned for help was a friend of Mrs Ganapathy's, Keith Roy, whom he had met at her flat in March 1964. Roy was Managing Director for India of Mercke, Sharpe and Dohme, an American pharmaceutical company linked with Tata. He was the son of an Englishwoman and a Bengali and had served with the ICS in Bengal and once worked with V.P. Menon in the States' Department. He gave Scott lunch at the Directors' Club in Belgrave Square in February 1965 and 'confirmed so many of the impressions I gained of India on my return visit'.[35] He was particularly helpful, too, with advice on the various legal provisions available to district authorities for the detention without trial of suspected subversives in 1942. He saved Scott from error in cases involving normal detention pursuant to Section 144 of the Criminal Procedure Code, detention in a period of emergency and under the Defence of India Rules. Scott felt that with his help he had dealt convincingly with the legal complexities, for 'although there may be some old India hands who will say, "No, he's got it wrong," there could be others who will say, "Yes, it worked like that in my district too." At least I hope so.'[36] Roy also contributed detailed advice on such matters as the surrender by Indians of imperial honours in 1942 and ecclesiastical arrangements.

5

When Scott first conceived the theme for *Jewel* he called it

> the English/Indian love affair. And what a curious love affair. In one sense India took the part of the woman, and can be said finally to have been abandoned by the lover *she* had grown tired of. Conversely place England in the situation of the woman and she becomes like an older mistress to a young man who eventually throws her off but remains faithful to her for certain useful lessons he has learnt about the art of loving and the art of life.[37]

Lady Manners, widow of a Liberal governor of the province, whom Scott describes as 'rather close to me as a character',[38] writes in such terms just after independence.

> Such a marvellous opportunity *wasted*. I mean for us, by us. Indians feel it too, don't they? I mean, in spite of the proud chests and all the excitement of sitting down as free men at their own desks to work out a constitution. Won't that constitution be a sort of love-letter to the English – the kind an abandoned lover writes when the affair has ended in what passes at the time as civilised and dignified mutual recognition of incompatibility? In a world grown suddenly dull because the beloved, thank God, has gone, offering his killing and unpredictable and selfish affections elsewhere, you attempt to recapture, don't you, the moments of significant pleasure – which may not have been mutual at all, but anyway existed. But this recapture is always impossible. You settle for the second-rate, you settle for the lesson you appear to have learned and forget the lesson you hoped to learn and might have learned, and so learn nothing at all, because the second-rate is the world's common factor, and any damn fool people can teach it, any damn fool people can inherit it.
>
> What terrifies me is the thought that gradually, when the splendours of civilised divorce and protestations of continuing as good friends are worked out, the real animus will emerge, the one both our people just managed to keep in check when there was reason to suppose that it was wrong, because it could lead neither rulers nor ruled anywhere. I mean of course the dislike and fear that exists between black and white. And this is a fifth-rate passion, appropriate only to a nation of vulgar shopkeepers and a nation of fat-bellied banias.[39]

Here was the theme of the novel, the problem of 'colour and invisibility', which 'it took me a return to India to realize was the vital one'.[40]

That realisation was heightened by events back in England, as he acknowledged in a lecture, 'Aspects of Writing', in August 1965:

> We have seen a lot in the last twenty years. . . . We have seen our voluntarily relinquished Empire disappearing into the mists of territorial fragmentation and dangerous racial

memory instead of arising into the reassuring morning of a common-wealth. We have seen, and have not forgotten, the communal massacre that attended the birth of Free India, a continent which for over 200 years was said to have enjoyed our unifying influence. We have seen the problem of colour . . . translated into a problem that might win or loss an election here at home.[41]

Scott was an active constituency worker for the Liberal Party at the October 1964 general election, putting in a twenty-one hour stint on polling day. He believed that 'behind Toryism is the old dream of master-race stuff'[42] but he was unprepared for the shame of Smethwick, the first seat to be won by a Conservative candidate on the issue of coloured immigration.

'Funny how a trip in 1964 sparks off a story set in 1942,' Scott wrote to Dorothy Ganapathy.[43] The emotional core of his trip was his village experience: 'It taught me, I think, more about the (cultural shock + fear = prejudice) equation than 20 years of liberal thought, Liberal assumptions (including 3 years of living in British India) ever did. . . . It is a salutary experience. . . .'[44] Much of the detail was incorporated in the novel: Daphne's visit to the Vaishnavite Temple and her suspicion that she had drunk cow urine; Robin White being shaved by the nai with water and razor only; Miss Crane seated on a chair by the roadside feeling like 'something in a zoo'; even the children she taught; all came from Scott's own experience at Timmapuram.[45]

By the end of *Jewel* it is clear that Scott intended Parvati to symbolise cultural integration, to be the living embodiment of the bridge between India and Britain. Daphne envisaged her baby as 'my own typically ham-fisted offering to the future'.[46] The name that he gave Parvati until the proof stage of the novel was 'Indira', whom he had wrongly thought was the goddess of rain. In his mind there remained the vague notion of a mango rain that watered the young fruit and symbolised the love that nourished relationships. The novel ends with the Stranger observing Parvati running down the steps of MacGregor House to a singing lesson with her guru. There is a 'promise of a story continuing instead of finishing'; of Parvati as 'another story, which is why her presence here is tentative'.[47] It was a promise never fulfilled.

4

Ruling Divided India

1

When Scott began *Jewel* he expected to write a sequel. *Jewel* would deal 'wholly with the Daphne Manners affair'.[1] Set in wartime India, it would be narrated through the Stranger's 1964 presentation of testimonies and reconstructions in order to elucidate the British–Indian affair. The sequel would deal with the affair 'as it is seen historically' and involve a 'repetition of earlier dramatic circumstances, e.g. a replay against the background of changed circumstances'. Scott was thinking literally of a dramatic replay of the 1942 Manners case, with Anne Poulson, 'the little daughter' of the Assistant Commissioner, playing Daphne. Here in vaguest outline was a prefiguring of the kind of re-enactment that Ruth Jhabvala employed in *Heat and Dust*, which won the Booker Prize in 1975.

However, no sooner had Scott completed *Jewel* than he disclosed other intentions to his agent in New York, Dorothy Olding of Harold Ober Associates. He now planned a sequel,

> taking the British Indian story up to Partition and Independence. There is all the Muslim thing still to be dealt with. And the Princes. I may introduce into the next novel my old Sir Robert Conway, the cold reserved father from *The Birds of Paradise* (which is why I mentioned that Ethel Manners went to live with him at the palace of Gopalakand in 1947, taking young Indira Manners with her).[2]

At the end of *Jewel* he had tried to lay the foundations for a sequel in Lady Manners's letters to Lady Chatterjee. The following passage from one dated 5 August 1947 is crucial:

> I have decided to leave 'Pindi. I refuse to live in a place

whose people at the stroke of a pen will be turned into enemies of India – the country my husband tried to serve – and you can count on it that 'enemy' isn't overstating the case. The creation of Pakistan is our crowning failure. I can't bear it. They should never have got rid of Wavell. Our only justification for two hundred years of power was unification. But we've divided one composite nation into two and everyone at home goes round saying what a swell the new Viceroy is for getting it all sorted out so quickly.[3]

Scott referred to this passage in a letter of 7 September 1965 that alludes to the opening of the India–Pakistan war the previous month: 'it is all our fault (as Lady Manners said in one of those letters to Lady Chatterjee)'.[4] Again, on 11 September he cited it in a letter to Mrs Ganapathy.

Scott opened a notebook on 8 September, 'Preliminary Notes for next novel in The Jewel in the Crown sequence':

Every aspect of this novel should be a variation on the general theme of our failure to unify. It should take into account the gradual fraction of the liberal left on the idea that India was a unity, as well as the idea, happily seized upon by the reactionary right that it never was and never could be.[5]

In his copy of Sir John Strachey's *India: Its Administration and Progress* (1888) Scott had heavily sidelined the statement 'that men of Bombay, the Punjab, Bengal, and Madras should ever feel that they belong to one great Indian nation is impossible'.[6]

The outbreak of war in the former princely state of Kashmir between the two nations carved out of Britain's Indian Empire gave point and poignancy to the project. He wrote to Mrs Ganapathy:

no one has yet traced that responsibility back to the failure of the British to consolidate and unite. No one has yet had the courage to say Divide and Rule has come full circle. At best, on the man-in-the-street side, there is a faded idea of paternalism gone wrong. I expect the Koi-Hais in

Cheltenham are talking about the Muslims of Pakistan as if they were still the favoured blue-eyed boys.[7]

He was appalled by the 'Labour paternalism' of the Wilson Government, which embargoed arms sales to India. Labour deluded itself that it had 'freed' India, whereas it had 'allowed Independence for its own political ends'. Now,

> They obviously imagine they are in a paternalistic position, vis à vis India. When they see 'the children squabbling' they get out the big stick. They get it out by saying 'No pocket money, and no sweets this week'. . . . What is clear to me is that in the end India must be reunited. Pakistan always was an impossible concept (politically and morally). . . . Has it yet struck you that the war with Pakistan is really an extension of getting rid of *us*? I'm sure Wavell is smiling in his grave, whereas Mountbatten is probably wearing a puzzled frown.[8]

At the end of September he anticipated 'making the time of partition the background' to the next novel.[9] A third and last volume would follow, on modern India, 'and that would probably mean making the main background one of the aftermath of the present hostilities'. Next month he repeated the intention to David Higham.

2

In his 'Preliminary Notes' for the second novel Scott ruminated, 'We are left, after the Daphne Manners novel, with certain signposts for further action'; and 'Certain residual aspects of the evidence arouse our curiosity'.[10] These included the 'mystery of what became of Hari Kumar'; 'the further history and death (murder?) of Ronald Merrick', the ex-Superintendent of Police; 'the life of Daphne Manners' illegitimate child'; and 'Lady Manners' disenchantment with the end result of her husband's life in India (partition and fragmentation)'. These situations suggested 'a culminating action in 1947', perhaps 'a ghost transference to the days of the Mutiny' or 'even to the Black Hole' of Calcutta.

'The Black Hole, the Retreat from Kabul, the Mutiny,' Scott wrote in a review of a March 1966 account of the catastrophic First Afghan War, 'each tragic and bloody incident hardened hearts on both sides.'[11] There developed through them a severe Anglo-Indian mindset: 'the stern righteousness of paternalism and sense of divine mission'; 'a sense of established, detached, authority that sought not to be questioned'; 'a hatred of liberal reforms which would weaken . . . defences'.[12] Scott laced his text with echoes of historical events that had contributed to British–Indian tension. The Bibighar of Kanpur, where Nana Sahib employed butchers to slaughter 200 British women during the Mutiny, became the Bibighar Gardens, scene of Daphne's rape at Mayapore. Scott had read of Bibighar in a 1963 study of Nana Sahib and checked with Mrs Ganapathy that the word meant women's quarters.[13] The Jallianwala Bagh of Dyer's Amritsar massacre became the Chillianwallah Bagh of Hari's humiliation.

Scott put down a title, 'A Division of the Spoils', and a suggestion: 'Possibility of this taking place in an Indian State, likely to accede to Pakistan (or India) with a fairly evenly divided population.'[14] He thought, too, of Merrick being killed at the time of partition, when he noted mistakenly that Sir Michael O'Dwyer, the Governor of Punjab at the time of the Dyer case, had been shot.[15] (O'Dwyer was shot in London in 1940.) At the end of the *Quartet* Merrick was to be murdered in an Indian state, and the word 'Bibighar' scrawled above his mutilated body.

Focusing on partition, Scott notes that the turning point towards it was the Cripps Mission of March–April 1942. Until then 'Pakistan was no more than a card the Muslim League played in the game of winning a career for Mr Jinnah in independent India'.[16] When he now, probably in October 1965, opened 'The Original Notebook', which he was to use until the *Quartet* was finished in March 1974, he observed that Cripps's proposals for India 'killed at one blow the myth of her unification'.[17] By permitting dissident provinces to opt out of its contemplated post-war Union, 'Britain officially recognises the likelihood of Pakistan'. By rejecting the plan and resorting to Quit India, which ensured that its leaders would spend the rest of the war in gaol, Congress 'left the field wide open to the megalomaniac Jinnah'.

3

Scott strikes the communal note at the very outset in his sequel. The Writer encounters a Muslim woman in a narrow street of the predominantly Hindu city of Ranpur. She wore the burkha, 'that unhygienic head-to-toe covering', emphasising her apartness.[18] It was Friday and perhaps she was bound for the Great Mosque. An account of the town with its depleted post-partition Muslim population follows. Scott acquired his knowledge of Islam almost entirely from books. His notes refer to Taqdir's *The Religion of Islam*, A.J. Arberry on Sufism, David Brown's *The Way of the Prophet*, and the Penguin edition of *The Koran*. He was to invent the poet Gaffur and his verses.

Where *Jewel* concentrated on an inquiry into events that occurred in a particular location over a few days, its sequel opened out in time and place, illustrating the many facets of Britain's failure to unify India. Inevitably the sequel would tease out the Muslim position as against that of the essentially Hindu Congress. It would also reveal the cleavage between the India of the autocratic princes and that of provincial self-government leavened by bureaucracy. A Muslim politician and an Indian prince would emerge. Their relations with the Raj as civil government and as paramount power would be important.

A book on the British–Indian affair that would trace out 'our failure to unify' must also explore the military means by which the Raj governed the divided subcontinent. Scott noted from Strachey's *India*: 'Britain created "India" by dominating it in its geographical entirety.'[19] Ultimately the Raj governed by force and Scott is concerned, mainly through the presentation of an Anglo-Indian military family, to show how it did so. The methods included paternalism and the preservation of social and racial distance. A major theme emerges with the Japanese recruitment of prisoners-of-war into an Indian National Army. The breaking of the moral bond of loyalty was a bitter blow to the believers in paternalism. The novel, which by April 1966 Scott was calling *The Day of the Scorpion*, exposes the inadequacy of the Raj either to unify India or to maintain the Empire much beyond the war.

The title of *The Day of the Scorpion* indicates Scott's initial intention to take the novel down to independence and partition in August 1947. He explains:

> Scorpions are very sensitive to heat, which is why they
> live under stones. The rains drive them out into the open.
> There was an old belief that if you surrounded them with
> a ring of fire they committed suicide. But actually they
> are shrivelled by the heat, and when they dart their tails
> they're not committing suicide but trying to attack. Well,
> that's what so much of the British in India was all about.
> They were driven out of their places in the end, by a number
> of pressures – and were scorched by fires they had really set
> light to themselves. . . . It's the Day of the Scorpion because
> this book is supposed to be taking us right up to the eve of
> Independence – when we were all flushed out from under
> our stones.[20]

Scott pursued the lives of his British scorpions in such detail that
he ran out of space before he reached 1945. A further volume was
foreshadowed.

Recharged by his Indian visit and relying on what he called
'automatic technique', Scott had written *Jewel* in a year. *Scorpion* would take him until December 1967 to complete. It became
'a very difficult book to write. . . . So many strands to sort out.'[21]
Its theme was not so much 'divide and rule' but ruling what was
divided. He explained to John Willey: 'I suppose the key idea in
Scorpion, or one of the key ideas, is that reference to India as the
place where the British came to the end of themselves as they
were. I am trying to illustrate the moral drift of history. Trying
to give it steel in its backbone was the reason it was so long in
the factory.'[22] The 'key idea' is introduced in the prologue by
the Stranger, after his brief encounter with the woman in the
burkha in Ranpur:

> If you look in places like Ranpur for evidence of things
> these island people left behind which were of value, you
> might choose any one or several of the public works and
> installations as visible proof of them: the roads and rail-
> ways and telegraph for a modern system of communica-
> tion, the High Court for a sophisticated code of civil and
> criminal law, the college for education to university stand-
> ard, the State Legislature for democratic government, the
> Secretariat for a civil service made in the complex image

of that in Whitehall; the clubs for a pattern of urbane and civilized behaviour, the messes and barracks for an ideal of military service to the mother country. These were bequeathed, undoubtedly; these and the language and the humpy graves in the English cemetery of St Luke's in the oldest part of the cantonment, many of whose headstones record an early death, a cutting-off before the prime or in the prime, with all that this suggests in the way of unfinished business.

But it is not these things which impress the stranger . . . . What impresses him is something for which there is no memorial but which all these things collectively bear witness to: the fact that here in Ranpur, and in places like Ranpur, the British came to the end of themselves as they were.[23]

4

Scott began research for *Scorpion* with Nehru's *Discovery of India*. There he read of the demise of the British inter-war experiment with unity, the 1935 Act to create an all-India federation of states and provinces. Negotiations to that end ceased at the outbreak of war. Congress, which had been governing most of the provinces, withdrew from office in protest at the vagueness of British war aims for India. Nehru, writing in 1944 during his long detention from August 1942 to June 1945, argued that between 1939 and 1942 the British should have called fresh elections in the provincial and central governments. But: 'Elections are not liked by the British Government. They spoil the routine of life and blur the picture of an India of warring creeds and parties. Without elections it is much easier to give importance to any individual or group who is deserving of favour.'[24] Between 1939 and 1942, Scott noted, the Viceroy should have moved towards a national government, as claimed by C.R. Rajagopalachari ('Rajaji') and supported by Congress. Instead, in the Congress provinces government was mostly resumed by the governors. Scott summarized Philip Mason's account of the outstanding inter-war Governor, Sir Malcolm Hailey, in a note headed 'Portrait of a Governor'.[25]

Scott now invented the character, Mohammed Ali Kasim (MAK), Chief Minister of the province of Ranpur, from 1937 until his 'resignation in 1939 on a point of principle for Congress

unity'. In 'The Original Notebook' he is described as siding with
Rajaji in favour of a national government between 1939 and 1942.
He was horrified during the Cripps negotiations when British
policy seemed to be paving the way for Pakistan. He makes
a violently anti-British speech that offends the British and the
Muslims and leads to his arrest in August 1942. However, he is
also dismayed by the drift to non-constitutional politics in India.
He stands for everything that the British and the old moderate
Swaraj section of Congress admired. Kasim is strategic to the
Quartet, for his relation to the Governor, Sir George Malcolm,
because his kinsman rules the princely state of Mirat and his
younger son works for its diwan, and because his elder son was
commissioned into the Indian Army in 1938, captured by the
Japanese, and recruited to the INA after he heard of MAK's
arrest.

Kasim was 'not based on anyone, nor is the province whose
administration he headed anything but an imaginary province'.[26] In November 1965, Scott wrote to Monica Felton for
advice on sources of 'authentic background information', especially on 'what it was like to be a detained prisoner under the
Defence of India Rules . . . stuck in some fort or other'.[27] Felton
observed:

> If your Congress Muslim prime minister is a man with
> any force of character he is going to take an awful lot
> of imaginative authenticating. A few months ago I had a
> long conversation with Rajaji and one of his younger col-
> leagues – a man who is still in the Congress – about some of
> the personalities who were prominent during your period.
> Both said that Jinnah was justified in calling the Congress
> Muslims 'showboys'. This wasn't so earlier of course.[28]

That is, by 1942 there were few Muslim political leaders of
stature in the Congress. Felton recommended that Scott read
A.K. Azad's *India Wins Freedom* (1959), the ghosted political autobiography of the Muslim who was president of Congress from 1940 to mid-1946. He was interned in 1942 with
Nehru and ten others in Ahmednagar, some 200 miles east
of Bombay. Felton also suggested the autobiography of Mira
Behn, the English woman follower of Gandhi, for details of the
August arrests, and the Government of India's White Paper,

Congress Responsibility for the Disturbances (1942), known as
the Tottenham Report. Scott borrowed these works from the
India House Library (where Keith Roy's brother worked) early
in 1966, finding Azad 'a horror', a man with a distorted view of
politics and an 'overweening sense of his own importance'.[29]
Clearly he was not the prototype for Kasim, though the fort
in which Scott placed Kasim, Premanagar, was worked up
from his reading on Ahmednagar. The only other fort where
Congressmen were detained was Lahore.

Kasim remained in Congress because, as he told Malcolm, he
was 'looking for a country'.[30] What mattered was the idea of
unity, the creation of a nation; 'the job that your Government
has always found it beneficial to leave undone, the job of unifying India'.[31] As Scott noted after reading the Tottenham Report:
'The Quit India Campaign certainly acted as a powerful *unifier*
(even Nehru was brought to heel). It bears out my feeling that
Ali Kasim *would* have continued in Congress because his desire
for unity had become central to his personal policy.'[32] The desire
for unity overrode his own aversion to Gandhi's unconstitutional
methods. The figure of Kasim is central to the idea of India as
a nation, not least as the embodiment of the rickety Congress
bridge over the Hindu–Muslim divide.

5

By the time that he created Mirat Scott was knowledgeable
about the Indian princely states. He had read of Forster's
experience in Dewas and of Penderel Moon's in Bahawalpur
at the time of partition. He had read Menon's *Integration of
the Indian States* closely and works by former members of
the Political Service. He had not managed to make the visit to
Bharatpur that M.M. Kaye had arranged but from her letters
and from Menon's book he learnt details of its communal troubles in 1947. The Jats killed many Muslims and Jinnah accused
the Maharaja of encouraging them. In March 1964 he spent some
days in Hyderabad.

Scott asserted that Mirat was 'politically . . . not connected
with a real state':

Geographically it has very vague connections with Hydera-
bad/Secunderabad. Between the City and the Cantonment

there is a narrow strip of land, a lake etc. As for my making Mirat a paradigm of political virtue – well, yes, why not. Quite a number of them were as virtuous as Mirat, if they were well advised and had progressively minded rulers and had a good Dewan or Wazir (of whatsoever national- ity). The thing is you seldom *heard* about them, because scandal and bad news are always more memorable than virtue and good news. If I had made Mirat a hotbed of autocratic corruption I would have thought myself guilty of following an easy, a popular line. Apart from which, of course, the State of Mirat obviously had to reflect the characters of the Nawab and Bronowsky, and – they being what I made them – the State of Mirat is as I had to make it because they had made it. Umh.[33]

There was no eponym for Count Dmitri Bronowsky. He was simply 'the kind of White Russian émigré you find cropping up in all kinds of places'.[34] He was the sort of man the father of the novelist Vladimir Nabokov, one of Scott's favourite authors, might have known. Nabokov senior was a founder of the Constitutionalist Democratic Party, a member of the short-lived Russian parliament, who was imprisoned for sub- scribing to a manifesto urging the people to resist the Tsar's order of dissolution in 1906. He escaped from Bolshevik Russia in 1919 and was assassinated by two Russian right-wing extremists whilst shielding a colleague in the Berlin Philharmonic Hall in 1922.[35] Scott's earliest note on Bronowsky was: 'At the bottom of Bronowsky's policy: a desire to turn all the differences in Indian life and culture to advantage: to see them as forming, together, a viable force – the almost anarchic force of energies opposed to each other.'[36] The contrast with the British rulers of divided India is unmistakable.

6

Scott's early reading for *Scorpion* included 'a rather poor biog- raphy of Subhas Chandra Bose'.[37] It was Hugh Toye's *The Springing Tiger* (1959), which concentrated on Bose's role in the formation of the INA. The INA was to be the aspect of history that Scott would research most thoroughly. At this early stage, with his focus on Kasim, he was mainly con- cerned to know when Kasim would, in historical terms, have learnt of his son's recruitment to it. The capture of Sayed by the British would trigger Kasim's release, for the British would realise that the old Swarajist could not condone his son's treason. When Scott put his question to Monica Felton she asked Mrs Ammu Swaminadhan, a leading post-war Congresswoman and post-independence parliamentarian. One of her daughters, Lakshmi, was the great heroine of the INA. She was practising as a doctor in Singapore when Subhas asked her to form the women's unit that became known as the Rani of Jhansi Regiment. She was arrested in March 1943 and her mother learnt of it soon afterwards. Scott could therefore date Kasim's knowledge of his son's defection any time he wished, allowing for security precautions at the fort. Scott suspended his knowledge until June 1944, after Sayed's capture at Imphal. *Scorpion* ends with a scene in which Ahmed tells Kasim of his brother's treason and Kasim walks out of custody, still wearing his white Congress cap, 'like a crown of thorns'.[38] Very soon after Scott began *Scorpion* he was confident of the development of Kasim's story to this stage, with which he would complete the book at the end of 1967: 'I think the situation I have been working up for my ex-Congress Muslim and his army son will be accurate enough.'[39] Though Scott began other INA research in 1966–7, largely through Keith Roy's help with books unavailable in England, much of it was premature.

7

Scott created the Layton and the Muir families, and Teddie Bingham, as his representatives of Anglo–India, especially its military side. They are at the centre of three of the book's five parts, 'A History', 'A Wedding' and 'A Christening', titles suggestive of the continuity or permanence of the Raj. Scott denied that they were based on actual people.

> I suppose every character has a flicker in him or her either of myself, or of people I've met, briefly, or known fairly well, or of all of them. I can for instance see that Sarah and Susan bear some physical resemblance to two girls I met in the NWFP whose father (a brigadier) was a prisoner of war. But that's as far as one can go. . . . And then of course people do tend, don't they, to fall defensively into recognisable roles: adopting a 'typical' mode of behaviour

and dress and attitude, so that you could look at a man
like Colonel Layton and say, Yes, of course, an Old Army
Man.[40]

In a very general sense, Scott drew on his own experience as the
father of two daughters, and on his mother's resentment – like
Mildred's – that her family lived in the lesser and two women in
the grander of two houses to which her husband had title.

Neither Susan nor Sarah, nor Mildred, has certainty of faith
in Anglo-Indian values. While Sarah is fit to bear the responsibility that reduced her mother to alcohol dependence and that
Susan cannot even contemplate, she feels the anachronism of
the Raj, its remoteness from the tides of history. Teddie was
'representative . . . of the very things which the English at home
were getting ready to destroy – a perfectly decent sort of man
but bone from the neck up, as it were'.[41] Scott confessed that
Bingham

> was partly based on a fellow I knew in the army, when I was
> only a private and he was an officer. (That was in England.
> . . .) He was such an awful fool on the surface that he made
> me miserable because underneath you could see how good
> he was. But nobody noticed it (except I suppose his mother,
> if he still had one). There were quite a lot like that in India
> too, and some of them got killed.[42]

Teddie most fully represented Anglo-India in the manner of
his death. Unable to believe in the ultimate disloyalty of two
members of his regiment who had gone over to the INA, he is
shot down at Imphal in the act of appealing to them to return.
Merrick describes the scene:

> He went down there for the *regiment*. I told you there was
> a touch of old-fashioned gallantry in it. All that paternalist
> business really meant something to him. *Man-bap*. I am
> your father and your mother. It would have been great if
> he'd gone down there and called as he did and if they'd
> come out, hanging their heads, and surrendered to him,
> trusting in the code, the old code. That's what he wanted.
> I don't mean there was anything vain or self-seeking about
> it. He wasn't doing it for himself or for them. He did it for
> the regiment. He risked everything for it, his own life, the

driver's life, Baksh's life, his job. So much. So much it's incalculable. Who knows, his going down there might have looked to that bunch of Jiffs and Japs, who'd been clever enough to get so near without being seen, like the beginning of an advance into the valley. It could have triggered the whole thing off. But in any case he was putting the regiment above his job. If it had come off he could have become one of those people a regiment remembers, celebrates, as part of their legend. . . .[43]

He defines the code: 'Devotion. Sacrifice. Self-denial. A cause, an obligation. A code of conduct, a sort of final moral definition, I mean definition of us, what we're here for – people living among each other, in an environment some sort of God created. The whole impossible nonsensical dream.'[44]

Merrick of course did not dream the paternalists' dream, and represents the racist critique of it, the affirmation that the Raj rested on force and contempt. The centrepiece of *Scorpion* is the long interrogation of Kumar by Nigel Rowan, ADC to the Governor of Ranpur, in Kandipat Gaol. In the course of it Kumar reveals that Merrick had tried to enforce on him an enactment of the reality of 'the situation' in British India:

He said for the moment we were mere symbols. He said we'd never understand each other if we were going to be content with that. It wasn't enough to say he was English and I was Indian, that he was a ruler and I was one of the ruled. We had to find out what that meant. He said people talked of an ideal relationship between his kind and my kind. They called it comradeship. But they never said anything about the contempt on his side and the fear on mine that was basic, and came before any comradely feeling. He said we had to find out about that too, we had to enact the situation as it really was, and in a way that would mean neither of us ever forgetting it or being tempted to pretend it didn't exist, or was something else. . . . He said the true corruption of the English is their pretence that they have no contempt for us, and our real degradation is our pretence of equality. . . . The kind really responsible was the one who sat at home and kidded himself there was such a thing as the brotherhood of man or came out here and went on pretending there was. The permutations of English corruption in India were endless – affection for servants, for peasants,

for soldiers, pretence at understanding the Indian intellectual or at sympathizing with nationalist aspirations, but
all this affection and understanding was a corruption of
what he called the calm purity of their contempt. . . . He
called the English admiration for the martial and faithful
servant class a mixture of perverted sexuality and feudal
arrogance.

And at the other end of the scale when you thought
about the kind of Englishmen who pretended to admire
Indian intellectuals, pretended to sympathize with their
national aspirations, if you were honest you had to admit
that all they were admiring or sympathizing with was the
black reflection of their own white ideals. Underneath the
admiration and sympathy there was the contempt a people
feel for a people who have learned things from them. The
liberal intellectual Englishman was just as contemptuous
of the Westernized educated Indian as the arrogant upper-
class reactionary Englishman was of the fellow who blacks
his boots and earns his praise.[45]

The other critique of Anglo-India in *Scorpion* is offered by
Major Jimmy Clark, the wartime officer who seduces Sarah in
Calcutta:

India and the honour-of-the-regiment. . . . Growing up with
all the other po-faced kids in a sort of ghastly non-stop
performance of Where The Rainbow Ends? Then having
to trot back for a time to a little island that's gone down
because it's become full of vulgar money-grubbers and
people without standards and all sorts of jacks-in-office
trying to paint out the pink parts of the map? . . .

Last Christmas . . . I was up in 'Pindi staying with a
friend of a friend back home who's been out here for about
ten years. And there they were, the man, the wife, and two
of the po-faced kids, and right from the beginning we felt
towards each other like I suppose those people do who suffer from that odd racial prejudice thing, as if in spite of our
being the *same* colour and class, one of us was black, me,
and the others white, them. We were tremendously polite
but simply had nothing to say to each other. I felt I'd met
a family who'd been preserved by some sort of perpetual
Edwardian sunlight that got trapped between the Indian
Ocean and the Arabian Sea round about the turn of the
century. . . .

You had a perfectly good thing going in that old merchant trading company who used to run things until the
industrial revolution. What you wanted then was a bevy
of steely-eyed brass founders and men of iron who'd have
ground the faces of the Indian peasants in the dirt, sweated
a few million to death and dragged India yelling into the
nineteenth century. Instead of which you got the people who
didn't like the smoke and the dark satanic mills because
that sort of thing was vulgar, and after them you got
the people who didn't like it because of the inhumanity
that went with it. What you didn't get was the damned
smoke. And that's the trouble. The Indian empire's been
composed exclusively of English people who said No. Out
here you've always had the negative side, the reactionaries
and the counter-revolutionaries, but you've never had the
bloody revolution. That's why an Indian urban dweller's
life expectation is still thirty-five and why people die of
starvation while the band plays at Government House. . . .
Well, at home after the war we'll cut your empire adrift
without the slightest compunction. It's a time-expired sore,
a suppurating mess.[46]

8

While Scott intended every aspect of *Scorpion* to be a variation
on the theme of Britain's failure to unify India, as its writing
advanced Anglo-India as such became his central concern.
The community appears aloof from the Indian society that it
manipulated and remote from currents of change in Britain.
Shortly after completing the book he wrote:

I do think . . . that it is probably important to remember
how cut off the imperialist British became from the general movement of their own Society at home. Their final
position was that of stranded whales, or minnows. I try to
illustrate something of that in the Scorpion book, particularly in poor Sarah.
On the whole you could say that the Turtons and Burtons
(or the more civilized Muirs and Laytons) simply did *not*
mix with Indians below . . . the Nawab/Judge/Governor
level. The Raj was an official society, civil or military.
Indians entered it to the extent that they were either official
or political.[47]

He denied that his characters were 'Forsterian', though they
seemed 'doomed to exist in a sort of Forsterian twilight'.[48] Whilst
there were many instances of genuine friendships between
Indians and British (and not merely in a master–servant relationship) 'these counted for nothing in the face of the community
attitude'.[49] This, as he later explained, had serious political
implications:

> . . . I think the British had a political responsibility that was
> never worked out; possibly because the majority of the Bri-
> tish felt there was an unbridgeable gulf between the British
> personality and the Indian personality. . . . The majority of
> the ICS identified with India but also held themselves aloof.
> It was part of the training of middle class Englishmen:
> never to reveal attachments/emotion.[50]

Scott relates the remoteness of Anglo-India from Indian society and society in Britain to the failure to unify. He asserts
that 'the partition was a logical consequence of the failure to
identify: also of the failure of the British at home to understand
the British in India'.[51] But this casts forward and is too cryptic.
As Scott was to realise, Anglo-India required a more micro-
scopic analysis if such themes were to emerge convincingly in
his epic.

Melancholy Exiles

1

When Scott reopened 'The Original Notebook' early in 1968 he entered the title 'Towers of Silence'. He sketched 'the main blocks of interest' as 'Indian nationalism and unity', encapsulated in Kasim, and 'English traditionalism' exemplified by the Laytons. A 'certain momentum' was generated by 'the pressure of events'. *The Towers of Silence* was to be the final volume of the Raj trilogy, extending in time from the end of war to partition: 'Hitler was dead, the war in Europe was won. In Burma British forces had taken Rangoon, the Japanese were scattered and their days in Malaya most definitely numbered. The years of humiliation were over but not for Barbie.' Barbie, of course, was the Bishop Barnard missionary teacher Barbara Batchelor, who had made a brief appearance in *Scorpion*. She had been a friend of Miss Crane's and in Scott's imagination was cognate in spirit to her and Daphne Manners, the third panel in a triptych inspired by Marcella Sherwood's ordeal at Amritsar in 1919. Scott intended that Barbie's story should open *Towers* much as Miss Crane's had formed an historical prologue to *Jewel*.

The year 1968 was disastrous for Scott as personal woes impaired his creative capacities. His wife, younger daughter and mother all suffered severe illnesses and he was hagridden by the costs of household repairs. He had also opened so many themes in *Scorpion* that he was groping for a way forward. The vagueness of his intentions is suggested by a letter to John Willey early in the year: 'Broadly, at the moment, I'm trying to say something about India as a historical environment of the British, affected by, affecting, the British character, and the Indian character.'[1]

Scott began with research on the post-war situation in India, focusing largely on the problem of the INA. Heinemann's had contracted to meet the costs of a research visit to India and he planned to undertake it early in 1969. At the end of 1968 the intended scope of *Towers* was still the post-war-to-partition period, as a brief for the press reveals:

> The novel on which Paul Scott is at work is planned as the third and final book. . . . [It] is planned to cover the period that began with the bombing of Hiroshima and ended with imperial abdication, partition of the sub-continent, and the lapse of paramountcy over the Indian Princes whose sovereign territories were subsequently absorbed by one or other of the two dominions.[2]

The book's title referred to 'the name given by the Parsees to the platforms on which the bodies of their dead are exposed, and devoured by vultures'. He was going to India 'for special research, among other subjects, into the controversial trials of Indian officers and men, ex-prisoners of war, who marched with the Japanese against the British'.

When he completed *Towers* in December 1970 a quite different book had emerged from the one originally planned. It had become the 'slow movement' of a quartet:

> I can't pretend to have set off with a clear idea of making it what it is, but I was trying to get down underneath all the previous material and come out with something coherent from the point of view of theme – clearing the ground for the action of the final part. Originally *Towers* was supposed to end the sequence with Miss Batchelor's story forming Book One, but it separated itself and once I admitted that it had I was able to ponder it all out and adjust the rhythm.[3]

Miss Batchelor's story was, as he told Gant, 'happier on its own'.[4] His fullest explanation of its development appears in his correspondence with John Willey. Whereas Barbie had previously appeared only briefly she became 'the central channel for the things going on in this particular section. In a way many of the old strings are gathered together again, but what we are trying to get at here, through Miss Batchelor, is a sort of synthesis of the currents of emotion in course. . . . The time scheme is 1939–45 beginning with the start of the War and the retirement of Barbara Batchelor.'[5] The motif that ran through the book became the distinction between the British at home and the British in India. Well. It is a quiet book. I've come to look on it, since finally admitting that there were going to have to be four books instead of three, as the slow movement; and perhaps when the whole thing is finished and if anyone ever reads it as all of a piece *Towers* will be the sort of contemplative pause that pushes everything in a bit deeper and from which all the themes etc. will emerge clearly enough to leave *A Division of Spoils* as far more a book of action.[6]

In *Scorpion* Clark had spoken of British India: 'it's all as dead as yesterday, isn't it? You ought to bury the body, or expose it to the vultures like the Parsees do. It didn't survive the Great War. It makes an awful smell. Of course there are still pockets of the stink at home. . . .'[7] In *Towers* the body of the Raj is laid out for close examination.

2

It was Scott's view that until the 1940s the British in India still bore a burden of experiences and attitudes that had long been discarded by the British at home. His understanding of that burden was deepened by a careful reading early in 1967 of the published diaries and correspondence of the secretary of an Edwardian Viceroy. He reviewed the work in a full page article, 'Anglo-Indian Attitudes', for the *Times Literary Supplement*.[8] It was *Servant of India: A Study of Imperial Rule, 1905–1910*, edited by Martin Gilbert. The 'servant' was Sir James Dunlop Smith, secretary to Lord Minto. His father had been a missionary, editor of the *Calcutta Review* and *Times* correspondent in India. Born in the year of the Mutiny, Smith had returned to India from Sandhurst in 1878 and transferred to the ICS in 1882. He served as private secretary to Sir Charles Aitchison, Lieutenant-Governor of the Punjab, and married his daughter. He was, in turn, a settlement officer, famine commissioner and political agent before becoming Minto's private secretary. He was related by marriage to the celebrated Butler family and R.A.B. contributed a prologue and an epilogue to the book. *Servant of India* is thus a splendid source-book on Anglo-India.

Scott observed Anglo-India's 'highly developed sense of community', to which three factors contributed. First, there was 'companionship-in-exile', an insular mindset produced by 'the

idea of resisting the dark tide' that might overwhelm frail
defences. Second, there was 'pride in experience' or 'secret
sharing', membership of an exclusive club whose dues were
twenty or thirty years of patient service. Third, and most dis-
ruptive to the machine of British parliamentary reform, there
was the possession of rights, or defence of obligations, that
companionship-in-exile and pride in experience were felt to con-
fer. The outsiders who threatened the Anglo-Indian community
were the British at home, especially in Parliament, and their
delegate to India, the Viceroy. Thus a man who had been too
long in India would be too partisan to serve the Viceroy well.
Minto took his chance with Smith but they achieved a rapport
in their response to the post-Curzonian challenges: demands
for quasi-parliamentary government; terrorist activity; and
claims to separate representation for the Muslims. They were
both gradualists and paternalists, and their essential policy was
to involve selected Indians in subordinate collaboration with the
Raj. Minto succumbed to Anglo-India. His viceroyalty made
a minor contribution to Indian self-rule. It was, rather, 'the
funnel' through which the agitations of Indians were forced, to
emerge 'carrying the seeds of republicanism and partition'.
Paternalistic imperialism manipulated to protect its rights and
defend its obligations against nationalism in India and liberalism at home.

Scott was led on to a rereading of the great novelist who
entered the Indian scene shortly after Minto left it and, on the
basis of his 1912–13 experience, published *A Passage to India*
in 1924. Scott, to his chagrin and disadvantage, was always
compared with Forster, and felt a compulsion to distinguish his
Anglo-India from Forster's. He had edited out of a March 1967
lecture, 'Meet the Author: Manchester', some comments that
revealed his irritation. First, 'Forster becomes in fact not only
the literary standard but the factual standard of comparison.'[9]
Second, 'few novelists of my age have had the misfortune to
be judged by the standard of a writer who is still England's
greatest living novelist'. In 1968 Scott analysed his approach
to Anglo-India in a lecture to the Royal Society of Literature,
'India: A Post-Forsterian View'.[10] It was really a clearing of his
conceptual decks, a preliminary necessary for the depiction of
wartime Anglo-India in *Towers*.

Scott views *Passage* as essentially a novel about the post-war liberal dilemma. The Turtons and the Burtons, the imperialist paternalists of the Raj, are challenged by the liberal humanists – Fielding, Mrs Moore and, initially, Miss Quested. Forster's concern was with the clash of ideologies. Scott admires the 'prophetic element' in the novel. Forster foresaw the inadequacy of liberalism to solve the problem of ruling India. Turtonism prevailed until Fieldingism's ascendancy in Parliament swept the Raj away in 1947.

Scott's own theme was quite different. It was the palpable anachronism of Anglo-Indian purposes and values in the face of inter-war and wartime changes at home. His characters suffer loss of belief in their inherited values and awareness of their irrelevance in the eyes both of Indians and of their own people in Britain. They are melancholy exiles. They are captive to their past. They are burdened by the crushing weight of their own history, caught in what Emerson had called 'the moral drift of history'.

Scott would show this through the consciousness of Barbie, who represents displacement and a sense of lost mission: 'my life here has indeed been wasted because I have lived it as a transferred appendage, as a parlour maid, the first in line for morning prayers while the mistress of the house . . . kneels like myself in piety for a purpose. But we have no purpose that God would recognise as such. . . .'[11] An historian might have made the point through the great and powerful. In February 1945 Winston Churchill wrote to his wife of 'the sorry plight to which we have reduced ourselves by losing confidence in our mission. . . . I have had for some time a feeling of despair about the British connection with India, and still more about what will happen if it is suddenly broken. . . .'[12] Being a novelist who saw his task as giving voice to the inarticulate, Scott made his point through a lonely and insecure retired missionary.

3

Among the attitudes that Scott now most wanted to inspect was the relation between British paternalism and Indian loyalty, especially in its military aspect. It was the doctrine of *man-bap*, that the government or an authority was all-in-all to its subjects as parents are to their children. Insight into this relationship, and its importance to Britons in exile, came to him on 26 January 1969 as he watched the Republic Day Parade in New Delhi. He describes the occasion in a review for *Country Life* of Philip Mason's history of the Indian Army, *A Matter of Honour* (1974). It was bylined 'Tradition and the Indian Army'. The sky was overcast:

> But instead of rain we had rose-petals: thousands of them, scattered from four helicopters that churned a couple of hundred feet above our heads, the whole length of the Raj Path. The thing to do was catch a few petals for luck. Those which fell on the road formed a thin fragrant carpet for the marching columns. . . . All in all it took about 90 minutes for the representatives of India's life and chivalry to flow past. Beginning with helicopters we ended with tanks and missiles and a v.formation of fighter–bombers which roared down the line of the processional route emitting broadening bands of smoke dyed to match the colours of the Indian national flag.
>
> A stirring sight; a moving occasion and, I thought, a very Indian one. I made a note (as writers do who find themselves not at their desks but idling, and feeling guilty) a mere phrase: Roses and Armour. The title for an article perhaps? It had a resonance. It seemed significant. . . .
>
> I wondered whether perhaps it didn't point to what was, what is, different about Indian militarism and any other, point to a certain equilibrium in the Indian character, an instinctive and distinctive balancing of the masculine and feminine; whether it was the sense of this that appealed to, helped to draw the best out of, the pinkest English youth who, with one pip on his shoulder, denoting a wholly male authority, nevertheless understood that he was expected to be both father and mother. *Man-Bap.* . . .
>
> The King-pins of the system, of course, were the mutual trust and respect between officers and men, and by and large in India these were to be found in a very notable degree. That this should have been so is, perhaps, something of a mystery and by no means to be explained as due primarily to the superior qualities of the English military man. . . .
>
> True, after the war . . . there was the grave problem of the applause accorded to men of the INA. . . . But today, in India, the memory of the INA has been swept under the carpet. Quite rightly. The Indian tradition – now harnessed

to a modern idea of Indian national identity and patriotism
– holds firm. To understand why it held so firm under the
raj one can't do better than look at this passage from
Mr Mason's closing chapter. The Indian Army, he writes,
'fitted something in the traditional structure of Indian life.
It provided a framework of discipline and organisation
within which the links of family and caste could play
their part.'

I think it also fitted something in the idealistic structure
of the life of the British abroad (an exile from other pressures). And remembering how I stood, in an enclosure off
the Raj Path in 1969, reaching for rose-petals, I feel I know
what that something was, but would be pushed to explain
it clearly.[13]

Scott had experienced the intimacy of *man-bap* with Dass and
Nimu during the war and represented it in Johnnie Brown's rela-
tions to his men in that first 'autobiographical' novel, *Johnnie
Sahib*.

4

The scene of *Towers* is Pankot, a north Indian hill station, summer capital of the province, cool-weather station of the Pankot
Rifles whose native soldiers were recruited from the surrounding hills. Scott's recent reading of Mollie Panter-Downes, *Ooty
Preserved: A Victorian Hill Station in India* (1967) presented
him with a strong impression of Ootacamund, in the Nilgiries,
and his imagination drew upon it avidly. He had not visited Ooty,
but he had seen Abbottabad and Murree and 'to have gone into
the hills at all is to have shared an experience with everyone
who did. . . . Ooty looks extraordinarily familiar, even to one
who has never been there.'[14] He notes the names on the gates of
bungalows (Apple Cottage, Ethel Cottage, Hopeful and Cheerful
Cottages) and, perhaps, Rose Cottage, Pankot – home of Mabel
Layton and from 1939 her paying guest Barbie Batchelor –
was created. Barbie had been in India for thirty years. The
Batchelors were 'very small lower-middle-class beer'.[15] Her
father, a solicitor's managing clerk in High Holborn, lost more
on the horses than he could afford so that her mother had to take
in dressmaking to make ends meet. They lived in Camberwell.
Barbie had succeeded Miss Crane at Muzzafirabad and she possessed a small copy of her allegorical print, *The Jewel in Her*

Crown, which depicted the sovereign, Queen Victoria, presiding over figures representing her brown/white subjects in unity.

Barbie hung the print above her writing desk at Rose Cottage and in her imagination the Queen became in turn Edwina guarding Chaudhuri's body, Daphne intent on saving Hari, and herself surrounded by children she had presumed to bring to God. The women were surrogates for God: 'From this there emerged a figure, the figure of an unknown Indian: dead in one aspect, alive in another. And after a while it occurred to her that the unknown Indian was what her life in India had been about.'[16] She had borrowed Emerson's *Essays* and absorbed the view that 'in her own experience lay an explanation not only of history but of the lives of other living people', including Edwina and Daphne.[17] In her dreams Chaudhuri and Kumar, both unknown Indians to her, had become one, common humanity. The contrast between the three loving women and the Raj as exemplified at Pankot is at once evident in a recapitulation of the Manners case. Brigadier Reid's brigade major arrives in Pankot and explains Daphne's behaviour in terms of her love for Hari. To Pankot 'the theory was peculiarly unacceptable'.[18] Racial distance destroyed the credibility of Daphne's love.

Edwina's suicide soon afterwards, in October 1942, convinced Barbie that the roadside image was not of love but of dumb despair – the Devil's work. The revelation uncovered Barbie's own despair. She fought consciously against admitting despair, on Christmas Eve 1943 questioning 'what gifts our mission had brought to the children of India, and if – among them – has ever been the gift of love. . . . Without that gift I doubt that any can be, could have been, brought to Jesus.'[19] She reflects on the division between Anglo-India and India:

> The division is one of which I am ashamed. I have done nothing, nothing, to remove it, ever. My poor Edwina sat huddled by the roadside in the rain, holding that dead man's hand. That, I continually see, was significant. For me that image is like an old picture of the kind that were popular in the last century, which told stories and pointed moral lessons. I see the caption, 'Too late'.[20]

Merrick had been responsible for investigating the circumstances of Edwina's death and associated the image of her holding Chaudhuri's hand with that of Queen Victoria in the allegorical print, *The Jewel in Her Crown*, which he found in her bungalow. He thought both, as also Teddie's manner of dying, represented *man-bap*:

> Man-bap. . . . It meant Mother–Father, the relationship of the *raj* to India, of a man like Colonel Layton to the men in his regiment, of a district officer to the people of his district, of Barbie herself to the children she had taught. Man-bap. I am your father and your mother. Yes, the picture had been an illustration of this aspect of the imperial attachment; the combination of hardness and sentimentality from which Mabel had turned her face. If Teddie had died in an attempt to gather strayed sheep into a fold she saw why Captain Merrick might remember the picture.[21]

But Barbie asserted that the image of Edwina was not *man-bap* but despair. She was confirmed in this view when Merrick himself told her that Edwina's suicide note said, 'There is no God. Not even on the road from Dibrapur.'[22]

For Barbie, as for Mabel, *man-bap* was a hard and sentimental doctrine, bespeaking loyalty not love. The allegorical print expressed it but, for Barbie, was on that account incomplete. The unknown Indian wasn't there. In *Towers* Barbie found her unknown Indian through Mabel.

Mabel Layton represented the old Raj, with its mission intact, the Raj at the far end of the Edwardian funnel, still believing in a brown/white unity under the Crown. When she died Barbie saw her body as the passing of the Raj. The British mission had expired with the First World War and the Amritsar massacre that occurred when India rejected the extension in the Rowlatt Acts of the discretionary wartime Defence of India rules. Mabel was haunted by the Jallianwala Bagh massacre, which Barbie heard as 'Gillian Waller' when she talked in her sleep. In protest against Anglo-India's lionising of Dyer Mabel had subscribed funds not for his benefit but for the Indian victims of his slaughter. Barbie found her unknown Indian in the child Ashok, whom she met on her daily visitations to Mabel's grave: 'Tu es mon Hindou inconnu. . . . Et tu es un papillon brun. Moi, je suis blanche. Mais nous sommes les prisonniers du bon Dieu.'[23]

Barbie passed from despair to purgatory before she entered

God's grace. Mabel's cadaver was her 'first authentic vision
of what hell was like'.[24] Her second was Mildred's 'joyless
coupling' with Captain Kevin Coley in a parody of divine creation. Next she saw Merrick as the Devil. Merrick's judgements
on the Manners case were diabolical. Hari Kumar was: 'The
worst kind of western-educated Indian. With all the conceit
and arrogance of the Indian whose family owns or once owned
land, plus the arrogance of the most boring and unprincipled
but privileged English lad who believes the world belongs to
him because he was taught at a public school to think he should
rule it by divine right instead of by virtue of a superior intelligence.'[25] Merrick was puzzled that Daphne 'fell for it' and found
the subject painful. He had been 'fond of her' himself but stopped
being fond of her when he 'realised which way she'd jumped'.[26]
Barbie caught the tone of sexual jealousy and racial contempt.
She 'knew that God had shone his light on her at last by casting
first the shadow of the prince of darkness across her feet'.[27]

5

In *Towers man-bap* is also explored through a recapitulation
of Teddie's death, which reveals its hollowness, and Mildred's
assuming the role of her prisoner-of-war husband in relation
to the villages from which Colonel Layton's regiment drew
recruits. Mildred was the one who most admired Teddie's hero-
ism, his 'blameless death, his praiseworthy sacrifice for a
principle the world no longer had time or inclination to uphold'.[28]
For Mildred, 'What Teddie tried to do was worth the whole
bloody war put together':

> As if aware of a special necessity, Mildred Layton now took
> a day off, put on jodhpurs, and accompanied by Captain
> Coley set out on horseback on a day's trek to the nearest
> villages to thank women who had sent little presents and
> messages of goodwill to Colonel Sahib's younger daughter
> and baby; to discuss with them the now excellent prospects
> of the early return of the long-absent warriors from across
> the black water. It became known, through Coley, that
> Mildred had gallantly drunk cup after cup of syrupy tea,
> eaten piping hot chappatis, a bowl of vegetable curry, been
> soaked in a sudden shower between villages, held squealing
> black babies, patted the shoulder of an ill-favoured looking

woman who was weeping because since her husband went
away she had grown old and fat; discussed the crops with
village elders, more intimate problems with the wives
and mothers, the hopes of recruitment with shy striplings
pushed forward by their old male relatives to salaam
Colonel Memsahib, and returned exhausted but upright
through one of the wet season's spectacular sunsets which
turned her white shirt flamingo pink and the shadows of
the horses brown.

There was a glow, but it was external to the affair; a bit
too theatrical to penetrate to the mind where it was needed.
It gave the performance qualities of self-consciousness
which made it look as if Mildred's main achievement had
been to draw attention to an undertaking whose only claim
was a nostalgic one upon the fund of recollected duties and
obligations which time and circumstances were rendering
obsolete; as obsolete as Teddie's gesture, of which the
division had taken a view of a kind it would not, in better
days, have taken, but with which one somehow could not
argue – considering the cost of a jeep and the shortage
of equipment, not to mention the escaped prisoner, the
burnt sepoy-driver and Captain Merrick's lost left arm.
The price of regimental loyalty and pride seemed uncom-
fortably high.[29]

The values encapsulated in the phrase 'the honour of the regiment' were time-expired. In a visit to the mess during Susan's
wedding party Mabel had conspicuously turned her back upon
them:

It had been a criticism of the foundations of the edifice, of
the sense of duty which kept alive the senses of pride and
loyalty and honour. It drew attention to a situation it was
painful to acknowledge: that the god had left the temple,
no one knew when, or how, or why. What one was left
with were the rites which had once propitiated, once been
obligatory, but were now meaningless because the god was
no longer there to receive them. Poor Teddie! His was an
end of an expository kind, like a last sacrificial attempt to
recall godly favour.[30]

Barbie saw Mildred's ride into the valley offering 'matriar-
chal wisdom to women older and as wise or wiser than she'
as 'an arrogance, the kind which Mabel always set her face

against'.[31] Belief in *man-bap* exemplified the distance between
Anglo-India and the realities of modern Britain.

6

The main point of *Towers* is to emphasise the distance that had
developed between Britain and Anglo-India. It had been made
explicitly enough by Clark to Sarah in *Scorpion*:

> Extraordinary, isn't it . . . that the people in this country
> who feel most like foreigners to each other are English
> people who've just arrived and the ones who have been
> here for several years. . . . It makes me want to say, 'Where
> have you all been? Come back. All is forgiven.'[32]

Sarah expresses for Scott 'the melancholy arising from too long
in exile, from too far a removal from the source of dynamic
native experience'.[33] In *Towers* Sarah reflected upon 'the tre-
mendous gulf' between herself and the sort of young men she'd
met at home before 1939 and recently in Calcutta.[34] Barbie
understood her sense of having 'no clearly defined world to
inhabit, but one poised between the old for which she had been
prepared, but which seemed to be dying, and the new for which
she had not been prepared at all'.[35]

The point is made directly through the 'senior woman' at
Pankot, the area commander's wife, Isobel Rankin. In her
'there resided in a highly developed form the animus of declining but still responsible imperialism':

> She was under no misapprehension about the mistakes
> made in the past and still being made by her own people
> in India but if she had been asked to say in what way India
> had most benefited from the British connexion, what it was
> that could be offered in extenuation of fault, error, even of
> wickedness, she would have been perfectly clear that it was
> the example so often given of personal trustworthiness:
> a virtue that flowed from courage, honesty, loyalty and
> commonsense in what was to her a single definition of
> good. She did not see how a person or a country could
> survive without it. . . .
>   She was in two minds about the benefit that might be had
> if the connexion with England were much prolonged. She
> accepted the fact that at home her own people had often

been indifferent to Indian affairs and that this indifference sprang from ignorance. But in the old days when the code by which she lived had been widely upheld in England this indifference to India had not mattered much, because those who came out to shoulder the responsibility could rely to a great extent on moral support at home. But of recent years, in England, she knew that these values had been eroded. . . .

She believed that through the business of attempting to divest old authorities of power the notion could become current that authority of any kind was suspect. To Isobel Rankin a world without authority was meaningless. There would be no chain of trust if there were no chain of command. She feared that in such a climate there could be a demission of authority in India by her own people that it would be possible only to describe as dishonourable, if by demission one implied as one should a full discharge of every obligation.[36]

In short, Isobel Rankin measured the distance between Anglo-India and home, recognised the moral drift against imperialism, but could not shed attachment to values incompatible with a transfer of power.

Scott's account of Pankot's view of the Cripps Mission is almost a parody of such 'responsible imperialism':

it was entirely to placate Roosevelt that Churchill (who knew a thing or two, including the fact that the Americans' only interest in India was that the sub-continent should remain a stable threat in the rear to Japanese ambitions in the Pacific) had sent out that Fabian old maid, Stafford Cripps, to do what Churchill knew couldn't be done: put pepper into Indian civilians and politicians by offering them what they'd been offered before, but which a pinko-red like Cripps, unused to office, would see as new, generous, advantageous, a Left-Wing invention. The farce of this particular confrontation between an English pinko-red and grasping Indian leaders had not been lost on the English community. Its total and inevitable failure had been a smack in the eye to Cripps who went home eating crow as well as his bloody vegetables. Given a chance to show that a modern British socialist could achieve what the old-fashioned Right had never achieved, unity among Indians and political co-operation between Indians and

English, he had also been hoist with the responsibility of office; a responsibility which meant, quite simply, having to make things work.

And he couldn't of course make them work because Indian politicians always wanted more if offered anything. Not understanding this he returned to Whitehall with that smile like a brass plate on a coffin and a conviction that while someone had been unco-operative it was not clear who.[37]

Towers ends with a brief appendix, an extract from a letter from Kasim to Gandhi in August 1945: 'I find myself uncertain which of two recent events – the election of a socialist government in London and the destruction of Hiroshima by a single atomic bomb – will have the profounder effect on India's future.'[38] Its point was, as Scott explained, 'to underline the motif that runs through the book, of the distinction between the British at home and the British in India'.[39] The scene was set for Labour's demission of power.

6

A Triumph of Principles

1

Scott opened a notebook for the fourth volume of the *Quartet, A Division of the Spoils*, on 4 February 1971.[1] He began by making a chronological summary of events in Indian history from Lord Linlithgow's departure as Viceroy in October 1943 to Jinnah's April 1946 appeal at an All-India Muslim League Conference for a full six-province Pakistan. It was essentially a summary of V.P. Menon's *The Transfer of Power in India* (1957), with interpolated speculations on Kasim's likely relation to events. He would, for example, have been infuriated by Gandhi's talks with Jinnah after his release in 1944 for they seemed to acquiesce in Pakistan. He would have felt that Jinnah's destruction of Wavell's Simla Conference over the matter of Congress–League parity in any interim government revealed that his dream of Indian unity was 'never based on fact or possibility'. On 14 July 1945 Wavell announced the failure of the Simla Conference.

Scott speculated on this turning point in history: 'When the war stopped, a Tory government, cock-a-hoop, might well have used the Muslim–Hindu detente as a prolonged excuse for doing nothing more. Therefore the British elections and the atomic bomb were the double headed deus ex machina that rushed in and completely altered the picture.'[2] Jinnah's ability to wreck the prospect of an interim government depended on the Tory Government's insistence on Muslim League entry to it: 'THE CRUNCH – CHURCHILL AND THE MUSLIMS', he noted. Churchill's biographer has recently quoted a letter that Churchill wrote in February 1945 after reading Beverley Nichols's *Verdict on India* (1944): 'It certainly shows the Hindu in his true characte. . . . However out of my shadows has come a renewed resolve to go fighting on as long as possible and to make sure the Flag is not let down while I am at the wheel. I agree with the book and also with its conclusion – Pakistan.'[3] Instead

of a Tory government continuing to rule divided India, from
August there was a Labour government determined to transfer
power. As for the atomic bomb, its sudden termination of the
war ended the need for British India as a support area for the
war in the East.

A note of 17 February 1971 reveals that Scott considered
opening *Division* on the eve of Wavell's announcement with
a meeting between Nigel Rowan and Bronowsky. Instead, he
begins with the failure of the Simla Conference and Churchill's
electoral defeat a fortnight later. Between these events Kasim
travelled from Simla to Mirat, his political future unclear. The
action of the novel starts on 4 August with a lecture to an infantry
battalion at Kalyan, near Bombay, by Guy Perron, a field security sergeant. The battalion was to be part of Operation Zipper,
an armada about to leave Bombay for action in the Far East.
Perron, who had been in India since 1943, expected to join it.
On 5 August, eve of Hiroshima, he was to attend with Captain
Leonard Purvis an evening party at a Maharanee's apartment
on Marine Drive to eavesdrop on loose talk about Zipper. He
discusses the future of the Raj with Purvis, an academic economist, in his flat in Queen's Road, opposite the Oval.

The opening of *Spoils* draws deeply on Scott's reading and
experience. The elements of the last stage of the Raj, from
war's end to independence and partition, are suggested, the
Hindu/Muslim conflict and the problem of the princely states.
The scene is one that Scott experienced in 1945, Kalyan and
Zipper, in which he was indeed involved. Purvis's flat is in
Mrs Ganapathy's block, but upstairs where he had never been
but had imagined. Even the Maharanee's party was based on a
recollection:

> The Maharanee *is* connected, but only very vaguely, with
> a shadowy figure (not the hostess) seen at a party in
> Bombay much in line with the one Perron goes to at the
> beginning of *A Division of the Spoils*. She was dancing with
> a woman. I asked someone, Who's that? The answer was,
> A Maharanee, but she's been divorced. I was 25 at the time
> which means it's thirty years ago. But there remained just
> a flicker.[4]

Scott denied that he was Perron but admits:

After all those tortured and tortuous three books one had
to find a way to come in from outside, roughly in one's own
persona: laughing at the whole thing, but knowledgeable
and involved. One had to wrap it up, as it were with a
smile, and a sense of openness. I needed and looked for a
positive man. I suppose every book has to criticize itself,
and Guy is the critic. But a kind and happy one. The sort
of man it would be nice to have a drink and a laugh and
a lunch with. You'd come away from that (at least that's
what I aimed at) feeling you'd had a good time but hadn't
destroyed anything.[5]

Unlike Scott he was public-school educated (Chillingborough)
until he was eighteen and went on to graduate in history from
Cambridge. He was born in 1918 and joined up in 1941.

Scott took the name 'Perron' from a prominent French mer-
cenary soldier in India during the late eighteenth century. He
encountered it in Shelford Bidwell's *Swords for Hire* (1971),
which he enjoyed reading in typescript and reviewing.[6] For
Scott the name probably connoted detachment from the Raj.
Also, after ten years in India the French Perron was still a
sergeant, Guy's rank when he was demobilised. Another of
Scott's devices to open up the view of the Indian scene was
his invention of a cartoonist, Halki, whose contributions to the
Hindustan Times he describes at great length. Halki was typical
of India's brilliant cartoonists, in the line, as Scott explained, of
R.K. Narayan's brother, or the famous Shankar.[7]

Scott was happy with the tone he struck in his first drafts, 'a
somewhat ironic one that should help to illustrate Britain's final
indifference'.[8] The writing would be simpler than it had been for
Towers. Yet it was not until his fifty-fourth birthday, 24 March
1974, that Scott would complete the book.

2

Much of *Division* is concerned with the Indian National Army, a
time bomb now to be detonated. In *Scorpion* Bingham's appeal
to two Jiffs (a corruption of JIFC, Japanese Inspired Fifth Col-
umn) at Imphal in 1944 is the cause of his death and Merrick's
mutilation, while MAK is released in 1944 consequent upon the
news that his son has joined the INA. In *Towers* Merrick delivers
a lecture at Mirat in 1943 on the formation and development of

the INA, which casts doubt upon the loyalty of the massive Indian component of the army upon which the Raj and the defence of India depended. The post-war treatment of the defectors, some 20,000 in all, would be central to the Raj's relations with the major Indian parties, which regarded the INA as a militant arm of the nationalist movement. The problem was crucial for Scott's further investigation of the main 'blocks of interest' that he had set down when he began planning *Towers* early in 1968: the Laytons, representing traditional Raj values (such as paternalism); and MAK, standing for long-established Indian nationalist values (unity and freedom through peaceful processes). The subject appealed strongly to Scott's imagination as another side of the theme of betrayal that had led him to Britain's treatment of the princely states in *Birds of Paradise*.

Scott's emotional connection with the INA goes back to 1946 when he was responsible for guarding an INA officer in Bihar. He was on his way from Malaya to detention camp in Delhi to face charges of brutal treatment of men who had joined or refused to join the INA.

> The only I.N.A. man I ever met was a young Muslim officer whom a fellow-officer and I were once asked to guard, when under canvas near Ranchi, in January 1946. He was on his way to internment or trial. My friend and I were revolted by what we were told (by the officer who deposited him with us) of what he was charged with. We guarded him overnight and, I'm afraid, didn't speak to him. At dawn he suddenly rose and went out of the tent and we followed, in some panic, empty pistols. But he had only gone outside, with his mat, to pray. It may have been from that moment that my emotional interest in the situation began. Perhaps not. The I.N.A. was part and parcel of the movement of India from the nineteenth to the twentieth century.[9]

He could not remember when he first heard of the INA but believed that knowledge of it was more widespread than British versions led posterity to believe.

After his early 1966 inquiries of Monica Felton about when MAK would have heard of Sayed's defection, Scott sought books at his local library, the India Office Library, and the India House Library. He asked Keith Roy's help to secure Shah

Nawaz Khan's *My Memories of the I.N.A. and its Netaji* (1946),
K.R.Palta, *My Adventures with the I.N.A.* and *Two Historic
Trials* (accounts of the trials at the Red Fort in Delhi of the
INA officers in 1945 and of the last Mughal Emperor, Bahadur
Shah, in 1858). Roy spoke to Krishnan Churamani of Allied Publishers, who borrowed Shah Nawaz Khan's book from a friend,
Dr P.C. Gupta of the History Department, Jadavpur University,
Calcutta. The rather frail copy reached Scott in April 1967 and he
found it 'invaluable'. Churamani observed that Gupta had lent
the book 'out of appreciation of your earnestness to present only
authentic materials in your novels about India'.[10] Scott wrote
to Gupta: 'My interest in the INA is, in a sense, relatively
marginal to the book I am writing, but I hate guessing, or
relying on an increasingly uncertain memory, when putting
anything into a book, even though that book is only fiction.'[11]
He pressed Gupta for information lacking in the book: would
an INA officer captured at Imphal have been held without court
martial until after the war? Gupta advised that such prisoners
were returned to India, interrogated and detained until after the
war.[12] Such information sufficed for Scott to conclude *Scorpion*
in 1967.

Towards the end of 1968, still expecting to complete the
sequence as a trilogy, Scott sought *Two Historic Trials* and
other works on the INA from Leon Drucker, a London bookseller.
Drucker offered him several volumes held by an Ahmedabad
colleague and Scott bought A.B. Saqui, *Facts about I.N.A.*
(c.1946), Bhulabhai Desai, *I.N.A. Defence* (1945), *The I.N.A.
Speaks* (1946) and V.S. Kulkarni and K.S.N. Murty, *First Indian
National Army Trial* (1946). The following February he declined
Drucker's offer of *Two Historic Trials*. He had just returned
from a research visit to India: '. . . I am now sure that I have
enough actual documentation – moreover I have valuable stuff
from my trip in the form of notes I took at an interrogation of
three ex-INA men, laid on for my benefit by a fellow writer,
Manohar Malgonkar. I'm also in touch with one of the (then)
young barristers who worked for the Defence Committee.'[13] The
copies of the five books of primary reference that he thus secured
are held at the University of Texas. The Khan and Desai volumes
are heavily sidelined and underlined in pencil. Notes from Khan
and Kulkarni and Murty appear in his notebook. These were

certainly Scott's main written sources, Khan for the history
of the INA and Kulkarni and Murty and Desai for the defence
of the three officers, a Hindu, a Muslim and a Sikh, who were
tried in the Red Fort at Delhi in November 1945. As chief counsel
for the defence Bhulabhai Desai had led a distinguished array of
barristers.

3

Scott's research on the INA, especially on the controversial Red
Fort trials, was a major reason for his planning an early 1969
visit to India. A page from 'The Original Notebook', headed
'1969 Indian trip: Questions', lists five items. Two concern the
INA: 'Disposal of captured I.N.A. officers and men before end
of war and I.N.A. trials. How many trials? Were all officers
cashiered?' And: 'The Red Fort in Delhi. Scene of trials'. The
other questions concern rank in the Indian Medical Service, his
wish to collect 'Partition stories', and 'Parsees in places other
than Bombay. Towers of Silence?'. When he acquainted Mrs
Ganapathy of his trip he simply wrote that he had 'things to look
into in regard to the next and, I think, final volume'.[14] He insisted
in November 1968 that he wanted to see the Republic Day parade
in Delhi and there 'to do some research (Red Fort, etc, actual
background for the I.N.A. trials, that sort of thing)'.[15] It was to
be 'something of a working trip'. He would arrive in Bombay
on Sunday 5 January and visit Delhi and Agra (to see the Taj
and Fatehpur Sikri). In the event, he stayed a week in Bombay,
then a week in Delhi (12–17 January), proceeded for a few days
at Agra and Jaipur, where he stayed with the Nello Muckerjees,
returned to Delhi, and visited Belgaum in early February en
route to Bombay and London.

Just before he left Bombay for Delhi Scott wrote to Gant
that he hadn't settled to much work but was making some
ground with the INA 'if only confirmatory'.[16] He had met a general who seemed unnerved by what was still 'a tricky subject'
'that Indians were very reluctant to discuss'.[17] In Delhi, where
he stayed with the Nag Chaudhuris, his 'not very thrusting
attempts . . . to be shown pertinent archives were not successful'. He asked, but failed, to see the rooms in the barracks at the
Red Fort where the trials had been held.

At Belgaum Scott stayed overnight with the Indian novelist,

Manohar Malgonkar. He owed the introduction to an admirer of his work, John Morris, formerly of the Indian Army and the BBC. Malgonkar arranged a meeting with three former sepoys of the INA, 'a valuable interview'. Scott also spent a night at Green's Hotel where he made a new friend, L.J.C. ('Peter') Goodbody (Wellington and Sandhurst), formerly of the British Army in India. Goodbody had 'stayed on' with his Eurasian wife, Maisie. They lived in the hotel's annexe. Goodbody knew Bhulabhai Desai's son, Dhiru, well.

Either Goodbody or Malgonkar set up an interview with Dhiru Desai in Bombay but it fell through because of a curfew. So did an intended meeting with S.S. Batlivala, one of the INA's defence lawyers, whom a friend of the Nag Chaudhuris suggested he meet. He subsequently sent Batlivala a set of questions about the disposal of prisoners. The answers did not extend but rather confirmed his belief that officers were held and interrogated until after the showpiece Red Fort trial, from the public reception of which GHQ and the Government would be able to devise policy. He confirmed, too, the information he received from an INA sepoy recruited in Germany that he was repatriated to India in June 1945 and held for interrogation fifteen miles from Delhi.

Though such details would remain on file for use in *Division* two years later the 1969 visit was by no means unnecessary. Scott described it as 'a fine trip, and I believe profitable in the sense that I feel recharged'.[18] He had not been to India for five years, and, as he once explained:

> The thing is, for an Englishman, that however much or little experience he's had of India, however many years he's studied its political and social history, whatever view he's formed of it, to write about it effectively – well, to his own satisfaction – he has to keep on going back there, to sense where he's got it right and where he's got it wrong. Perhaps this is pure self-indulgence.[19]

Some self-indulgence was doubtless beneficial for Scott's writing in the domestic and financial circumstances that he faced in the late 1960s and early 1970s. His younger daughter's persistent and worrying illness, its emotional depletion of Scott and his wife, and an ever-falling real income taxed his concentration.

Roland Gant again helped by successfully recommending Scott for an Arts Council grant of £1000 in 1969–70.

4

By late 1971, as each page seemed to take longer than the last to write, Scott felt the need for a further Indian visit. The tone and scale of the first chapter of *Division* were established but a huge task lay ahead. In these circumstances, a British Council invitation to visit Delhi for an International Book Week and undertake a lecture tour came as a 'godsend': 'Had reached a stage in the last novel in the quartet when I realised how much I needed to go to India again,' he wrote to Gerald Hanley.[20] He offered John Willey another reason for accepting the invitation: 'It's a tour I must do because it's the first time the establishment has ever really noticed that I am here.'[21]

The British Council would pay expenses and find accommodation. There was also a fee of £50 a week, which, he reflected to Hanley, would keep him in liquor. The cost, of course, was the preparation of lectures, sometimes delivered at the rate of two or three a day. In November he told the British Council that he would visit Malgonkar and he asked for their Delhi representative to arrange a visit to the rooms in the Red Fort where the trials had been held.

Scott left London on 29 January and within a week had lectured to university audiences (undergraduate, postgraduate and faculty) and others (for example, Rotary) at Bombay, Poona, Baroda and Ahmedabad (where he visited Gandhi's ashram) in western India. On 6 February he had a day at Udaipur and the night at Jaipur (University Guest House). He then stayed five days at the India International Centre in Delhi and visited Chandigarh. From 13 to 20 February he was at the New Kenilworth Hotel, Calcutta, next to the British Council office. He spent a mere thirty hours in Madras, and went on to Mysore (for the first time), Bangalore, Mangalore, and then to Dharwar for his last lecture. On 27 February he was driven to Belgaum, where he wound down at the Malgonkars' for a couple of nights and again stayed a night at Green's and dined with the Goodbodys. He spent a further three days at Bombay and arrived home early in March. The guest lists that he submitted to the British Council for official occasions suggest that he saw most of his previous acquaintances. His lectures included revised versions of papers that he had delivered previously in England, notably of his 1968 'Post-Forsterian View'.

The tangible benefits of the exhausting five-week trip for *Division* are difficult to specify. As Scott did not keep a diary his activities in the interstices between his lectures are uncertain. But it is unlikely that he did not sometimes travel by train. The second chapter of *Division*, 'Journey into Uneasy Distances', was written in 1972 after his return. It is set largely on trains. Sarah and her father travel overnight from Ranpur to Pankot, after a journey from Bombay via Delhi. Sarah's conversation with Bronowsky when they met on the occasion of his seventieth birthday in the Nawab's coach at Ranpur station is recalled. Perron and Merrick join Rowan in the Governor's coach at Ranpur for their journey to Mirat. In 1947 Perron travels to Mirat from Bombay by train and the sequence ends with the last train from Mirat to Ranpur.

Scott was to write to Rebecca West:

> It would have been impossible to write properly about India without dealing with people on trains. One spent so much of one's time on them – hours, days. When you come to the end of *A Division of the Spoils* I expect you'll see how important it was to have established trains as part of the narrative pattern in this closing book. But I wonder if I'd have chanced my arm to such an extent if you'd not written *The Birds Fall Down*.[22]

He had been impressed by that novel when he read it in 1966, especially by the setting of important conversations in French trains in the early years of the century. Coincidentally, Rebecca West's heroine was Laura Rowan, and as Scott had married his Nigel Rowan to a Laura Elliott he was happy that such 'unconscious mimicry' might be taken as 'tribute'.

Visits to the former princely states and palaces at Jaipur, Udaipur and Mysore provided the atmospheric and architectural basis for the details of Mirat. And the experience of staying at the Poona Turf Club, which he had known during the war, would be useful for Perron's breakfast as a temporary member of the Mirat Gymkhana, which 'might have been a duplicate' of it.[23] Otherwise, details of Bombay might be confirmed.

Again, renewal and refreshment by exposure to the light and landscape of India, and the removal from his personal woes, were important. His daughter had miscarried in the psychiatric ward of the Middlesex Hospital the day before he left London. He was very hard up financially, resigning that year from the Society of Authors when it raised its dues. The British hardback edition of *Towers* sold only some 5000 copies in Britain. He unsuccessfully sounded out publishing contacts on the prospects of part-time work. Every second weekend he ground out a 2000-word review article for *Country Life*. The trip prepared him for the hard two-year slog on 500 pages that would complete the *Quartet*.

5

After sustaining the claustrophobia of Anglo-India in *Towers*, essentially by its self-examination through Barbie's consciousness, Scott has Perron view its society with the observations of an historian on field work:

> Their lives were not his affair. He had his own to live. Their dissatisfaction, their boredom, the strain they always seemed to be under, were largely their own fault. The real world was outside. . . . If you allowed yourself to sympathise too much they would destroy you. You would lose what you valued most. Your objectivity.[24]

Scott aimed 'to sustain the note of an underlying historical detachment from scenes which, every so often, are devised to come up from underneath, with all the involvement and emotion felt by the participants'.[25] He urged himself to 'Get *at the people*, come up from underneath them if you possibly can.'[26] The aim is an inner history of the Raj *in extremis*. Scott reverts to the method of *Jewel*, where the Stranger records testimony – Reid's memoirs, White's commentary, Daphne's letters and journal, and so on – but also reconstructs, as in the story of Edwina Crane and young Kumar. Virtually all of *Scorpion* and *Towers* are reconstructions, mostly from evidence supplied by Sarah and Rowan. *Division* reverts to a mixture of reconstructions and commentaries.

Division appears in two books of uneven size. The first is set essentially in the three weeks beginning 4 August 1945, the eve of the atomic age, and ending 26 August with the political future of Kasim decided. The second book of *Division* is set in the period June to August 1947, from Mountbatten's plan for a transfer of power to the dominions of India and Pakistan to partition and the accession of the princely states. The lacuna of twenty-one months was a period of intense political activity: the INA trials, the provincial and central elections and the mutiny of Royal Indian Navy ratings; the Cabinet Mission's long visit and Congress–League wrangles over its scheme; Wavell's establishment of an interim government and his replacement by Mountbatten; communal violence and the breakdown of law and order; the Attlee Government's decision on a time limit for ending British rule and Mountbatten's negotiation of a plan to give effect to it. The effect of the novel's structure is to emphasise that the INA problem undermined the Raj. This is a view rarely advanced by the British but it finds support in recent Indian research. Professor P.S. Gupta, historian of Labour's policies on the Empire, has argued persuasively that 'there has not been enough documentation on what a dent it made in the imperial mind'.[27]

In Book One Perron and Purvis both present critiques of Britain's Indian Empire, while at the Maharanee's Perron meets three of the *Quartet*'s leading characters, Sarah, Merrick and Bronowsky. Sarah is in Bombay to meet her father (just arrived from a prisoner-of-war camp in Germany). Merrick is there to examine a havildar from Colonel Layton's regiment who went over to the INA. Sarah and her father travel to Pankot, followed by Merrick and Perron (who has been transferred to his staff), ostensibly to undertake interrogations relating to the INA. En route Perron meets his old schoolfriend, Rowan. The Governor has asked Rowan to arrange a meeting with Kasim at Mirat. While the first two chapters are reconstructions the next two are accounts by Perron and Sarah, which reveal Merrick's scheme of an alliance with the Laytons by marrying Susan. Colonel Layton, acutely aware of returning to a new world in which the INA had shaken belief in *man-bap*, accepts Merrick as an agent of the Raj's continuity. The first, 450-page book of *Division* ends with another reconstruction. This is a major section of the whole *Quartet*, the long-expected interrogation by Kasim of his INA son, Sayed. The interview convinces Kasim that he must now stand down from politics. He cannot condone Sayed's betrayal, though both Congress and League would defend the INA. Neither could he abandon Congress for the League as Sayed suggested. Scott comments:

> it is my intention to try to show how M.A.K. – a politician like that with a long and honourable career – is in pretty much the same sort of fix as that, say, a man like John Layton, Colonel of the Pankot Rifles is in. All these old Sahibs and all these old Congress warriors are time-expired. The future belongs to a different generation. Sayed is a forerunner of it. Not so much a traitor as a prototype of the Indian wheeler and dealer, the Indian man of the twentieth century.[28]

Book Two is a mixture of reconstruction and Perron's diary: 'we are now at the climax of the book . . . I have chosen [to set it] in Mirat because it is a Princely State and it was in such that the absolute indifference to the obligations of history is most clearly stated or exemplified.'[29] The theme of *Birds of Paradise* thus reappears. Scott fills the lacuna between September 1945 and June 1947 with lengthy descriptions of Halki's cartoons, which offer ironic comment on the main historical events. Perron arrives at Mirat as Merrick's funeral is in train. He uncovers the story of Merrick's marriage to Susan, his appointment by Bronowsky to the state's police, and his murder. Mirat accedes to India. He witnesses the slaughter of Muslims, including Ahmed, in a train out of Mirat.

6

Scott explains the novel's title: 'The spoils we are dividing are moral spoils – the remnants of an old nineteenth century morality and notion of what we are in the world to do, either as a good Fabian, a good Indian, a sensible Englishman, a bitter reactionary or a weeping colonel. Upon this division the workaday world casts a casual eye . . .'[30] The division represented a 'triumph of principles': Pakistan for the Muslims, freedom for Congress, and the fulfilment by Britain of her promise of self-government.[31] In the division hundreds of thousands of people died – 'Massacred by other principled people'. Scott and Perron quote Emerson: 'Nothing can bring you peace but the triumph

of principles.'[32] But for Sarah, Scott's authentic voice, the lapse
of responsibility overrides fidelity to principle:

> The massacre itself must have been a retaliation for the
> killings and burnings the night before in Mirat when Mus-
> lims attacked Hindus because Mirat was going under Con-
> gress rule. I suppose Ahmed was marked out as a victim
> not just because he was a Muslim but because the people
> who killed him didn't want Muslims in the Congress, or
> didn't trust Muslims in Congress and his father was still
> in Congress. And perhaps because they knew his brother
> was a rabid Pakistani and perhaps because on top of that
> they hadn't forgotten that Ahmed's father hadn't stood by
> the INA, which made it senseless anyway because Sayed
> had been INA. But it was all so senseless. Such a damned
> bloody senseless mess. The kind which Ahmed tried to shut
> himself off from, the mess the *raj* had never been able to
> sort out. The only difference between Ahmed and me was
> that he didn't take the mess seriously and I did. I felt it was
> our responsibility, our fault that after a hundred years or
> more it still existed.[33]

Both felt the break from the past: 'We recognised in each other
the compulsion to break away from what I can only call a
received life.' In any event, a shared moment in time, the
British–Indian affair, was over, except for the few who stayed
on – in fact or in spirit.

The Prose-Poet of the Raj in Decline

1

Reviewers invariably applied the very highest critical standards to Scott's novels, whilst often conveying the impression that they did not quite achieve them. His pre-*Quartet* work earned him a steadily growing reputation among a limited readership. In 1960, John Davenport commended Scott as 'a writer's writer' who was becoming a 'reader's writer'.[1] In the late 1950s and early 1960s he was variously praised for the veracity of his backgrounds, his narrative skill, his delicately managed time sequences, his high seriousness, his rich characterization and powerful storytelling.

Jewel remained in the top-ten fiction sales lists for several weeks. Robert Nye wrote in the *Guardian* of its consolidating his position as 'the prose-poet of the Raj in decline', 'a born storyteller'.[2] In the *Daily Telegraph* Iain Hamilton described it as 'a breathtaking accomplishment', 'portraying the epic movements of the time in terms of fully realized individuals'.[3] Now Jocelyn Brooke referred to Scott as 'something of a novelist's novelist in . . . his elaborate narrative technique', but believed that he was really writing a sort of 'politico-sociological history' in novel form.[4] The *TLS* was less kind about 'pages and pages of all too solid discussion about the condition of India past and present'.[5] It complained that Kumar and Merrick were too unusual to be representative figures and that as a study of Anglo-Indian relations *Jewel* was disappointing. In the *Sunday Times* John Raymond praised the 'sum effect' of 'an absorbing series of tableaux of the Indian scene'.[6] However, Scott wrote to protest at his allegation that Daphne resembled Adela Quested in Forster's *Passage*.[7] There were comparisons with American authors: *The Times* saw in *Jewel* 'some of the intensity of Faulkner';[8] the *New York Times Book Review* saw Kumar as a Brahmin version of the black author–hero of Ralph Ellison's

Invisible Man (1952);[9] the *Listener* discerned a 'Dreiser-like accumulation of detail'.[10] However, Orville Prescott lamented that in the USA it had been 'generally ignored or briefly and obscurely praised'.[11] He viewed it as 'a major work' by a man of 'blazing talent' who wrote of a wide range of characters caught in an historical situation not of their own making. The review that pleased Scott most was Richard Lister's in the *Evening Standard*, which made much of the 'absorbing and brilliant' use of the rape to establish the racist mentality.[12] 'At the end we feel we have got as close as possible to a comprehension of this tragic episode in our history.'

Scorpion fared less well. Again it was almost ignored in the USA. 'They hate sequels,' Scott reflected.[13] There was some carping in Britain. In the *New Statesman* Gillian Tindall mused that Scott 'must have considerable faith in his audience's fidelity'.[14] He was greatly annoyed by Maurice Capitanchik's criticism in the *Spectator*: 'This very long tale is, at bottom, North-West Frontier flag-waving for moderns – it is tedious.'[15] The characters were 'speechifying stereotypes', the novel 'rather literal', 'social history-cum-myth, without the sparkle of life'. He was puzzled by John Raymond's latest comparison of Sarah with Adela Quested, who was 'only a casual visitor to India'.[16] Many reviewers dismissed *Scorpion* in a few lines, though three weeks after its appearance it did reach third place in the best-sellers' list. Again Iain Hamilton accorded high praise to 'a work of literature informed by honesty, understanding and love', of 'moral and aesthetic integrity', whose scale and effect were Tolstoyan.[17] It was 'just about everything that the most voguish fiction of the day is not. . . . What an opportunity for an able writer to employ every weapon in the armoury of denigration, to reinforce success with contempt for the past, to lay down a smoke screen of inverted racialism, and finally to break through into triumphant sensationalism behind a barrage of pornography and sadism.' Scott had neglected all such easy opportunities.

When the reception of *Towers* was more disappointing, it was clear that the *Quartet* would bring Scott neither the immediate literary acclaim nor the financial independence for which he had hoped. The publication of *Division* was the occasion not only for its review but for a critical assessment of the sequence as a whole. In *The Times* David Pryce-Jones acknowledged the underestimation that Scott had so long suffered, and suggested reasons for it:

> Lead reviews and critical essays and the newest jack-in-the-box professors turn a blind eye to Paul Scott. Partly, I think, because his subject is India, a country which has dropped out of our national view as if it had never been in it. Also partly because he writes about people at a time when symbols are supposed to matter more. *A Division of the Spoils* completes his quartet of Indian novels, altogether in heroic contrast to the private rigmaroles of modern fiction.[18]

In May 1975 Scott was to enjoy his best press yet.

2

On the day of its publication in *Country Life*, Scott responded that H.R.F. Keating's review was 'the best and most perceptive I've ever had. . . . Not only that, you ask the major question, Why India? why India then? And answer it better than I could have hoped anyone could or would.'[19] Keating, the creator of the fictional Bombay detective, Inspector Ganesh Ghote, knew his India:

> These are imaginary people and imaginary events, but the framework in which we read of them is, as Mr Scott says, 'as historically accurate as I could make it', which is to say about as accurate as any fallible mortal is likely to get. Indeed, taken solely as a history-book *A Division of the Spoils* is marvellously informative and accurate, and a good deal more attractive reading than most works of history, even popular history. . . .
> Why India in this day and age? What relevance in the Raj?
> India today for almost everyone in Britain is no more than one exotic area of the world to be enjoyed or dismissed at whim, merely another Mexico. But Mr Scott is right to have devoted so much of his life to recreating one short period of Indian history. In the not so distant past he writes about, India was nothing less than the great testing ground of all that was the British attitude to living, even all that Western man stood for, since (let us admit it, though it is

unfashionable) not that long ago the British attitude was the leading point of Western civilization.

The notions of honour, of decency, of being right and doing right, which today have been all but swallowed up in the seas of 'situation ethics' and a fluid morality, were then the highest point of what man could achieve. And in India these values were supremely tested. They did not in the end pass the test, or Englishmen would be honoured administrators in India today. They were not quite capable of encompassing everything the sub-continent asked of them. But there was a titanic struggle when the test came. It was a struggle that called for a superb chronicler. In Paul Scott it found one.

A similar note was struck a few days later by Phillip Knightley in the *Sunday Times* when he applauded 'a literary triumph of the highest order':

Although the characters dominate the story, the backdrop of a world at war is always present, so that at the end a picture of those fateful years in the destinies of two great nations should have been composed and Emerson's belief – 'The persons who make up a nation today, next year die, and their experience with them' – should have been proved wrong. If Scott were able to achieve this, then a history student years from now should be able to say to his professor, 'Yes, but what was it really like in India in the last days of the Raj?' and be told, 'Read these four books and you'll not only know, you'll understand.' A slice of history, and the experiences of everyone, English and Indian, who lived through those years are here in these pages.[20]

Scott felt 'vindicated' by Knightley's review.[21]

In the *Telegraph* David Holloway essentially endorsed Keating and Knightley: 'In 100 years' time when men are wondering what India in the 1940s was like, they should read Mr Scott's quartet. It will not only describe events but, far more important, will give, by its shambling bulk, its hesitancies, its repetitions, headlong rushes and *longeurs*, a portrait of the real India in a way no formal history could.'[22] In the *Guardian* Christopher Wordsworth saw the *Quartet* as a 'recessional' by 'a writer whose sense of historical responsibility' was intense.[23] Here was

to be found 'the true ghost of the Raj'. In the *Sunday Telegraph*
Francis King (India born) praised 'the skill of an accomplished
historian'.[24]

3

However, Scott felt that some of the adverse comments by
reviewers failed to understand him. Within a month of *Division*'s appearance he wrote to Storm Jameson, a great admirer
who had written long letters of fulsome praise to him: 'I've
decided I hate being published. I end up by feeling dirty, I don't
know why. Only letters from friends mean anything, and I've
had few enough of those.'[25] One of Pryce-Jones's comments left
him doubting whether he knew anything about women:

> Perhaps [wrote Pryce-Jones] too many lonely bachelors
> are defined by their jobs, and not much else. The women
> are kept in their proper place while the men get on with
> politics and power. So large and Tolstoy-conscious a book
> ought to have made its declaration somewhere that human
> beings are motivated by love of the opposite sex. Had this
> masculinity been broken, the book would also have lost a
> sameness of tone.

Scott protested: 'I thought this was what Sarah was about, and
Ahmed, and Perron. And Daphne and Hari (and on the arcane
side, Bronowsky and his invisible boy friends).'[26] In the *TLS*
J.G. Farrell complained of signs of weariness in the writing of
Towers and of the whole work's confinement: 'And demanding
as the work already is for someone interested in India, there
is a risk that the reader without such an interest will find it
claustrophobic.'[27] Scott was disappointed at Farrell's failure to
see his point:

> Claustrophobic I'd accept (I think that to an extent any
> good novel is), but difficult because of lack of interest in
> the subject is a criticism I'd have thought Perron himself
> takes some pains to criticize. No reviewer has actually
> yet picked up the point that the tragedy of British–Indian
> history was the indifference shown by Britons at home both

to Britons abroad and Indian subjects. Not even Cameron in the *New Statesman*, who is a political and not a literary journalist.[28]

It would be a little while before Scott's central historical themes would be discussed (and longer still before they were evaluated!).

4

With time for reflection it rankled with Scott that the stature of the *Quartet* as literature remained unrecognised. In August 1975 he wrote to Elizabeth Cadell: 'Kind as the critics were, I can't help wishing they'd said more about the characters and less about the history. Overall they gave the impression that the thing was history students would be able to learn something from 100 years from now. Which is nice for the students.'[29] And to Jean Crowcroft: 'Somehow . . . writing about India in this country brands you as an historian, rather than as a novelist. As a novelist you find yourself contending with the people who wrote about India 40 years ago or more.'[30] He confided to friends feeling not elation at the completion of his masterpiece but 'bereft, deprived, worked out', unable to put one sentence in front of another.[31] He wrote to Dorothy Ganapathy: 'The one thing I've had to fight here is the awful English literary–academic fixation on Kipling and Forster. For heaven's sake! Did nothing happen between 1924 and 1945?'[32]

Scott was mortified when James Cameron, the experienced journalist on India, accused him of derivativeness. 'It was history,' he responded, 'rather than Forster's fiction, that left me with my own Protestant missionaries and Daphne. . . . Sherwood is certainly my blueprint for Miss Manners, Miss Batchelor and Miss Crane. A triptych. One hates to be suspected of borrowing other people's fiction. Using and refurbishing history is a different matter.'[33] Cameron apologised profusely, adding: 'There can be no doubt that your India and mine are the same, though your monumental achievement makes what I have done look pretty puny.'[34] Nevertheless, Cameron's subsequent comments were ungenerous and sometimes silly. He complained of the repetitiveness of the *Quartet*, believing one book would have done as well as four. And confused by Granada's translation of

Mirat to Udaipur, he complained at the transformation of the latter's Maharaja into a Nawab.[35]

Scott had sold his manuscripts to the University of Texas because no English university had ever approached him. He wrote to Dorothy Olding: 'Here there isn't a bleep from universities . . . they are still convinced that Forster = India = Forster.'[36] And to Dipali Nag: 'The English academics remain indifferent, but then the English have never been the slightest bit interested in India. So long as they had Kipling and Forster to refer to they seem or seemed to think that was enough in regard to *that* part of the world. How insular we are, as a people.'[37] Scholars in Texas, Washington and Illinois were 'ahead of anyone here in thinking my stuff is worth looking at and studying'.[38] In Washington D. M. Burjorjee, who taught English Literature at Montgomery College, Maryland, was planning a book on Anglo-Indian fiction whose centrepiece would be a study of Scott. At the University of Illinois Francine Weinbaum was well advanced with a doctoral dissertation on the *Quartet*. In August they helped arrange a lecture tour for him. Morrows opened their New York apartment for his use and both John Willey and Dorothy Olding travelled to Washington for a celebration arranged by Burjorjee. In Illinois he stayed with the Professor of Literature, Bernard Benstock. At Austin, Texas, he gave the first paper, 'The Raj Quartet', to a now famous Faculty Seminar on British Studies. He stayed with a good friend from his agency days, Peter Green, now Professor of Classics. He had the satisfaction of viewing his working papers and manuscripts in the magnificent Harry Ransom Humanities Research Center, 'beautifully catalogued and preserved', adjacent to the papers of Bernard Shaw.[39] He signed the door that bore the signatures of authors such as Tennessee Williams and William Faulkner and came away satisfied 'to think my stuff is there, for everyone who in the future may wish to consult it'.[40] There were, he told Mrs Ganapathy, 'literary and academic areas in the U.S.A. much more alive to our conjoint, though opposed histories, than there are in this country, where you might expect them to exist'.[41] Americans were 'not smothered by the Kipling/Forster tradition'.[42] Sadly, American interest was too exclusively academic. Sales of *Division* there were no better than in Britain. Scott's three-week lecture tour earned a mere $1230 gross ($583 net). Still, it boosted his morale. And he indulged an old passion, dancing the band out with Dorothy Olding to good trumpet at the Rainbow Room.

5

Soon after he returned to London Scott was interviewed by Caroline Moorehead for a long profile in *The Times*. It was bylined 'Getting engrossed in the death-throes of the Raj' and appeared on 20 October under a photograph of him at ease in his garden. Miss Moorehead remarked that though he had strong admirers, was well reviewed and sold respectably, if not widely, he 'remains surprisingly little known, and has on occasion been dismissed rather summarily as the Nevil Shute of India'. This, she thought, was partly because of his nature – 'a retiring, pensive man, a worrier, with a slow quiet voice, a long nose that gives him a mildly melancholy air, and a rather subdued charm'. He lived unobtrusively, seldom leaving his house. But she believed the real reason for his relative obscurity was his chosen subject. 'The English', he is reported as saying, 'are very insular, and extraordinarily uninterested in India.' He was ashamed at Britain's ignorance of India and shuffling out of responsibility for it. 'I do not', he said, 'see how you can rule for 200 years until midnight August 14, 1947. And then stop.' Moorehead reiterated his admitted dominant concern: 'The terrible thing is the indifference and the ignorance' of the British towards an empire that had provided them with the benefits they so long enjoyed. He also condemned 'the new slave trade'. The British admitted formerly colonial peoples after the war and 'then want to kick them out'. At the end, Moorehead most praised Scott's characters: 'They are real people and you believe in them. And you also believe in the moment at which he has chosen to freeze them.' Of this he said: 'You have to get the historical framework right. So that the action grows both out of the characters and the pressure of history.' Scott observed a few errors of fact in the story but commended it as 'a fine job'.[43]

6

Scott was greatly pleased to hear that Max Beloff, Principal of the new private-enterprise University of Buckingham, proposed to write a review article on the *Quartet* for *Encounter*. Beloff was a Fellow of All Souls College, formerly Gladstone Professor of Government and Public Administration at Oxford University, and was engaged in writing a two-volume history of the decline of the British Empire. Here was 'the first sign of academic interest' in Britain.[44] He wrote enthusiastically to Charles Pick, managing director of Heinemann's:

> American academic interest has been growing of late – and that is why I'm so chuffed about Beloff on this side. . . . I've been very much aware of a gap in British reaction (in spite of those reviews) – and this is something Beloff might help to begin to fill. To be taken seriously by an establishment literary-historian could just start the ball rolling in the right way.[45]

The article, 'The End of the Raj: Paul Scott's Novels as History', appeared in May 1976.

Beloff was primarily concerned with 'the historian's questions': 'Has Paul Scott succeeded in making Britain's retreat and the partition of India that followed it . . . more directly intelligible than these events might otherwise be to us? Can he convey both what these events meant to those affected directly by them and their wider significance?' He answered that Scott reveals 'the relative insensitivity of Britain (and of Britain's new rulers in 1945) to their own responsibility for the human tragedies on a major scale that were the product of Britain's precipitate departure and of the abandonment of their implied pledges to the rulers of the Indian States and their peoples'. Scott does convey 'the full tragic significance of the combination between a sense of duty and a sense of permanent alienation from those to whom the duty was owed'. History, Beloff argued, was still being written by the generation that voted Attlee, Cripps and Bevin into power. Historians were circumscribed by the closure of relevant archives and were apt to see what happened as inevitable. Time was required before they could appraise the actions of the policy-makers. Scott, with a novelist's imagination informed by a solid groundwork of study, had achieved an understanding of the partition in terms of Britain's past inadequacies, notably the garrison-like existence of the Raj and the ignorance and indifference of the

British at home. He had widened the reader's 'moral sensibilities' towards Britain's role in the subcontinent's independence and partition. 'His achievement is on any count a major one.'

Here was high praise indeed, and insight into Scott's essential purpose. He thanked Beloff profusely: 'I really am profoundly grateful to you both for the review itself and for the time and thought you have devoted to four very long books. It has been especially encouraging to have these novels discussed in terms of history as well as works of imagination, and it delighted me to find so many aspects that were important to me as themes being isolated and emphasised.'[46] Scott expressed his appreciation to Gant: 'What a good piece it is. He homes in on every point one could hope for, looking at the book as history and not just literature.'[47] And to Dorothy Olding: 'I'm glad to have had the thing assessed as history as well as literature, and he's done it in just the proper sober and enthusiastic way.'[48] Scott met Beloff in the company of Gant and Pick at the Garrick Club. He sought him out for more intimate conversation over lunch at L'Epicure.

Beloff was eloquent on the capacity of the novel as compared with historical writing to elucidate the relationship of the British with India:

> the subject is one to which the historian's techniques, however refined, may not be able to do justice. For, in the end, what was decided by governments depended upon their response to a whole series of pressures, some of them no doubt at least in theory identifiable and even quantifiable, others, however, much less easy to grasp and define. What the British thought and felt about India between 1935 and 1947 was the product of a great many personal experiences of civilians and soldiers, of businessmen and reporters, of missionaries and policemen. And it was not only their own experience that counted but that of earlier generations who had come to India and grown to love or hate it, and of all those who had never been to India but whose first glimpse of the exotic had been in the pages of *Kim*.
>
> For these reasons, the role of the novelist in exploring the relationship between the two peoples has always been a crucial one; and novels are an historical source that we are only now beginning to exploit. For the novelist has the freedom both to present the circumstances of the case, and through his personages to evoke either directly or through

symbolic reference the complex of feelings, physical and moral, that go to make up the experience as a whole.

This opinion has recently been endorsed by an American professor of literature, David Rubin, who extols Scott's novels as 'a striking justification of the novel genre . . . as opposed to what is generally called history. His fiction . . . explores universal human potentialities and destinies for which history can provide only a deplorably inadequate record.'[49]

7

Scott would have prized the appreciation of the author, R.K. Narayan, whom he met, liked and greatly respected. Narayan has written that Scott's 'perceptions are subtle and penetrating; his descriptions display a remarkable understanding – more accurate than any British writer on Indian themes'.[50] Malgonkar wrote of *Scorpion*'s 'disquieting inner knowledge of the Indian character which only Forster among non-Indians had'.[51] He applauded *Towers* as the best novel published in 1971 and wrote: 'I who have lived through those times cannot help feeling amazed at your knowledge of them. Barbie, unlikely creature, lived and made one feel sad when she stopped fluttering.'[52] Mrs Malgonkar added: 'What dreadful —es the other women were, anyway, they *were* all like that here with such few exceptions.'[53]

M.M. Kaye was not convinced of the representativeness of Scott's main characters. She has been critical of his memsahibs, in particular, but appreciative of his insight into the last years of the Raj: 'This was the epoch that Paul saw and wrote about: and if, in a hundred or three hundred years from now, any one wants to know exactly how it was then, they will be able to find out by reading "The Raj Quartet". It is all there. . . .'[54]

The celebrated travel writer, Freya Stark, was in India for five months towards the end of the Raj. After reading the first half of *Jewel*, she wrote to Scott: 'I can't begin to tell you what I feel about its *greatness*; the sweep and vision.'[55] She read the remainder of the *Quartet* in three weeks and wrote of it as 'a really great monument'. She concurred with his emphasis on the paternalism of the military system and its centrality to the Empire: 'Even the army wives as far as the soldier *families* were concerned and the Colonel's wife was Mother.'[56] In her book about army wives, *On the Strength* (1975), Mrs Veronica Bamfield – one herself – wrote that Scott's 'magnificent sequence paints a truly representative picture of the last days of the Raj and the army in India'.[57] Wartime officers with experience of 'aid to the civil power', of preparing counter-propaganda against the INA and of the internal situation and the general milieu, wrote to Scott to applaud his achievement.[58]

8

Many readers of the *Quartet* have found 'their India' in Paul Scott's Raj. Mrs Ganapathy and Keith Roy felt they knew the characters in *Jewel* and had talked with them. D.M. Burjorjee claimed an identikit likeness to Kumar. He had been born in Burma in 1923, served in the Indian Air Force and was married to an American. He wrote of 'the plight of a second career Harry–Hari who, like others of his ilk, is as "homeless" here as he was in India'.[59] An American correspondent, Catherine Bates Shiraeff, wrote to Scott of her husband, '*my* Hari Kumar', a Hindu from Assam who was a member of Mensa.[60] Scott was cheered by such assurances of Hari's reality, for he felt deeply such critical comments as that of an English school teacher who told him that she could not believe in it.[61] In 1968 he read the autobiography of Sasthi Brata, Calcutta born and London resident. Brata was the thirty-year-old son of a Bengali Brahmin who had admired English education and business methods. In his review for the *TLS*, Scott quoted: 'The deepest tragedy of British Rule in India is that it succeeded in producing individuals like me who can neither feel an identity with their own people nor accept . . . the West. We are left crying in the wilderness and are forced to adopt the horrifying vulgarity of the stranded pose.'[62] The complex fate of the déraciné westernised Indian was real enough.

So too was that of the INA traitor–hero. Mohan Singh himself, organiser of the INA after his capture in northern Malaya, appreciated Scott's 'attempt to convey the INA situation fairly'.[63] In 1976 he was in the Rajya Sabha and invited Scott to be his guest and the guest of the Punjab Government on his next visit to India. He sent Scott an inscribed copy of his memoirs, *Soldier's Contribution to Indian Independence* (1974).

Scott was delighted that John Morris, the BBC's reviewer

of *Jewel* and formerly Controller of the Third Programme, recognised his India in *Jewel*. For Morris had served in the First World War and later as an Indian Army officer with the Gurkhas. He believed that Mayapore 'might be almost anywhere in northern India and its inhabitants, both Indian and British, are described with such acuteness that time and again I felt that I was reading about one or another of the several familiar places in which I spent some years of my own earlier life. These were all people, I felt, that I actually knew.'[64] A reviewer in the *Illustrated Weekly of India* presumed that Mayapore was in Bihar and wrote of the topographical details of the cantonment as 'excessive'.[65] Scott commented on speculation about it: 'I think the thing is that English cantonments, and Indian towns, tend very much to look like one another. But it's always a compliment to be told that a reader feels he has recognised his own (perhaps) favourite place, or one he knew well.'[66]

Like all of Scott's locations, except the cosmopolitan British–Indian cities of Calcutta and Bombay, Mayapore is fictitious, 'an amalgam'. The province of Ranpur lies between Delhi and Calcutta. Its capital of the same name is nine hours from Calcutta by rail, beyond Benares. Pankot is a few hours by train to the north of Ranpur, Premanagar 200 miles to the south-west en route to Mirat. Mayapore is east of Premanagar. In geographical terms, Scottland is therefore in the United Provinces (or Uttar Pradesh). Yet Scott's knowledge of the UP was slight. He never visited Lucknow, nor probably Kanpur nor Allahabad. From his post-war encampment at Chas and Lohardaga he knew the bordering eastern province of Bihar better and drew on his recollections of its summer capital, Ranchi, and perhaps its capital, Patna. He told an Indian journalist that Mayapore was in the eastern UP/Bihar border area.[67] Scott follows UP nomenclature for official appointments but a Merrick, who scraped into the Police Service, would probably have been posted to Bihar.

Anglo-Indians and members of their families applauded the *Quartet*, though Scott's correspondence contains letters from one descendant of a long military and proconsular line that complain of his undue emphasis on the 'evil' in their lives.[68] Scott rejected the judgement vigorously. One son of an Indian

Army brigadier saw his father in Brigadier Reid.[69] Another
Anglo-Indian son exclaimed, 'By God, you've caught the types
of the British in India. I've known them all my life.'[70] Several
had known Miss Crane and Lady Chatterjee. It was certainly a
compliment to Scott that Mr W.H. Saumarez Smith asked him
to write the introduction to his book, *A Young Man's Country:
Letters of a Subdivisional Officer of the Indian Civil Service,
1936–1937* (1977).

In a long article for the *Listener* Richard Rhodes James
acknowledged that Scott had 'pinned . . . down with a marvellous precision' those who were 'a part of the Raj'.[71] He was born
in Burma in 1921, as was one of his brothers, whilst his sister and
two other brothers were born in India. Aunts, uncles, cousins
and grandparents were scattered through the subcontinent. His
father, like John Layton, won the MC in Mesopotamia in the
First World War. His sister was Susan's age and, like her,
returned to India just before the Second World War. Rhodes
James joined the Indian Army at home and landed in Bombay
a year ahead of Scott. He recalls meeting a spinster missionary like Miss Crane who also admired Gandhi, entertained
young British soldiers and similarly lived on the margins of
the memsahibs' society. Scott, he writes, 'fixes beautifully the
rootlessness that we felt', the difficulty of identifying with the
country. He served in north Burma, was involved in Operation
Zipper, and corroborates Scott's detailed account of the landing
near Port Swettenham. He recognises Purvis's critique of the
'reactionary' Raj and Perron's derision at Merrick's accept-
ance of 'Kiplingesque double-talk'. He finds 'reality' in Scott's
account of murder, rape and racism at Mayapore. His parents
were caught in the Anglo-Indian time warp and returned home
in winter 1946–7 to feel 'perplexed by the new rulers of England'.
When his mother wrote to compliment Scott on his remarkable
accuracy of detail, he replied: 'It's important to get the small
things right.' Rhodes James concludes: 'He got us right, in the
big things and in the small, in the traumas as well as in the tea
cups. . . . Now, if we are asked what it was really like, we can
say with confidence, "Read Paul Scott". He has ensured that our
past will never be wholly lost.'

An Anglo-Indian 'who really knew the score', Sir Herbert
Thompson, KCIE, wrote to Scott at length in June 1975, 'amazed

and full of admiration . . . at your achievement in volume after volume – for I do regard your four novels as . . . history in the guise of fiction'.[72] He had gone out to the ICS after the First World War and was a sub-collector in South India when *Passage to India* appeared in 1924. He had transferred to the Political Service, hoping for postings to the states; but in fact he had spent long years on the Frontier. In 1939 he was Political Agent in Jaipur. Thereafter he was Deputy Secretary in the Political Secretariat, Delhi, Head of the NWFP Civil Service, Resident in Kolhapur and the Deccan States, and then in the vast Punjab States (extending from Karachi to Tibet). He ended his career as deputy to Sir Conrad Corfield, head of the Political Department. He had had the sort of career that Scott had accorded to Conway and Rowan. He thought that Gopalakand might well be based on Gwalior and Mirat on Bhopal. Here, indeed, was verification of Scott's fictional representation of the princely states and their relations with the Political Department. Scott wrote that it was 'marvellous to feel, at 55, that you've got an old and retired and expired man's life right enough for him to write to you to say so'.[73] And 'to have earned the approval of such a distinguished Indian Civilian means far more to me than whatever the literary critics say or don't say'.[74]

9

Though Scott was himself a theorist, as his lectures amply reveal, he was sometimes impatient of literary criticism as a genre. He complained about a lengthy analysis of the *Quartet* by Benita Parry in *South Asian Review*, the journal of the Royal Society for India, Pakistan and Ceylon.[75] Benita Parry wrote of the *Quartet* as 'a muted celebration of a concept rather than a critique of a reality', a '"tribute" to a segment of the British middle class', of 'what the British–Indian relationship might have been', an imperial dream rendered 'irrelevant' by the exiles' unawareness of currents of historical change. Furthermore, the limitations of Scott's concern for India only in its relation to the British exiles rob his work of 'a total authenticity'. For Scott, this piece by a 'blue-stocking' was 'much too intellectual for me to understand'.[76] Or rather, he wrote to Francine Weinbaum, those parts he did understand 'immediately seem cancelled out by the next paragraph'.[77]

Whilst he kept at arm's length prospective authors seeking biographical details, he was forthcoming to serious students of his work, such as Burjorjee and Mrs Weinbaum. He kept up a frank and lengthy correspondence with Mrs Weinbaum and talked openly of his work when they met at the University of Illinois, Urbana-Champaign. He was, indeed, protective of her interests. 'What I said to you is for you,' he wrote after their meeting.[78] Mrs Weinbaum's doctoral dissertation, 'Aspiration and Betrayal in Paul Scott's *The Raj Quartet*', was presented in mid-1976 and she has since published articles based upon it.[79] Her interpretation draws on psychoanalytical insights, an approach of which Scott was sceptical. When a correspondent had written to him of the Oedipal relation between Bill Conway and his father in *Birds* Scott repeated his description of it in the novel – a 'label'.[80] More recently an American scholar has written on 'Love, Sex, and History in *The Raj Quartet*', viewing thwarted love as Scott's metaphor for the failure of imperialism, and homosexuals as his realists and seers.[81]

There have now appeared two short volumes intended to introduce Scott's fiction to a wider audience. Both are laudatory. Dr K. Bhaskara Rao's volume in the Twayne's English Authors series ranks Scott as 'far superior to Kipling and Forster' and close to Tolstoy, Henry James, Conrad and Madox Ford; as the benchmark for all writers on the British experience of India.[82] Dr Patrick Swinden wrote his thoughtful and enthusiastic volume from 'guilt at failing to notice the work of a fine writer before he died; to draw the attention of other people professionally concerned with literature to the great merit of Paul Scott's fiction; and to try to encourage a wider public to read . . . some of these splendid novels'.[83]

Recent academic comment on Scott has generally elevated his status. In 1983 M.M. Mahood of the University of Kent complained of the 'small heed' that 'serious literary critics' had paid to the *Quartet*, and suggested 'that it aspires to be an imaginative recreation of Tolstoyan breadth and depth'.[84] David Rubin accords Scott's corpus pre-eminence in his study, *After the Raj: British Novels of India Since 1947*:

Let me say at the outset of my discussion of Scott's Indian novels that they are far and away the best fiction dealing with Anglo-Indian relations not only since Independence but since the very beginning of such fiction. 'Best' comports two specific areas of excellence: first, the depth and breadth of understanding of the British who lived and worked in India; and second, still more important, the sheer novelistic power and technical resourcefulness grounded in an observation of manners both objective and compassionate – the qualities one often thinks of as specifically Tolstoyan.[85]

10

It seems sad that despite his long absorption with the last years of the Raj Scott never encountered British scholars professionally engaged in the subject. Whilst he laboured in isolation in his study at Hampstead Garden Suburb, a few miles away at the University of London in Bloomsbury and at the India Office Library in Blackfriars Road major projects on the partition of India and the transfer of power were proceeding.

In late 1965, as Scott committed 'every aspect' of *Scorpion* to exploring Britain's 'failure to unify' India, Sir Cyril Philips, Director of the School of Oriental and African Studies, inaugurated a seminar to bring together the testimony of British, Indian and Pakistani witnesses and academic studies of the partition. It met fortnightly until summer 1967 when an international conference was assembled for a whole week. Some of the participants were contemporaries of Scott whose experience of the Indian Army in wartime had similarly led them on to a lifetime obsession. Others included British politicians, former members of the ICS, judges and governors of provinces, a Muslim Raja, Congressmen and leading Muslim Leaguers. Scott would have contributed wisely and enjoyed the company, though he declined an invitation from the *TLS* to review the published collection of the papers that appeared in 1970, *The Partition of India: Policies and Perspectives, 1935–47*, edited by Sir Cyril Philips and Mary D. Wainwright. He found Sir Conrad Corfield's chapter useful and sidelined it in his copy, but he dismissed the book as 'an awful hodge-podge . . . "awful" in the overall sense of its losing attempt to make sense'.[86]

Partly as a consequence of the interest aroused by the project, in March 1966 the Wilson Government reduced from fifty years to thirty the closure period for official archives and in the following year decided to publish an extensive series of documents on the transfer of power. This massive enterprise, which would eventually extend to twelve volumes, was to be edited by Professor Nicholas Mansergh, Master of St John's College, Cambridge, Mr E.W.R. Lumby, formerly of the India Office, and Sir Penderel Moon, whose *Divide and Quit* Scott had reviewed in 1961. It began with Scott's own turning point to partition, the Cripps Mission of 1942, the opening year of the *Quartet*, and finally ended in 1983 with his terminus, August 1947. His belated awareness of the series in 1976 is mentioned below.[87] There is indeed an insularity in the life of a nation when the fictive and academic analyses of its history run on parallel lines at the same time without meeting.

Someone with Power who Rules

1

The only major character to appear in each of the *Quartet* novels is Ronald Merrick. He represents the continuity of the Raj in the maintenance first of law and order, and later of military authority. He is central to the Raj's responses to the Quit India movement, to the INA problem, and, in the end, to communal unrest in an Indian state. He is important in the definition of moral issues such as race relations, *man-bap*, loyalty, the imperial idea itself. As Perron explained to his stepson, Edward Bingham, Ronald meant 'someone with power who rules'.[1]

The creation of Merrick has been hailed as a major achievement. Francis King saw him as 'subtly ambiguous' in everything yet wholly real, while Pryce-Jones described him as an 'enigmatic figure' whose activities touched upon everybody.[2] Farrell traced his progressive revelation as 'a pathological case', a narrow-minded policeman in *Jewel* who becomes 'a monster to rank with the Master of Ballantrae'.[3] Storm Jameson wrote of Merrick as 'one of the most horrifying characters in any novel'.[4] Balzac would have 'coarsened and so diminished him morally, intellectually'. Merrick 'evolved', whereas Dostoevsky would have presented him fully fledged at the start. In any case, Merrick was not really a monster, for at the end the reader, like Bronowsky, feels 'compassion' for him as a man whose every chosen and perverse principle fell away as he experienced love.[5] The love of an Indian boy finally destroyed his racist–imperialist philosophy. Much earlier, too, as Scott's notes explain, his nightmare of the bicycle bespoke his burden of guilt, 'centred on the object that points him to his own capacity for unjust dealing and prejudice and envy'.[6]

Whereas all of the other major figures present themselves in some form of testimony – as the Stranger or Traveller gathers his evidence from memoirs, letters, journals and conversations with survivors – Merrick alone is represented solely through the records and recollections of others, from which the Traveller creates his reconstructions. Scott replies to Jameson: 'There is not a single paragraph in the entire million words written from his point of view. He is peripheral, marginal. But central. And of course you pounced on that other key word – compassion – at the end, when Bronowsky described Merrick's death to Perron.'[7] Scott acknowledged that Merrick represented something essential to his exposition of the Raj, the psychology that underlay its 'coalface' dealings with Indians. Jerry Tallmer of the *New York Post* asked about Merrick's sado-masochism: 'Is his quasi-homosexuality supposed to lie at the root of what was British rule in India?' Scott replied: 'I wouldn't quarrel with that. I think there is something perverted about imperialism. But it's sort of an echo. Sort of a reflection on me as well – the bad characters and the good ones. It's all an author can do – expose himself each time he writes a chapter.'[8] For the creation of Merrick Scott could draw on his own early homosexual leanings and experiences. He told Caroline Moorehead that he got under the skins of his characters 'by trying to get under my own'.[9] Merrick emerged from Scott's getting under his own skin, and finding an arcane side that appalled him. As Sarah said, Merrick was our 'arcane side', and he appalled her.[10]

As with so much of the *Quartet* Merrick emerged from Scott's 1964 visit to India, his response to the racism of the new generation of sahibs and memsahibs from Stevenage and Luton, and especially from his Andhra village experience. His stay with Dass revealed to him his 'sahib's face'. He told Weinbaum in 1975: 'When I go to India now I am, I have to admit, distinctly aware of a sense of superiority, of having once been a representative of a people who were once in control. It's hateful. But you can't duck out from under it. It's what I call Sahib's face.'[11] Scott's village experience and his expression through Merrick of the role of racial distance and even contempt contribute to an understanding of the mechanics of the Raj, the means of governance. *Jewel* suggests the inadequacy of liberal administration to the challenge of Quit India, whilst *Scorpion* exposes the insufficiency or anachronism of *man-bap* paternalism for imperial continuity. Merrick is made the mouthpiece for the realities of empire.

When a reader complained that there was not enough revealed about Merrick in *Jewel* to explain his hatred of Kumar, Scott emphasised that Merrick was 'only marginally established' there.[12] In *Jewel* we see Merrick only through the eyes of Daphne and, to a lesser extent, Sister Ludmila. He is the voice of racial apartness in conversation with Daphne. In *Scorpion* he enacts contempt for Hari and seeks to provoke his fear in exemplification of 'the situation' of British–Indian relations. In the underground interrogation room he experiences a long night of the soul, 'revealing things to himself about himself'.[13] The enactment pricks his conscience, reveals an underlying sense of common humanity and his latent homosexuality.

Through Merrick's association with Bingham, Scott builds him up 'from a more intimate angle'.[14] Merrick risks his life attempting to save Bingham and momentarily accepts the paternalistic, missionary myth of the Raj. He has several weeks in hospital to reflect and further reveals himself in conversation with Sarah: 'Merrick, of course, is (a) trying to create an impression on Sarah, inviting her *in*, as it were, and (b) trying to talk himself out of his bad conscience while at the same time preening himself. He's also hamming a bit, enjoying the wounded-soldier gambit. Given half a chance Merrick will always gab.'[15] From the conversation Sarah felt that Kumar and his aunt lay as victims 'like a weight on that conscience of his which he said he could examine but give a clean bill to'.[16] Perhaps 'the way in to him [was] to become his victim and then to haunt his conscience'. She could not bear the prospect, proposed by Susan, of his becoming godfather to Bingham's child. He was the dark side of the Raj, drawing down the shutters of its crumbling house against all of India.

2

Merrick, then, is not a monster but Scott has made him to give voice to the monstrous underside of imperialism in India. Scott was always troubled by the silence that Anglo-Indians had pre-served about their work. He wrote to Sir Herbert Thompson: 'Nothing is more maddening to me than the lack of printed evidence of how men like you actually spent their day. From chota hazri to sundown. Minute by minute, hour by hour.'[17] Official Anglo-India was 'the silent service'. Even a great man like Wavell was 'inarticulate' in relation to Indians, whom 'he wasn't quite able to like'. *'That's* what I'm after. Should be most grateful if you would help me understand this problem.' He acknowledged that he had given a voice to the ordinary English missionary like Barbie who had lost faith in the imperial mission. She was one of the inarticulate for she never stopped talking: 'The inarticulate have always fascinated me – and the overarticulate are of course (I think) only a variation of that kind of person. Actually I think one writes novels to give ordinary people a voice they don't possess in life.'[18] Scott espoused T.S. Eliot's maxim that literature was 'a raid on the inarticulate'. In 'The Original Notebook' he wrote of the novelist: 'He is there, often, to say the things that are not said in life. . . . He tries to make articulate the silences that exist between people.' Merrick was there to express the unstated assumptions of an empire ultimately founded on force. In Perron's words: 'There he is, the unrecorded man, one of the kind of men we really are (as Sarah would say).'[19]

In *Division* Perron the historian and Bronowsky the seer expound the significance of Merrick. He is the 'invisible' man in England, of humble social background, in search of a persona. As an arriviste on the imperial stage, he invents his own role, and lacking established connection defines himself by choosing his supporting cast. Lacking class distinction he supports his role by exaggerating racial differences, enacting his white contemptuousness to draw envy and fear from his victims, yet also to provoke them into retaliation. Hari is beaten and abused sexually, subjected to humiliation, invited to hit back. The INA havildar, Karim Muzzafir Khan, is shamed and insulted until he commits suicide. The boy Aziz, with whom Bronowsky believes he first finds peace, is beaten as Merrick courts his own destruction through retaliation. Perron believes that Merrick has chosen him for his predictably persistent antagonism or insubordination, so that Merrick can define himself adversarily.

Perron sees that Merrick chose a social definition that was anachronistic, alliance with Anglo-India in its decline. Merrick hoped not to be drowned by the tides of history: 'But he will be. Can't the fool see that nobody of the class he aspires to belong to has ever cared a damn about the empire and that

all that God-the-Father-God-the-raj was a lot of insular middle-
and lower-class shit?'[20] Merrick believed that the British had
'abandoned the principles we used to live by, what he would
call the English upper- and ruling-class principle of knowing
oneself superior to all other races especially black and having
a duty to guide and correct them. He's been sucked in by all
that Kiplingesque double talk. . . .'[21] He coveted everything that
Colonel Layton had and was but despised his lack of nerve and
guts to live up to it, his sentimentality towards Indians.

Bronowsky saw that 'Merrick without question was a man of
the past', believing implicitly in both the real and the imagined
virtues of the Raj, possessing an 'unshakable sense of his own
authority'.[22] His style was suited to the ambiguities of politics
in Mirat on the eve of independence. He saw his own career
as continuing after independence in Pakistan, 'somewhere like
Peshawar, near the old North-West Frontier, where administration was much more of a question of off-the-cuff decisions
and not of just going by the book'. [23] Bronowsky attributed to
him a hope 'that his murder would be avenged in some splen-
didly spectacular way, in a kind of Wagnerian climax, the *raj*
emerging from the twilight and sweeping down from the hills
with flaming swords'.[24]

Perron, as the historian casting a backward glance from
the vantage point of the early 1970s, ruminated on the fateful
meeting of the types of Kumar and Merrick: 'they had met
before, countless times. You can say they are still meeting,
that their meeting reveals the real animus, the one that historians won't recognise, or which we relegate to our margins.'[25]
This was a comment on the essential racialism of the Raj
and on its persistence in contemporary Britain. In a July 1971
review of Ursula Sharma's *Rampal and His Family*, a socio-
logical study of an immigrant Indian family, Scott wrote of
the pressing need for 'the clarification of a subject increasingly
vexed by the obstinate refusal of people of one colour to recognise their own aspirations in people of another. Meanwhile,
presumably, we must all limp on, wearing the thick boot of
envy at the end of one leg and the iron of contempt on the
other.'[26]

Of Scott's critics, Tariq Ali has most perceptively recognised
Merrick's significance:

Merrick was the fictional representation of a genuine phenomenon. He was not just one bad apple. . . . He was a type
and there were facsimiles in every town. In fact Merrick
is a powerful and contradictory character, displaying all
the vices of the English petty-bourgeois, but in a different
context each time. At home in England he would be bitter,
but loyal, loathing his social superiors, but accepting their
right to rule and extremely fearful of the class below. In
India the inhibitions disappear. It is, after all, a large and
liberating sub-continent. There are countless incidents of
sexual and wanton brutality against Indians by British
soldiers and officers throughout the period of British rule.
India affected a layer of the English petty-bourgeoisie very
deeply. That is why I have always thought that it was a bit
of a cop-out to kill Merrick off at the end. Surely he returned
to Britain after Independence, joined the Conservative
Party, became a Cabinet Minister and then began to be
haunted by the sight of odd Asian faces in *his* sweet and
pleasant land. His racial obsessions gained the upper hand.
He confesses to a radio interviewer that the job he would
most like would be the Viceroyalty of India (this was two
decades after India became independent). He breaks loose
from the patrician constraints of his social superiors. He
sees 'rivers of blood' on Mondays and Fridays and 'excrement pouring through letter-boxes' for the rest of the week.
It was, of course, Asian excrement. He could tell the difference. He had stirred it long and often in India. In other
words, racism in contemporary Britain is closely related
to the colonial experience.[27]

The proposition is that Merrick expressed the racial prejudice that, after April 1968, was most publicly represented by
Enoch Powell. There is good reason to probe, in due course,
Powell's view of the Raj, as well as Scott's concern at the rise
of Powellism in Britain. First, however, Merrick's career as a
Police Officer involved in suppressing the Quit India movement
requires scrutiny.

3

Merrick was born in 1916, the same year as Nigel Rowan, the
son of a north London newsagent–tobacconist. His parents were
killed in an accident while he was at grammar school and he
owed his Indian career to an encouraging assistant headmaster

who took him in as a ward. After matriculating he scraped in to the Indian Police, around 1936, a stage when the British Government was having difficulty attracting recruits. Candidates were chosen by competitive examination and interview, and had to pass a riding test. As Merrick told Barbie, riding was important to him (perhaps as a social accomplishment). He would not have passed out high enough to secure appointment to the plum provinces, UP and Punjab. The Bihar service would have matched his examination performance. He was appointed Assistant Commissioner of Police on two years' probation and addressed by the Secretary of State for India, Lord Zetland, who urged the recruits to keep up the traditions of the service. He probably sailed P & O from London for Bombay and arrived in 1937. Like the chronicler of the IPS, Martin Wynne, a few years before, he might have been given his 'first lesson in British arrogance' by a shipboard companion who advised him not to give way to an Indian on the sidewalk but crowd him into the street.[28] He then went on his first long train journey, to Hazaribagh, Bihar, for Police Training School.

There were some 600 members of the Police Service, two-thirds of them Europeans. The probationer was required to pass examinations in Criminal Law and Procedure, the Police Regulations, two languages and police practice. After three or four years as an ASP an acting short-term appointment as superintendent was common. A permanent appointment would follow soon afterwards. Merrick would have been DSP Mayapore for perhaps a year before the Quit India movement. As such he would have been responsible for one of sixteen districts in Bihar, with an average police strength of some 800. There was one policeman to each 2625 of the populace of Bihar in 1939.[29]

Ronald Merrick entered an administrative context in which the racial superiority of the British was taken for granted. Recent British scholarly studies document that fact, notably Kenneth Ballhatchet's *Race, Class and Sex under the Raj* (1979) and David Potter's *India's Political Administrators, 1919–1983* (1986). Ballhatchet's study surveys the nineteenth century and culminates in the Edwardian twilight, with Curzon's close attention to preserving racial distinctions even at the level of the Indian prince. Ballhatchet introduces his theme: 'Racial feeling among the British became more explicit and more aggressive in the course of the nineteenth century and reached its peak during Lord Curzon's viceroyalty, between 1899 and 1905. The Mutiny of 1857 showed them the insecurity of their military power.'[30] The social hierarchy was made to correspond to the political hierarchy, with sexual behaviour subordinated to both. The official elite established itself at the head of the social hierarchy, and 'English class attitudes are transformed into racial attitudes in an imperial setting.'[31] Perron's observation rings true: in England the social status of Merrick and Kumar would have been reversed. In England a prince might be a favoured guest at Windsor and Sandringham; in India he would feel it a high honour to be received at Government House. The Anglo-Indian elite distanced itself from the Indian populace socially and as a political necessity. Britishers who threatened to bridge the distance aroused concern. Ballhatchet concludes that 'to the end of British rule the authorities would discourage such unions. All members of the ruling race were supposed to keep their distance.'[32] At the level of the prince, Churchill's wartime Secretary of State for India, Leopold Amery (1940–5) lamented, with no less racist sentiments, the consequence of this policy in October 1943:

> If India is to be really capable of holding its own in the future without direct British control from outside, I am not sure that it will not need an infusion of stronger Nordic blood, whether by settlement or intermarriage or otherwise. Possibly it has been a real mistake of ours in the past not to encourage Indian Princes to marry English wives for a succession of generations and so breed a more virile type of native ruler. Perhaps all that may yet come about.[33]

Against this the Viceroy noted an appropriate expletive: 'Hell!'
Potter found that in India the esteem of the British public school – the dominant catchment area for the ICS – for the idea of service 'tended to accentuate a feature less noticeable at home: racial superiority'.[34] Its breeding ground was the very superior status of official Anglo-India as compared with that of the service class in England. Sir Percival Griffiths (ICS, Bengal) remarked: 'There's no doubt you did feel you were the ruling class. . . . We did, no doubt, tend to get aloof and

perhaps a little bit conceited.' David Symington (ICS, Bombay) agreed: 'We realized that we were members of a very successful race; we realized that we were working in a country which was as pre-eminently unsuccessful as we were successful. . . . We tacitly – not explicitly – felt ourselves to be rather superior people.' In an Indian setting, Potter argues, 'such beliefs were translated into a sense of racial superiority'.[35]

As with other assumptions, for the official cadre did not learn its demeanour from books, racial superiority largely defies precise reference. But there is clear evidence in private documents. John Orr (ICS, Bihar) notes overhearing Justice Herbert Meredith in the locker-room of the Bankipor Club, Patna, in the early 1940s, vent his feelings about two Indians whom Orr had proposed for membership:

> They were the same racialist feelings which had sustained the empire-builders and administrators for generations. . . . [There] was a rejection by India, or at least by all self respecting Indians, of British rule because of its implicit assertion of racial superiority. It strengthened my sympathy for the Indian cause . . . but in those days this was a feeling which one kept to one's self. . . .

Andrew Hume (ICS, UP) wrote home that his Collector was 'not a bad fellow', but 'rather one of the "big stick" type, with a deep-rooted contempt for the "nigger" whom he abuses in language not always very choice'. As a young man Hume himself believed that 'the Indian is at heart a funk, i.e. the Hindu', and that 'it is indeed a consideration whether one would care to work a life time subject to "popular wog" control'. Michael Carritt (ICS, Bengal) observed that in Midnapur in 1930 T.B. Jameson (ICS, Bengal) had 'an almost pathological contempt for Indians in general and a desire to make them suffer. His judicial sentencing was notoriously severe.' John Maher (ICS, Madras) admits that when he arrived in India in 1928 he felt 'contempt' for Indians generally 'due partly to youthful arrogance, but mainly to youthful ignorance'. Potter generalises that 'probably a majority of ICS men held more or less strong feelings of racial superiority *vis à vis* the rest of Indian society and culture'.[36]

Between the wars European recruits to the Indian services

were assured that 'medical officers of their own race would
be available' to them and their families.[37] It is true, as Scott
believed, that official relations between British and Indian
members of the services were close at work, but that racial
distance was general in their social relations. Marriage with
Indians was discouraged and rare. With Quit India it is said
that in Bihar and the UP a 'great divide' occurred, 'a complete
social separation of the Indian and the British officers in the
Civil Service'.[38] It has been suggested that the ferocity of the
Quit India movement in eastern UP and north and western Bihar
was compounded by anti-white fury among Indian evacuees
returning there from Japanese-held South-East Asia.[39] Scott
recorded that there were said to be white and brown escape
routes from Burma. One British official, Robert McGuire (ICS,
Burma), recalled:

> One of the worst features of the evacuation was the haphaz-
> ard trek of Indian native soldiers armed with their rifles
> and ammunition. . . . With a few notable exceptions, Bri-
> tish officers preferred to help no one but themselves, to
> ignore the men and make their own way out as quickly as
> they could. Civil officers, again with exceptions, were just
> as bad. It was altogether a disgraceful exhibition of rotten
> morale and it was no wonder that the native soldiers – and
> for that matter most of the comparatively small number of
> British soldiers on the route – became increasingly aggres-
> sive and difficult to control.[40]

4

In a brilliant account of 'Empire and Sexual Opportunity' Ronald
Hyam observes the shyness of imperial historians about putting
sex on their agenda.[41] Characteristically the popular radio series
Plain Tales from the Raj, subsequently edited and presented
as a book, skirts the unmentionable. A 1981 biography of the
Raj's last Commander-in-Chief, Lord Auchinleck, 'almost hys-
terically' denied that his interest in Indian boys had an active
sexual side.[42] Hyam believes that 'crossing the colour line was
sometimes done in contempt, with cynicism, and racial discrimination', which lends credibility to Merrick's treatment of
Kumar.[43] The contemptuous Papua New Guinea White Women's
Protection Ordinance (1926), which imposed the death penalty

for blacks who attempted to rape a white woman, but which neglected to protect black women, is an interesting comparative case. Hyam contends that sexual relations and taboos soldered the invisible bonds of empire.

Evidence of sexual, as of racial, attitudes is under-recorded, and often survives only when something went wrong. Suicide was the sequel to the revelation that Lewis Harcourt (an ex-Colonial Secretary) had exposed his 'stalagmite' to a thirteen-year-old Etonian, and to disclosure of the Anglo-Boer War hero, Sir Hector Macdonald, as a paederast. Merrick's relations with young boys at Mirat emerged only through his cabalistic murder, a death Bronowsky believed he had courted. The Mutiny hero, John Nicholson, enjoyed boys as his principal solace. Apropos of Bronowsky's theory that Merrick's fulfilment through Indian boys threatened the edifice of racialism on which his imperialism depended is Barry Smith's linkage of the Purity Campaign in late-Victorian England with fears of imperial decline: 'This grand fear directly linked sexual pollution with the threat of social chaos and the fall of the Empire.'[44] The plausibility of the homosexual Bronowsky's life in an Indian state is also endorsed by the confession by E.M. Forster (ex-tutor to a crown prince) of his intercourse with an Indian boy in 1921.[45] One can but speculate about the young Merrick's relationship with the schoolmaster whose ward he became; but surely the early death of his parents may be related to his observed 'hollowness'.

5

The racist–imperialist contempt that characterised Merrick's treatment of Indians had long festered under the Raj. Churchill, whom Lord Halifax believed had never shed the prejudices of a late-Victorian subaltern, spoke of the 'gross, dirty and corrupt . . . baboos' and thought they 'needed the sjambok'.[46] In 1942 Viceroy Linlithgow was Curzonian in his contemptuous dismissal of Congress leaders save Nehru as 'a collection of declining valetudinarians who have no grip on the country', and who 'could never run straight'.[47] Soon after the outbreak of war, the head of the Home Department, Sir Reginald Maxwell, saw in Congress opposition an opportunity to bring down emergency legislation that would enable the Raj to 'crush the Congress finally as a political organization'.[48] As for the Indian Army,

Auchinleck could look back to 'the great bitterness bred in the minds of many Indian officers in early days of "Indianisation" by the discrimination, often very real, exercised against them, and the discourteous, contemptuous treatment meted out to them by many British officers'.[49] Indian officers had been seg-regated into separate units, suffered differential rates of pay and terms of service and 'the prejudice and lack of manners by some – by no means all – British officers and their wives'.[50]

During the Quit India movement there were indeed Merrick-like servants of the Raj willing to resort to cruelty. The initial concern of the Indian National Congress when it met in Sep-tember 1945 for the first time since August 1942 was to condemn the excesses of over-zealous officials who suppressed the Quit India movement. Sir Francis Wylie, post-war Governor of UP, recalled that there had been officers who 'used on occasion methods which I cannot condone and which, dragged out into the cold light of 1946, nobody could defend'.[51] Wavell found Nehru 'reasonable' and opposed to any general inquiry but he argued for the retrenchment of certain individuals against whom there was strong public feeling and well-substantiated evidence.[52]

In the week following the arrest of the Congress leaders the Superintendent of Police at Hazaribagh in the Bihar Province, Lawrence Russell, handled the threat of a crowd to a police station severely:

> Russell decided that corporal punishment inflicted on the ringleaders in public would have a salutary effect and discourage others from making further attacks on gov-ernment buildings and explosive magazines in the mining area. It might, of course, precipitate an immediate attack upon the police, but that was a risk that would have to be taken. He gave all 28 of his prisoners ten lashes with his dog whip in the presence of the crowd before sending them off to the Central Jail at Hazaribagh. This was undoubtedly illegal and maybe cruel, but there was no further trouble throughout the district.[53]

Russell was supported by higher authority and awarded a medal. An intelligence report gives an account of the restoration of order in the Ghazipur District of Eastern UP by Michael Nethersole, ICS, officiating Commissioner in the UP.

After this display of non-violence for ten days the government started its show of violence and the first victims of this violence were its own supporters. Commissioner Nethersole and Civil Guard Commander Marsh Smith entered the district with British and Indian troops. The first place they visited was Rampur – a village near the Railway Station Orihar. There they got hold of Thakur Sheo Shanker Singh ex-chairman of the District Board, a staunch supporter of the government and the worst enemy of the Congress. He and his brother's son-in-law were publicly whipped. Similar treatment was meted out to many others. Even the elders of the village were not spared. Seeing Baldeo advancing towards them with a mob, they flew away to Irihar where they indiscriminately beat members of the public. Post Master Ram Rakha Pathak was also beaten. In Saeedpur, Commissioner Nethersole greeted the Tehsildar with a couple of kicks. He also laid waste the market and had several persons whipped publicly. A patriot was stripped naked and tied to a tree and they started beating him with thorny bamboo sticks. He was asked to repent for being a Congressman and to promise that he would never put on khadi again. They whole of his body was terribly bleeding but he went on shouting patriotic slogans till he was unconscious. The president of a Congress Committee Sjt. Har Prasad Singh was similarly tied to a tree and beaten with thorny sticks until his body was all wounds and pieces of flesh were flying on each stripe. When he fell unconscious they applied salt over his wounds and sent him to prison. Sjt. Vikrama Dutt Singh, the correspondent of the Benares Daily 'Aj' was also similarly beaten and is now lying in the Ghazipur jail.[54]

At Nagpur, where a curfew had been declared, it was recorded that Michael Sullivan, Under Secretary to the Government of the Central Provinces, 'boasted at the club in the evening that he had jolly good fun having shot down 24 niggers himself' – mill hands, milk-maids and newspaper boys who were in the street too early that morning.[55] In his study of the Quit India movement, the American scholar F.G. Hutchins writes:

The mood of underground workers was also expressed in a widespread preoccupation with the threat of rape. Rape always accompanies the chaos of warfare, resulting from military bravado or the desperation of sick and vengeful men. The incidence of British rape at the time of the Quit India movement cannot account, however, for the pervasiveness of Indian anxieties. The British and their allies, it was held, were everywhere indulging in rape with phenomenal determination. Agitators had long portrayed British exploitation of India's resources in metaphors of sexual violation, to suggest British contempt for all standards of civilized conduct, and to induce Indians to respond to a political challenge as they would to a family insult. With an added access of anger, natural British propensities would, it was feared, inevitably engender unprecedented atrocities.[56]

Mr M.L. Saksena, a Congress Member of the Legislative Assembly, complained to Linlithgow:

From what I have seen in places I have visited as well as from reliable reports received by me, I am convinced that the country has witnessed a regular 'black and tan' regime and even worse. Jallianwalla Baghs have been enacted at more than one place. To cite only one instance from my own constituency I may refer to Sitapur. Peaceful demonstrators were fired upon to teach them a lesson, and at the lowest computation the number of killed, I am informed, is sixty, besides many more injured; although the official report gave only 5 killed. Those killed were removed in lorries and disposed of by the police without any post mortem. Two of the litigants received shots in the court room and were killed and their dead bodies were removed by the police in defiance of the order of the Judge directing them to be taken to the hospital. Worse scenes are reported to have been enacted in the Eastern Districts of these Provinces and Mr Nethersole has been posted at Benares with full powers of the Government to deal with the situation, and I am informed he has been doing so with a vengeance. Railway men belonging to repair gangs have been shot at from the patrol trains and one or two have even been killed. Life has become very cheap specially after the local Government's communiqué issued here, as in other Provinces, that there was not going to be held any judicial enquiry or even any formal inquest into all such happenings. . . .

How have Government been treating thousands of those arrested and detained in connection with the present movement? Perhaps you are aware that they are not allowed to have even interviews with wives and children nor are they

permitted to write even business letters. Further they are
not allowed even their clothes and beddings from outside
nor are they supplied with any newspapers. Besides this
they are being subjected to other pin pricks.[57]

The punishments inflicted during the movement included
generalised collective fines (not related even to alleged specific crimes but intimidatory), the destruction of dwellings
and contents, the quartering of troops on villages, exemplary
beatings, mutilation, torture and killings. Captured rebels were
treated brutally and the rate of deaths in custody was abnor-
mally high.[58] Apart from Bihar, by 5 September the police
had killed some 340 Indians, the military 318.[59] Scott's source,
Amba Prasad, quotes the following overall statistics released in
Parliament: police and military firings, 538; total killed, 1028;
sentences of whipping (excluding UP), 958; arrests, 60,229;
machine gunning from the air, 6.[60] He states that whipping
was cruelly administered by a rattan cane half an inch thick,
and that the police were accorded wide discretion.[61]

Fifty-seven battalions of troops were deployed to restore
order in what Linlithgow regarded as the 'most serious rebellion' in India since the Mutiny.[62] In the context of the rebellion
Merrick's maltreatment of Kumar and the prolonged detention of six innocent youths for their suspected involvement are
plausible. Merrick's transfer to the Indian Army (1st Punjab
Regiment) in 1943 and rapid rise to the rank of colonel by 1945
is not surprising. Another Englishman of modest origins, with
whom Scott associated an anachronistic imperialism and racial
prejudice, enjoyed a similarly meteoric ascent.

6

Enoch Powell had already scaled the heights of academe when
he enlisted in 1939. Born in 1912, the son of schoolteacher parents, he was Professor of Greek at the University of Sydney
at the age of twenty-five. After service in the Middle East and
North Africa Powell went to India as lieutenant-colonel on the
staff of Major-General Walter H. Cawthorn, the Director of
Military Intelligence, in August 1943. He was to organise joint
service intelligence. At once he fell 'hopelessly and helplessly
in love with India', felt that India was a Briton's patrimony, felt

needed and called, and if there had been a foreseeable future in
the Indian Army would have opted to 'leave my bones there'.[63]
There was no future and he returned home in February 1946,
while Cawthorn, 'almost a second father' to him, stayed on in
Pakistan. During his Indian period he became, like Merrick,
proficient in Urdu and developed a passion for riding. He read
Kipling voraciously.

In spring 1944 Powell joined Auchinleck's staff at Dehra Dun
as a brigadier – the youngest at thirty-two in the British Army –
and a member of the Army Reorganization Committee, chaired
by Lieutenant-General Sir Henry Willcox, which was charged
with planning the Raj's post-war army. He wrote the long report
'Reorganization of the Army and Air Forces in India', all but
single-handed as Willcox acknowledged.[64] He argued from the
premise that India lacked sufficient officers of character and
education to achieve military independence for twenty years:
'If therefore the Indian Army is to reach and maintain its present size in war at any time in the next 15 or 20 years, at least 17500
emergency commissioned British officers will be necessary to
make up the requisite 35000; in other words, at least 50 per cent.
of the emergency commissioned officers will have to be British.'
In view of danger of war, especially from Russian aggression,
the Raj must remain for at least twenty years.

7

Back in London in February 1946, Powell joined the Conservative Party Secretariat. By the end of the year he had prepared a
single-spaced fifty-foolscap-page study of the Indian problem.[65]
It is a remarkable document, as the preface signals:

> The background assumed in this study is that a general
> collapse of law and order in India, accompanied by a
> mutiny of the armed forces, has occurred and that Britain
> has interposed to restore the situation by force of arms. In
> the areas affected by the collapse, which amount to most
> of the country, military administration is still in control;
> but a stage has been reached where civil government and
> administration can be reintroduced.

Powell begins by assuming 'a fresh start', a return to first principles. He claims

the advantage of breaking once for all through the atmosphere of hallucination which surrounds Indian politics.
Political progress in India has consisted largely of rearing
up one superstructure of words and forms upon another,
until little correspondence remains between realities and
the political organization which appears to have been
attained. As long as this hallucination is unbroken, politics and political forms, which should be only the means
to social and economic ends, will continue as now to be the
be-all and the end-all. By breaking the spell, or assuming
it broken, we escape back to real objects, real factors and
real methods.

The reality that Powell invokes is essentially economic and
most of the study concerns economic planning, proceeding from
efficiently organised agriculture, industrial development and
the extension of such services as power, communications and
transport. Much of the rest of the paper advocates central control and administrative efficiency to achieve these goals. The
states/provinces division will be replaced by logical regional
units of administration. The key to 'the full exploitation of the
country's resources as a whole' was investor confidence, but no
regime since the early years of the century, whether central or
provincial, had provided the 'assurance of permanence' essential to that confidence. Britain was the only source from which
stability and confidence could be provided: 'The predominance
of the British military and police power has long been accepted
throughout India as something axiomatic. A scheme of reform
supported by the associations of permanence and power which
attach to the British authority would have the best prospect
of being accepted and worked.' Powell applies the same logic
to the need for British civil administration that he had to the
military. The narrow base of education and experience meant
that 'on grounds of qualification alone the administration must
for decades contain a large non-Indian element'. It followed that
'the final control of Indian affairs must . . . be vested in the
United Kingdom Government'.

Powell judged India to be quite unfit for self-government. The
existing electorate was neither in a position to express itself
on the economic and social issues that constitute the subject
matter of politics, nor did it divide on these issues: 'The fact

that the so-called Indian political parties are with unimportant exceptions fixed and unchanging communal bodies would render any system of self-government unworkable.' Powell was winding back India's political advance, from the 1946 breakdown of Congress–League negotiations, through the Act of 1935, the Montagu–Chelmsford and Morley–Minto reforms, to the Curzonian obsession with imperialist efficiency. History was to be erased, and the reintroduction of forms of self-government must await a time when communal differences were overlaid by political differences. A 'moratorium' must be placed on representative self-government, though government might be made 'responsive' to Indian opinion and prejudice: 'It is a form of government such as Lord Curzon at the beginning of this century conceived to be alone suitable for the India of the coming decades.' In the interests of centrally controlled and imperially administered economic development there must be a 'deliberate and complete cessation of political and constitutional activity as it has gone on in India for the past four decades'.

Powell sent his extraordinary document to R.A. Butler on 3 December 1946 as an elaboration of a policy that he had adumbrated on the day that Labour's Cabinet Mission scheme had been announced, 16 May 1946: 'Britain must institute a social and economic revolution in India before she can bring about a satisfactory constitutional settlement.'[66] His approach thus preceded the breakdown of Congress–League negotiations that the scheme provoked. The breakdown that he invoked as his preface was not an actual collapse, but a device through which the realities of the Indian problem might be arrayed for inspection and treatment. A breakdown would necessarily take Britain back to first principles, but they were the right starting point breakdown or no breakdown. Powell's approach bears a significant resemblance to one option enumerated by Wavell in an evaluation of policy alternatives in a memorandum that he gave to Attlee on 3 December: the restoration of British rule for a substantial period of years. Labour dismissed it summarily. In view of Scott's strictures on Labour's manner of transferring power, it is an option of some interest.[67]

It is not surprising that Powell resigned as secretary of the Conservative Party's India Committee in protest against its acquiescence in Indian independence. He recalled 'walking

about the streets all night trying to digest it'.[68] Powell has
recently written of 'the dream that the British and the Indians
dreamed together for so long, a dream unique in human history
in its strangeness and its improbability'.[69] It was a dream of
British brotherhood with a united India under the Crown. 'The
Raj itself . . . was a mirage.' The 'imperfect dream' was 'bound
to break one day . . . though some of us, under the influence
of our love affair, dared to believe otherwise'. In a recent
interview Mr Powell has amplified his meaning to include the
paradox or unreality of a parliamentary democracy governing
India paternalistically or despotically.[70] The parliamentary tradition is of the essence of Britain's history and some day the
anachronism of a paternalistic Raj must be submerged in the
flow of that history. In Powell's phrases there are unconscious
echoes of Merrick's moment of sharing 'the whole impossible
nonsensical dream' as Teddie dies faithful to his belief in the
doctrine of *man-bap*. When Merrick was created in 1964–5 Scott
knew nothing of Powell's views on immigration. As he wrote in
another context, that was 'too early for Powellism to have had
any effect and add bite' to racialism in Britain.[71] But in his own
mind there would develop a link between Merrick's racism and
Powell's campaign in the late 1960s.

8

In November 1969 Scott delivered a lecture, 'Enoch Sahib: A
Slight Case of Cultural Shock', to members of the Commonwealth Countries' League in London.[72] The previous month he
could not say 'how largely Mr Powell will figure in the talk itself'
but thought the title summed up 'the general drift' of his talk.[73]
'Enoch Sahib' gave a contemporary context for what he had
since his village experience of 1964 called 'Sahib's face'. For Mr
Powell the Commonwealth was 'a gigantic farce', 'a disastrous
encumbrance from which Britain must break free'.[74] Common
citizenship of the Commonwealth was 'an outworn fiction', for it
embraced peoples who had cast off allegiance to the Crown. 'To
have our laws so far out of relation with realities was the cause
of the massive coloured immigration in the last decade which
has inflicted social and political damage that will take decades
to obliterate.' In his infamous speech at Birmingham on 20 April
1968 he had reported anecdotes that inflamed the issue, such as

that of the old white woman of Wolverhampton whose coloured neighbours pushed excreta through her letter box and who suffered abuse as a 'racialist' from 'charming, wide-eyed, grinning piccaninnies'.[75] For Powell the Commonwealth in whose name coloured immigration occurred was ultimately 'not a political entity, or indeed an entity at all except in make-believe'.[76]

For Scott the Commonwealth was 'a warming concept, a splendid example to the world of interracial co-operation', and Powell's Birmingham speech was 'a noxious emanation'.[77] But the main point of his lecture was not to attack Powell. It was rather to probe the source of the 'defeatism' of his policies and the 'insularity' that distinguished 'the British race from races less surrounded by water like Piglet in *Winnie the Pooh*'.[78] He found the source by probing his own village experience. 'India', he confessed, 'always did, still does and probably always will bring out the Enoch in me.'[79] Cultural shock of the sort he experienced at Timmapuram went a long way to explain the form of Anglo-Indian society under the Raj and the tendency of colonial immigrants to 'herd together'. He recounts his precipitate withdrawal from Timmapuram with a sense of shame. He condemns Powell's 'policy of non-involvement with international human problems' and his activities as a threat to the moral standards of the nation.[80]

9

The Raj at Work

1

'Why do you, as a modern English novelist of serious pretensions, bother to write about the time-expired subject of the British Raj?' Scott posed the question for himself in a lecture that he gave in Bombay in 1972, a reworking of his 1968 address to the Royal Society of Literature, and retitled 'After Marabar: Britain and India, A Post-Forsterian View'.[1] 'Because', he answered, 'the last days of the British Raj are the metaphor I have presently chosen to illustrate my view of life.' He acknowledged the definition of the novel suggested by the English critic, Walter Allen, as 'an extended metaphor of an author's view of life'. After a brief rehearsal of the themes of his pre-*Quartet* novels, he summed up their common thread as an 'obsession with the relationship between a man and the work he does'.[2] Life, he argued, was 'most nearly itself when here and now . . . are governed by a philosophy in pursuit of whose truths and rewards men know they can honourably employ themselves'.[3] Scott's view of life, as expressed in the British-Indian metaphor, was of 'the importance to a man, or to a woman, of engaging himself honourably . . . in work or acts that are not, to put it simply, entirely selfish'.[4] What he was saying as an author was that contemporary society offered few rewards to the man or woman 'who feels he must do work of some positive value . . . in the context of the philosophy on which that society bases its aspirations'.[5] As a people who worked in fidelity to liberalism or imperialism, it was in India that the British came to 'the end of themselves as they were'.

Scott extended his view of British India into a severe criticism of Forster's *A Passage to India*. He admired *Passage* as a powerful and prophetic representation of the liberal dilemma, of liberalism's inability to resolve the contradictions of the necessity of resting on force an imperial government ostensibly dedicated to Indian freedom. Yet he felt that sociologically something was missing from Forster's characters, the Turtons and the Burtons, that during his war service in India he had never actually met anyone quite like them. In *Passage* the Raj seemed 'notably *unoccupied* by anything so much except the need to take up a stance or attitude'.[6] There was lacking any reference to the 'concern and belief in occupation' that underlay the observed rigidity of the Raj. Forster, Scott told Caroline Moorehead, denied his characters 'one dimension – their work – a dimension that dignifies people'.[7] It was for this reason that Scott described his view of the Raj as 'post-Forsterian'.

Scott admitted that when he first went to India he felt alienated from Anglo-Indians. They seemed 'more foreign than the Indians whom I met in ante-rooms and messes, on parade, in a daftar, in shops, railway stations. . . . Because they seemed unself-conscious, a bond of common humanity was much more easily formed between myself and the Indians I met in these ways than between myself and the sahibs and memsahibs who were always, I thought, conscious of having to represent something. . . .'[8] He would then have endorsed Forster's characterisation of Anglo-Indians. But: 'Later on – when I learned something about the kind of work they did – and what it meant to them – although they seldom spoke about *that* – I felt that some of them were my kind of people after all – ordinary English people in exile.'[9] He summed up his change of outlook to a group of American students: 'I never was a Kiplingite. In my youth I was a Bloomsburyist – a Liberal Humanist. I didn't believe in the British Empire. I went to India with a Cadet group . . . who mostly felt as I did. Here I began a movement from Bloomsburyism to uncertainty. I found I couldn't denigrate the Kiplingites. They were doing good solid work. I came to appreciate the Sahib.'[10] The extent of his move through youthful 'uncertainty' towards a mature endorsement of the Raj dignified by work is revealed by his capacity to lampoon and yet redeem the sahib.

The lampoon first appears in Scott's 1968 lecture to the Royal Society of Literature:

In Anglo-India, surely, the Sahib was shaved while he still slept, then led, stupefied, to the gusl-khana, folded into his tin tub, doused, dried, powdered, dressed; creakily mounted on a no less creaky, stupefied pony, and pointed in the direction of the daftar (which is Anglo-Indian for office). Arrived there, with sleep receding and temper rising, he would dock his clerk a week's pay for losing a file, order four peasants out of his sight, three fined, two rigorously imprisoned, and one to District and Sessions for deportation; and then address himself to the more agreeable business of writing a sharp minute to the Divisional Commissioner about the Civil Engineer's plan to drain the marsh out at Burrapore for a scheme that would improve agricultural conditions but drive out the duck and ruin the shooting. Thus kindled for the day, he would return to his bungalow, riding his pony to a lather of terminal fever, kick the syce in the seat of his pants for not catching him as the loyal beast fell dead at the foot of the bungalow steps, then stump up to the veranda in full view of the whole vast retinue of his servants, but shouting *Koi Hai* in response to some deep reflexive notion of the protocol to be observed, then clatter into the dark polished dining-room and sit at the end of the long dark polished table where for a moment he would be puzzled by the presence of a sour-looking woman reading letters at the other end of it. Then, remembering it was memsahib he would mutter, 'Hullo, old thing', and bury himself behind the pages of the *Civil and Military Gazette*.[11]

The redemption follows:

even if that cartoon were the truth, you would say that man had a philosophy and was emboldened to act thus by the knowledge that others shared it and that through acts and attitudes like these the truth of this philosophy would be revealed and its rewards shared out. The cartoon conveys that man's view of life, and the cartoonist's, who clearly holds a different one.[12]

Sahib and memsahib, bearing the insignia of the Raj, the solar topi and the fly-whisk, are dignified as surely as were Lucy and Tusker Smalley enthroned on their twin thunder-boxes in *Staying On*.

Scott echoes such statements in his book reviews. When *Plain Tales from the Raj* appeared in 1975 he complained that of more than 220 pages only ten were concerned with the work routine of the Raj. 'How did it *work*?' he carped, 'there is hardly a book anywhere that tells you'.[13] He wrote an enthusiastic introduction to an edition of W.H. Saumarez Smith's letters as a subdivisional officer for this reason:

> the job was there to be done by someone and it has for a long time seemed to me that in this situation there was a moral challenge met rather well by the people who accepted it, as a job of work, and who are in danger of disappearing into the mists of history and anonymity because they have seemed to think that readers would be bored by accounts of what the job was and how it was done, and so have in general preferred to write memoirs of princes and palaces, tiger, duck, viceroys, pro-consuls, punkas, polo and poodle-fakers, temples, monuments; and tell plain tales from the hills: all of which leave an erroneous impression that no young Englishman, or aging Englishman, or his wife, had in mind, in heart, on the conscience, the workaday affairs of the workaday Indian world.[14]

Sadly he did not live to see the compendious *The District Officer in India, 1930–1947* (1980), the collation by Roland Hunt (formerly ICS) and John Harrison (formerly Indian Army) of recollections of the pleasures and pains of an ICS career by some seventy-three administrators. In a review of a biography of Curzon, bylined 'A Glittering Disaster', Scott was scornful of the Viceroy's failure to appreciate the servants of the Raj: 'behind the machine, attempting to serve it, there were scores of quiet and sober men, strangers to chicanery, innocent of jobbery, guilty neither of murder nor rapine, who diligently performed their tasks to the best of their capabilities; unsung, unheralded, above all unknown to the aloof Curzon'.[15] He became lyrical and sentimental in a review of Veronica Bamfield's 'enchanting' book, *On the Strength: The Story of the British Army Wife* (1975).[16] The author had lamented that 'war, the army, and the British Raj are dirty words'.

> In the old United Services Museum in Whitehall there was a pair of pink satin slippers, a relic of Cawnpore. I used to go in every so often to look at them because I wasn't quite sure what they meant to me. Mrs. Bamfield's book has supplied the answer.

The slippers are symbolic not of a young girl's martyr-
dom but of what a man and a woman can mean to one
another when they work together, sharing the same beliefs
and notions of service and duty. Prejudice, snobbishness,
bickering, excessive attention to petty details of protocol
and seniority, a ridiculous sense of superiority, a rigidity
of mind coupled with an unwillingness, and inability, to see
beyond the end of the nose – these are all faults of which the
service wife (and her husband) has been, both justly and
unjustly, accused. But behind the faults, common enough
in life anyway, has always lain a virtue. What virtue? I'm
not sure it's wholly identifiable but I think it's something
to do with the impression one has that to the question, 'Any
complaints?' Mrs Bamfield, and those she has spoken up
for, would answer, 'None'.

Scott had acquired a certain regard for the memsahib:

Nowadays there is a commonly held belief that most of the
Raj's faults arose from the attitude of its women. Certainly
no one was more adept at making an Indian feel like
something crawling from under a stone than Memsahib
and she it was who, creating a home from home and
solemnly observing the rites of Camberley in the heart
of Mudpore, ensured that the community of the Raj should
never develop along lines that could lead to an English
sense of identity with India. But the Raj did not come to
an end because it treated Indians badly, and having given
the subject quite a lot of thought I've come to the conclusion
that the women made a vital contribution to the important
and lasting impression India has of the way an Englishman
did his job, because of the indispensable part that used to
be played by women in the Englishman's image of himself.
. . . She and she alone really brought out what was good in a
man. Sharp-tongued, hard-bitten, handy with rifle and gun
she might be – he might hate the one he had – but the notion
that a woman was 'sort of sacred' was inseparable from the
image.[17]

2

In 1970 Scott accepted the meagre fee of £50 to write a light-
hearted chapter on the mystique of the Raj for a volume, *John
Kenneth Galbraith Introduces India* (1976). Scott likened the
India of the Crown to a private company, with the great British

public typically indifferent shareholders concerned only with dividends. The Raj represented what the English people were when they last believed in the value of their product: rule, in the form of benevolent despotism or paternalism. Belief in that product did not survive the First World War in Britain but it lasted until the 1940s in India.

Scott made the discovery that even in 1945 a pamphlet was issued to attract suitable English and Indian recruits, then in the armed services, to the ICS, the Political Service and the Police. As late as 1986 a scholarly monograph on the ICS referred to the 1945 resumption of recruitment as a 'little-known activity'.[18] It was generally believed that recruitment was last undertaken in 1943. Scott quotes from the Secretary of State for India's foreword to the pamphlet, which admits that in view of Britain's commitment to self-government the careers of appointees might be prematurely terminated. Yet: 'At the same time it is my belief that when that time comes opportunities for continuing to render good service to India and Burma will not be lacking to men whose devotion is to the peoples of those countries and whose capacity for efficient and disinterested service has already been proved.'[19] Scott's discovery validates his account of the activities of Colonel Grace in Calcutta and Bombay, where he was representing to service-men the attractions of an Indian career. A number of applicants were brought back to London. One of them, Professor Hugh Tinker, writes of being put through a 'Country House Party' form of interview at Anna Pavlova's house in Hampstead.[20] In March or April 1946 he was told that he had been successful and might soon expect to return to India. By early summer some seventy-three Europeans had received offers and fifty-four had accepted. Exactly a year before independence, on 14 August 1946, Cabinet decided to cease recruitment to the ICS and the Police. All offers were cancelled. For Scott, the 1945 recruiting pamphlet was 'an embodiment of the Raj's illusion of its own permanence'.[21]

3

Behind the illusion persisted the belief in the value of pater-nal imperial rule and India's need of it. Paradoxically, the 'Indianisation' of the services meant 'the Anglicisation of Indians, their metamorphosis into what Macaulay called brown English-men'.[22] After a century of providing English education essentially on the model that Macaulay had advocated surely the Raj should have worked itself out of a job. In Scott's view, until about the First World War the 'company man' and his wife in India, like the British 'shareholder' at home, continued to believe that 'the Raj was doing its job and turning out clever Anglicised Indians . . . who could one day take over'. But thereafter

> the Raj took a different view, one that inclined them to
> believe that too many of the clever Anglicised Indians
> were exactly what India did not need because they were
> being Anglicised in the wrong way, being fed with ideas
> that questioned the value of the product and which were
> threatening to influence young people at home, too. . . .
> India was not composed of clever English-speaking chaps
> who played cricket, read Shakespeare and studied law.
> That pleasant fellow one had met at Balliol seemed differ-
> ent when he turned up in Mudpore, claiming acquaintance.
> It was pretty rotten not being able to treat him as decently
> as one wished but one had to be careful. He might want
> something it would be impossible to give. For the job's sake
> you simply had to be detached, disinterested, and think of
> the country as a whole. The Indian chap's parents were
> stinking rich, too, and probably didn't care tuppence for
> the poor old peasant who called you Sahib. And then of
> course Hari was a Hindu (a Rajput at that) and most of
> the peasants in this sub-division were Muslims.[23]

After the war paternalism deepened, and 'central to the Raj's image of itself was the belief that it held the balance of power between otherwise irreconcilable forces who would lose no opportunity to cheat, threaten or slaughter one another'. The old altruistic liberalism of Lady Manners and Mabel Layton became *passé*. Indians were still thought to be 'incapable of correct (i.e. English-style) government' and it seemed best 'to rule what was divided for as long as that seemed necessary'.

Scott acknowledged that the work of the Raj had long included such aspects of unification as the introduction of a single rule of law, a common language, a subcontinental network of rail-ways and communications. But it had shrunk from seeking the emotional unity of Indians, for their combination against itself was a frightening prospect. The insecurity of a people in exile fed a psychology of *divide et impera*. Folk memories of the Mutiny reinforced the Fort mind, the Cantonment mind, the Hill Station mind, the Club mind. The mindset of the Raj could parody the Raj's highest objectives. Hari Kumar, the paradigmatic brown Englishman, became invisible. Merrick, symbolic of the Raj, could prove the law an ass. An insecure Raj must needs exercise caution with the two-edged swords of unification and Anglicisation.

4

The essay, 'The Raj', written at the midpoint in Scott's ten years' hard labour on the *Quartet*, emphasises the First World War as the great divide between the attitudes of Britain and Anglo-India:

> After the 1914–18 war the divergence of opinion between the people at home and the members of the Raj about what Indians were capable of became so wide that the two lines of belief never met again. At home the idea of what an Englishman was had begun to undergo radical changes. There in your Bloomsbury bed-sitter you sat round the popping gas-fire toasting crumpets and observed that the old world was dead and the old England with it and that it was quite wrong to go on exploiting countries that were capable of exploiting themselves. But in Collector Sahib's bungalow things looked very different, because Collector Sahib sat on his verandah and gazed at his darkening garden, sniffed the ancient smell of cow-dung fires in the ancient villages, thought of his 4,430 square miles of territory and the souls entrusted to him and observed that *his* world hadn't changed at all.[24]

The divide is encapsulated in the novels by references to the Amritsar massacre that resonate through echoes of Jallianwala /Gillian Waller, Dyer/Reid and Sherwood/Crane/Manners/ Batchelor.

The references extend back to that other divide, the Mutiny, through the association of the Bibighar massacre at Kanpur in 1857 and the Bibighar rape at Mayapore. In *Division*, the historian Perron claims the twenty-five years preceding the Mutiny

as his 'period', the decades of Anglicisation pressed too hard
and too fast, from Macaulay's Education Minute to Dalhousie's
Doctrine of Lapse. That, says Perron, is when things began to go
wrong.[25] In 'The Raj' Scott tells us that 'the period between 1833
and 1857 was one of such single-minded imperial expansion that
the Indians took fright at last and rebelled'.[26] The lasting effect
of the Mutiny on race relations in India is scarcely calculable.
'One cannot overemphasize the importance of the Mutiny,' Scott
notes in 1973.[27] In a passage of Viceregal Lodge at Simla there
still hang photographs of eminent servants of the Raj. One of
them is an unforgettable group picture of the Viceroy's post-
Mutiny Council, men old before their time, weighed down by
the burden of their responsibility, their grave faces haunted
by memories of recent events. In 'The Raj' Scott describes
'Sahib's face':

> This was neither suntanned nor (as in the cartoon) red-
> dened by drink, spiced food and self-indulgence. It was
> pale, grave, withdrawn; and the mouth when it smiled
> did so with reluctance so that the corners, anchored by
> the determination not to see anything funny in what was
> patently very unfunny, turned down instead of up. The
> movements of the limbs became slow, studied. Heat and
> humidity contributed to the lethargy but it was mainly a
> reflection of the deliberate slowing down of responses as
> an understanding was reached of the very narrow channel
> there was through which one could steer a safe course
> between the rock of contagion and the more dangerous
> rock of irreversible error of judgment and action.[28]

The injunction never to forget the Mutiny was symbolised at
Lucknow by the flying of the Union Jack, night and day, over
the ruined but carefully preserved Residency where the British
suffered heavy casualties during an eighty-seven-day siege. In
a letter to Scott in 1975 Sir Herbert Thompson endorsed Scott's
view of the persistence of Mutiny memories: 'My generation in
the ICS (survivors of World War I) went out to India as a sort
of new generation and I was fortunate to begin in Madras . . .
and so have avoided meeting the Mutiny hangover which still
hung about the U.P. and even the Punjab until I was experienced
enough to realize it for what it was.'[29]

Scott's essay is about the mystique of the Raj. Locating it meant communing with ghosts, remains, emblems and echoes. He found it in its attitude to work, and summed it up in the word 'integrity', which 'seems to fit because nowadays that is what we say people have when they don't seem to have enough of anything else to get by, when they do good work withdrawn by circumstances or temperament from contact with those abrasive elements that make life an emotionally and intellectually dynamic, dangerous and altogether very uncertain affair'.[30]

5

On the first page of *Jewel* Scott writes of 'an imperial embrace of such long standing and subtlety it was no longer possible for them to know whether they hated or loved one another'. The embrace, he realised, was the key to the mechanics of the Raj, which were not confined to the deployment of superior force and racial distance, though those weapons are the dominant ones in *Jewel*. By contrast, the opening scene of *Scorpion* shows the importance for the Raj of its attachment of loyal Indians to the processes of imperial rule. As striking as the Amritsar sequence in Attenborough's *Gandhi*, but more difficult to represent, is Scott's interview between the Governor of Ranpur and the former Chief Minister. In its comprehension of the 'embrace' it is light years removed from Attenborough's caricature of a nameless, Blimpish 'Governor'.

Tariq Ali has written appreciatively of the opening dialogue in *Scorpion* as 'central to an understanding of Scott's project and explaining the peaceful transition of power from the ruling race to an old/new ruling class'.[31] Malcolm appeals to Kasim:

'. . . you're still a pillar of the Congress Party, one of its most famous favoured Muslims, good propaganda and apparently living proof of the truth of their claim that they're an all India party, the sort of man who's influential enough in this province for me not to think twice about locking you up as a potential inciter of riots and strikes, because your party, your party, Mr Kasim, yesterday committed high treason by conspiring to take steps calculated to aid and comfort the King–Emperor's enemies. And the one big question in my mind is why is it still your party, Mr Kasim? What official policy or policies has it

adopted and pursued in the last three years that you have hon-
estly felt to be either wise or expedient?'

'Perhaps none,' Kasim said.

'Exactly. And so, my dear Kasim, don't go into the wilderness
with the rest of them this morning. However long it is, and my
guess is it's for the duration, what a waste of your talent, what
misplaced loyalty. Get out now. Write to Maulana Azad. Write
this morning, write here and now. Send in your resignation.
What more suitable moment? And the moment you write your
resignation I tear up this stupid document authorizing your
arrest. There's not a single act committed by you since you
resigned office in 1939, not a speech, not a letter, not a pamphlet,
not a thing said in public or overheard in private that warrants
your being locked up. All that warrants it now is your continued
allegiance to the Congress, your continued standing as a leading
member of an organization we're outlawing.'

'I quite understand, Sir George.'

The Governor studied the expression on Kasim's face. Then
he got up, walked to one of the long windows, looked out, and
came back again, pacing slowly. Kasim waited, his hands still
folded on his lap.

'I want you on my executive council,' the Governor said. 'If it
were constitutionally possible for me to re-establish autonomy
in this province I know whom I'd invite to head the administration. Short of that I want you *in*, I want to use your talents, Mr
Kasim.'

'It is very kind of you, Sir George. I am immensely flattered.'

'But you refuse, don't you? You refuse to resign. You insist on
going to jail. Forgive me, then. I hope you don't feel insulted.
That wasn't my intention.'

Kasim made a gesture of dismissal. 'Please. I know this.'

The Governor sat down, took off his spectacles and played
with them as before, but with both hands, leaning forward, with
his elbows on the desk. 'Waste!' he exclaimed suddenly. 'Waste!
Why, Mr Kasim? You agree with everything I've said, but you
don't even ask for time to consider my suggestion. You reject it
out of hand. Why?'

'Because you only offer me a job. I am looking for a country
and I am not looking for it alone.'

'A country?'

'To disagree about the ways of looking for it is as natural as you say it is to squabble about how power will be divided when it is found. And as you say, I have disagreed many times about these ways, and people have many times expected me to resign and change my political allegiance. And if ways and means were all that mattered I expect Congress would have seen the back of me long ago. But these are not what matter, I believe. What matters is the idea to which the ways and means are directed. I have pursued this idea for a quarter of a century, and it is an idea which for all my party's faults I still find embodied in that party and only in that party, Governor-ji, nowhere else. Incidentally, I do not agree with you when you speak of Indian independence having become a foregone conclusion. Independence is not something you can divide into phases. It exists or does not exist. Certain steps might be taken to help bring it into existence, others can be taken that will hinder it doing so. But independence alone is not the idea I pursue, nor the idea which the party I belong to tries to pursue, no doubt making many errors and misjudgements in the process. The idea, you know, isn't simply to get rid of the British. It is to create a nation capable of getting rid of them and capable simultaneously of taking its place in the world as a nation, and we know that every internal division of our interests hinders the creation of such a nation. That is why we go on insisting that the Congress is an All India Congress. It is an All India Congress first, because you cannot detach from it the idea that it is right that it should be. Only second is it a political party, although one day that is what it must become. Meanwhile, Governor-ji, we try to do the job that your Government has always found it beneficial to leave undone, the job of unifying India, of making all Indians feel that they are, above all else, Indians.'[32]

Ali comments: 'The meeting ends with Kasim refusing an offer he cannot accept as an individual (acting as a broker between imperialism and the insurgent masses), but which his party will later implement voluntarily. It is this side of the British/Indian connection, which has hardly ever been seriously discussed in fiction or history, that gives the *Quartet* its edge.'[33]

Scott's recognition of the crucial role of Western-educated intermediaries in the mechanics of the Raj, its rule and its demission of power, is indeed impressive. The process that he observed was described in a term that entered Raj historiography in the year of *Scorpion*'s publication: 'collaboration'. Anil Seal's *The Emergence of Indian Nationalism: Competition and Collaboration in the Later Nineteenth Century* (Cambridge, 1968) analysed the growth of a new phenomenon, the Western-educated Indian, who appeared as a nationalist opposed to the Raj, but in fact competed for its favours against longer-established 'elites' in society. Early 'nationalists' were presented as collaborating with the Raj in return for professional and political advantages: 'By cajoling the Sarkar they could . . . enter its offices and then bang the doors in the faces of aspirants from circles other than their own.'[34] Of course the Raj had always enlisted collaborators, in particular nawabs or rajas with whom it entered treaties, landholders through whom it collected taxes, and the peasants who formed its armies. An empire run through British military and civilian agencies never could pay its way.

As Western-educated Indians achieved prominence in the administrative and political process the recruitment of collaborators became a subtle game. Seal was arguing that the Westernised elites that dominated the Indian National Congress were engaged in mock conflict with the Raj, 'tentative', 'limited' and 'inconclusive': 'Many of the battles which the Raj and the Congress waged were mere feints . . . a Dashera duel between two hollow statues, locked in motionless and simulated combat.'[35] Their aims 'had much in common'. As Tariq Ali observed, Malcolm and Kasim discussed the Congress's Quit India resolution 'almost as if they belonged to the same party'.[36] Kasim declines to collaborate on this occasion but he had served the Crown as Chief Minister of Ranpur, with a wholly Indian Cabinet, from July 1937 until November 1939.

The enticing idea of 'collaboration' to help explain how the people of a small island ruled a subcontinent 6000 miles away, and how they finally transferred imperial power to friendly successors, emerged in the late 1960s from the long partnership of John Gallagher and Ronald Robinson. The pair shifted the locus of inquiry in imperial history from the dominance of the metropoles to the dependence of their local agents on indigenous intermediaries. The idea was not floated in print as a general interpretation until Robinson's essay, 'Non-European Foundations of European Imperialism: Sketch for a Theory of Collaboration', appeared in 1972.[37] Several years earlier Scott had set about inspecting the mechanics of the Raj and presented, independently of the scholars, a powerful account of how Britain ruled India for so long and finally escaped with goodwill. While the account documented racial distance, repression, *man-bap* paternalism and the preservation of princely autocracy and communal divisions, in its centrepiece, the treatment of Kasim, it anticipated the emphasis that historians were to place upon collaboration. As early as May 1967 Scott condemned as 'rotten psychology' the imperialist–paternalist belief that 'the right sort of Indian' might be taught to 'collaborate in the business of wielding' power.[38]

6

The recognition of collaboration as essential and intrinsic to the Raj places a premium upon loyalty. Malcolm alleged that with the Quit India resolution Congress committed 'high treason by conspiring to take steps calculated to aid and comfort the King–Emperor's enemies'. This was a charge that both Gandhi and Congress President Azad denied vehemently.[39] The 8 August resolution sanctioned 'for the vindication of India's inalienable right to freedom and independence, the starting of a mass struggle on non-violent lines on the widest possible scale'.[40] As the Raj's pre-emptive strike removed Gandhi and the Congress leaders from the scene, there was need to establish the responsibility of Congress for the widespread violence that occurred and the intention to aid the Japanese. From August 1942 the intelligence organisations of the Central and Provincial Governments were engaged in collecting evidence of Congress responsibility from every possible source. The Government's pamphlet, *Congress Responsibility for the Disturbances*, which Scott read in 1965, was supplemented by the report of Mr T.D. Wickenden, ICS, a judge in the Central Provinces.[41] Wickenden was charged with making an independent judicial study of the large volume of evidence available, and with reporting on how far the unpublished material corroborated the pamphlet's conclusion and established the responsibility of Congress. Wickenden endorsed the conclusion that the movement contemplated by Gandhi was of the kind that occurred; and that it was planned beforehand. But he believed that the movement was not intended to assist Japanese operations against India. There was no direct evidence of intention to facilitate a Japanese invasion. The Government concluded that at law 'it could not be established that the deliberate object of the rebellion was to help the enemy'.

The evidence thus supports Kasim's clear distinction between the Quit India protest and the INA's treason. In his first interview with Malcolm in *Scorpion* he asserts that Sayed would appreciate the difference between resigning his military commission in defiance of an oath of loyalty to the Crown and his own resignation from office in 1939 in protest against an imperialist war. When he learns from Ahmed of Sayed's capture as an INA officer Kasim is first incredulous and then distraught:

> . . . Sayed would not be fighting and killing Indians. He would not be helping the Japanese to invade his own country. . . . You are calling your brother a traitor? . . . You forget that Sayed is an Indian officer. He holds, unless he is dead, the King–Emperor's commission. . . . It is a contract, a contract. All of Muslim law is based on the sanctity of contract, of one man's word to another. . . . I do not know that kind of India, I do not know that kind of man. He is not Sayed. He is not my son.[42]

Towards the climax of the *Quartet* there is a big scene, long anticipated and long planned, between Kasim and Sayed.[43] It is by way of a trial, the substitution of the Congressman father for the Raj as the prosecuting counsel. For many years Scott had sought information about the infamous INA trial at the Red Fort. It underlines his whole account of the British–Indian affair as an embrace that Kasim should now speak against his son as if for the Raj, and accuse him of cowardly self-interest, self-promotion and bearing grudges against the British. He advises him to plead guilty to treason and explain his reasons. Sayed replies as if briefed by the INA officers' defending counsel at the Red Fort trial, Bhulabhai Desai and his team, for it is their arguments that he uses: that he was fighting with a properly constituted army for a provisional government of Free India in exile, like De Gaulle's; that his decision to do so was consequent

upon the imprisonment of Congressmen for the Quit India resolution, whose counterpart it was. Kasim expects that his traitor
son will be a national hero for a day, but will never be admitted
to the army of independent India. He declines to defend a son he
would not readmit to the army.

7

That Scott got the psychology of the old nationalists right is
suggested by the judgement of Gandhi upon Second Lieuten-
ant Charles Napier. He was a regular soldier who had entered
Sandhurst in 1938 and joined the Northamptonshire Regiment
in India in 1939. He was, indeed, a descendant of Sir Charles
Napier, conqueror of Sind in 1843 and thus author of the famous
telegram 'Peccavi'. By 1940 he had reached the conclusion that
there was no justification for British rule. The Empire was 'an
association for the making of money, propagated by merchants
in England under a hypocritical screen of "Empire glory and
the betterment of the native races"'.[44] As his views were incompatible with the retention of his commission he asked to be
discharged. He was aware of the cost to himself but India's
'freedom is the most important thing'. Nehru wrote to Gandhi
that his heart 'went out to this young and terribly sincere boy'.[45]
After reading the letter and a statement of Napier's Gandhi
replied simply that he was referring 'the matter to the Viceroy':
'It is a pathetic case.' In due course Napier was discharged.

The narrator of this curious tale, Professor Christopher
Thorne, explains Gandhi's response by his 'strong aversion
to anything smacking of disloyalty to a person's own nation
or sworn duty'.[46] Gandhi would similarly deplore the INA's
activities. Professor Thorne observes that while in 1942 Nehru
rejected collaboration with the Japanese, in 1946 he applauded
the INA's activities as 'a brave adventure' in 'the cause of Indian
freedom'.[47] In the book that he wrote during his detention in
Ahmednagar, *The Discovery of India*, he called the INA officers
'the symbols of India fighting for her freedom'.[48] But the acute
Guy Perron observed Nehru's 'shrewd fence-sitting' in his 1946
foreword to a book by one of them, Shah Nawaz Khan's *My
Memories of I.N.A. and its Netaji*. For Nehru had there written
that he had 'not been able . . . to read through this record'.[49]
Rowan realised that they were 'only heroes for a while . . . folk

heroes. People in a story or legend. When it comes to finding places for them in the world of affairs it's a bit different.'[50] Sayed Kasim and others convicted of treason were cashiered. The three officers tried at the Red Fort had been sentenced to transportation but Auchinleck had remitted their sentences. Only officers convicted of brutality were punished as criminals. INA officers were not admitted to the army of free India.

India has never had a military dictator, a fact that British observers have often explained in terms of the successful introduction of liberal political institutions. It is arguable that greater importance should be attached to the Raj's tradition of a loyal army. The Indian Army was partitioned but survived. Not only was Enoch Powell astray in his prognostication. So was that seasoned 'viceroy at bay', Lord Linlithgow, who wrote at the end of 1947:

> I do not believe that Nehru's Government or any successor Government will be found under test capable of holding the country together. The Indian Army has ceased to exist. What remains on either side of the line [of partition] is likely to prove venal and corrupt. Soon it will dawn on men that the power behind the Government which for so long has been the British Army is no longer effective. Ambitious men will be tempted to challenge the authority of existing administrations and will make their bid for armed support. Power politics will be the order of the day.[51]

The Historian's Novelist

1

The narrator of *The Raj Quartet* is bound to excite fellow feeling among historians. Appearing in *Jewel* as the Stranger or the Traveller, his interest in the Manners case of 1942 has been aroused in the early 1960s by Brigadier Reid's unpublished memoir. Events at Mayapore recall the darkest moments in British-Indian history by the racial passions they arouse. Quit India was the greatest crisis since the Mutiny and Reid's treatment of it at Mayapore evokes memories of Dyer at Jallianwala Bagh. The Stranger visits India and collects written and oral testimony that he includes in *Jewel*. Historical truth is the quarry. Asked whether he was the Stranger, Scott answers:

> No, not quite. Nearly. But not. He's certainly the chap who's writing the book. Doing all the leg-work. I don't think I should go much further into that. But I'll say this: he turns up elsewhere, in each book, as 'the writer', 'the traveller' – and he has obviously talked to all the people who matter who are still alive, which is why he sometimes says, 'Sarah writes', or 'Sarah has said'. Basically, this writer/traveller/stranger is a mechanism for achieving both detachment and involvement.[1]

Scott is the novelist, controlling the narrator/historian.

At the end of *Jewel* the Stranger flies to Calcutta to have another look at 'mouldering missionary relics' at the headquarters of the Bishop Barnard Mission.[2] These are Miss Crane's effects and include letters from Barbie. He does not use this evidence until he begins *Towers*, but Barbie's letters lead him to contact Sarah Layton (now Perron) back at home. She and Nigel Rowan are the sources of the narrator's construction of *Scorpion*. Early in *Towers* the narrator's presence is apparent

from his description of effects (especially a photograph) that
Sarah inherited from Barbie (including her letters intended
for Sarah).[3] Again, the book is the narrator's reconstruction of
events from correspondence and testimony. In *Division* the narrator employs a further source, the oral and written evidence of
Perron the historian. It combines the narrator's reconstruction
and the direct presentation of accounts by Sarah and Perron.

The method of the narrator of the *Quartet* is that of historical
inquiry, extending over the decade following 1964. The concern
is with what happened to those involved in the Manners case,
its ripple effect on their subsequent lives, and its utility as a
mirror of the long British–Indian affair. The case study in its
widest dimension leads on to findings about a major turning
point in history, about why Britain quit India in 1947 and why
India was partitioned. Scott summed up his general conclusion
for Roland Gant:

> The overall argument of the sequence is that the greatest
> contribution to the tragi-comedy of Anglo-India was the
> total indifference to and ignorance of Indian affairs of the
> people at home, who finally decided to hand India back in
> as many pieces as was necessary so long as it was got rid
> of. Which is what happened. No one, that I know of, has yet
> said so.[4]

He explained to Francine Weinbaum that 'the partition was a
logical consequence of the failure to identify [with Indian aspi-
rations]; also of the failure of the British at home to understand
the British in India'.[5]

2

On 25 October 1965 Scott opened a notebook and wrote playfully:
'Well it is my obsession to tell stories. Does it matter whether
they are true? History is always being re-written. Once done
with a fiction is inviolable. So.'[6] Ten years later, Scott affirmed
on television in Illinois that his novels were not historical. The
comment puzzled Francine Weinbaum, who thought his novels
more historical than any that she had ever read. Scott explained
that 'a historical novel is a novel concerning a period during

which the author did not live'.[7] In this sense, only brief episodes in the *Quartet*, such as the early history of the Laytons, or Miss Crane's girlhood, were historical. He utterly refused to be classified as an 'historical novelist', perhaps because the term conjured up for him such 'commercial' historical romances as M.M. Kaye's, which he distinguished sharply from 'straight' or serious writing.[8]

Scott denied employing historical methodology. He insisted that he did not analyse movements of social change philosophically, or equate them historically with other movements. Rather, he recalled and celebrated movements and events of his own time and life, and his images were 'those of one who was/is emotionally involved. It isn't an "historian's" view.'[9] Again, he wrote to Storm Jameson that 'one belongs as much to one's parents' generation as to one's own', which he felt made him a mid- to late-Victorian and an Edwardian: 'I certainly don't think of the latter part of the 19th Century as *history*. (Unless my own.)'[10] As he planned *Towers* in 1968, he wrote of his sequence of novels as 'a coherent whole of more than merely historical interest'.[11] The next year he declined to attempt a straight historical essay on the Raj for *Galbraith Introduces India*.[12] When his chapter was complete he felt that he had put the Raj 'historically and emotionally into perspective' in 'an original and potentially controversial appraisal'.[13] Even when he faced a financial crisis he refused to use his immense knowledge to write a short history of the Raj 'to appease the bank manager', preferring if necessary to return to publishing as an editorial consultant.[14]

Scott never shirked the labour of getting the historical context and the details right. In an Author's Note for *Division* he wrote of the sequence: 'The characters were imaginary. So were the events. The framework was as historically accurate as I could make it.' The name of a cinema in Calcutta or a chemist in Bombay, the words whispered by the Thugs as they prepared to break their victims' necks, the caste or communal significance of names, the complexities of arranging a Hindu marriage, wartime Indian attitudes to royal honours, procedures for presenting war decorations, the words of a raga, the date of a music-hall song, minutiae upon minutiae, all were investigated tenaciously. He was severely critical of less meticulous authors.

His review of Stanley Wolpert's novel about the assassination of Gandhi, *Nine Hours to Rama* (1962), complained of such inaccuracies as the use of the term 'Viceroy' in 1948, the substitution of 'Gupta House' for 'Birla House' and the breakdown of Godse, who had in fact been unrepentant: 'In cases like this an author's note adumbrating liberties taken with fact would not be out of place.'[15] Again, writing of *The Journey Homeward* (1961), a novel set in an Indian state in 1947 by his friend Gerald Hanley, he comments that 'there are matters of fact absent from it that worry the pseudo-historian in me'.[16] Yet in the end he asserts that 'Jashimpur must be allowed to exist in the way Hanley says it did at that time.' He explained to Hanley: 'I wanted to point out that in novels history is what the novelist says it is.'[17] Ultimately Scott was pursuing and defending a truth that is not wholly accessible by historical inquiry: 'Finally one just uses one's instinct, intuition, imagination: and hopes that out of this combination may come something which reaches beyond one's actual personal experience but which can be recognised as containing something of the truth about things.'[18]

Roland Gant believes that 'what interested him most of all was trying to understand why the British presence in India, which should have been a successful partnership, ended in recrimination, departure, division and bloodshed'.[19] The *Quartet*, and Scott's occasional non-fictional writings, provide a coherent, original and important statement on the later history of British India.

3

A celebrated Oxford philosopher of history, R.G. Collingwood, asserted, 'Every new generation must write history in its own way.' Reviewing a biography of Robert Clive by the mercurial Nirad Chaudhuri, Scott concurred: 'One thing . . . that worries Mr Chaudhuri but doesn't worry me is that "history seems to change as moral judgment varies". For me this is what makes it continually alive.'[20] He identified contemporary problems as 'rotten logs' in the 'moral drift of history', that 'moral continuum of human affairs' which he mentions at the start of *Jewel* and elaborates in Emersonian terms from time to time in the *Quartet*.[21] In the 1930s 'the rotten log of Fascism and anti-semitism', at other times religious bigotry, industrial slavery, superstition and so on, clogged the river bed. Throughout the period of the *Quartet*'s creation the log damming up the stream was racial prejudice and Scott felt that his fiction reduced 'the weight of ignorance' that produced it.[22] Like a good historian Scott was seeking to illuminate a contemporary problem by probing its past. How was racial prejudice to be explained?

The other major problem of the 1964–74 period that preoccupied Scott was international relations on the subcontinent, the 1965 Indo-Pakistan war and the 1971 Bangladesh crisis. Like the massacres of summer 1947 they lay heavily on his conscience as a Britisher, for they too were consequences of partition. How was British shuffling out of responsibility for it to be explained?

Scott answered the questions about racial prejudice and abandoning responsibility for India's unity in much the same way. Anglo-India pursued the 'rotten' gradualist road to Indian freedom because it did not identify with India's nationalist aspirations. The road meant inviting the 'right sort of Indian' to 'collaborate' with paternalistic government. The Raj sought not to unite Indians but to attach them to itself. In essence the British were too 'insular' to be able to identify with an alien culture. Racial distance and repose on the cushions of authority were their response.

From Scott's reviews one can but glimpse the emergence of racism as concurrent with the Mutiny. He wrote of the 1830s as a period in which 'the colour bar had not yet taken hold'.[23] He did not regard the British as an imperial people and endorsed James Morris's suggestion that the age of imperialism was limited to the twenty years preceding the Boer War.[24] He believed that they were profoundly indifferent to the subject Empire and remained ignorant of it. The epithets 'insular', 'indifferent' and 'ignorant' echo through his lectures, reviews and novels to describe the British at home. He elevates the conviction into an explanation of India's independence and partition and the betrayal of the princes.

4

Scott's explanation of the British departure in 1947 is radical in its Anglocentrism. The viewer of Attenborough's *Gandhi* receives the impression that it was the Mahatma and his non-cooperation movements that won freedom. Scott describes Gandhi's contribution as a 'sustained act of public relations' that ensured the Indian cause a continuing place on the agenda of British reformers, or Liberal Humanists.[25] Had he been a reformer–collaborator independence would have come no sooner but there may have been no partition. It was on the reformers' agenda for twenty-five years, waiting with social injustice, poverty and class privilege for action at Westminster by those who saw the Raj as a symbol of middle-class pretension, Empire as wrong and unnecessary. Their moment came with the return of Attlee's Labour Government in 1945. Dispossession seemed morally right though not one in a thousand of the electors was concerned about India. Scott answers those doubtful of such Anglocentrism with a question: Would a Churchill government have quit India? He clearly believes it would not.[26]

Partition sprang from the same context. In a note that he made in 1969 Scott writes of voters

for whom getting rid of the White Man's Burden, and all its vulgarities, had been an article of faith, a *sine qua non* of the British pursuit of happiness and social justice at home. . . . Twenty years after one sees that the act of political withdrawal from India was carried out with a resolution as implacable as any in our imperial history. Indian independence was not I have come to believe won by Indians in revolt, but enforced by the British who were in pursuit of a new image of themselves. In 1969, loving India, I have been trying to imagine the effect on both nations if for once in 1947 we had acknowledged the difference between principle and responsibility. What I find extraordinary is that in India we are respected and the Pakistanis hated. To me, Pakistan is the price freely extracted from India for our reputation as a nation that made amends, and the price still being paid, politically, for our good name in the form of proliferating nationalism.[27]

The argument is developed in a long review article in the *TLS* that year on B.N. Pandey, *The Break-Up of British India*, and H.V. Hodson, *The Great Divide*.

The article, 'The End of the Raj', is crucial to an understanding of Scott as an historian *manqué*.

It may be that the question – was partition inevitable or an impracticable reactionary solution? – cannot be answered by concentrating on the internal politics of Anglo-India but by dismissing them as, in one sense, irrelevant, and looking to British home politics for a satisfactory explanation . . . Indian independence was an article of faith with the British Labour movement . . . [The *raj*] if it did not actually divide and rule its jealously held possession, did more to assist division than it did to encourage unity.

But was this *raj* the body-politic from which the Indians wrested their freedom? The situation is clearer if we ask what would have happened if in 1945 a British electorate – for the most part ignorant of or indifferent to the jewel in the old imperial crown – had voted Churchill back in? . . . The Indians were denied the opportunity of a real postwar confrontation with the *raj* by Smiths in Pinner and Browns in Bolton, who gave their vote to Attlee. From July, 1945, Indian freedom was merely a matter of careful arrangement, and for this both the Indians and the *raj* were sadly unprepared. But Attlee was determined; hence the sacking of Wavell (the last Englishman, surely, to have pondered the complex problem in purely Anglo-Indian terms?) and the appointment of the time-and-motion-study expert who came, saw, and arranged. Through that glamorous vice-regal figure, the methodical Attlee cut through the Anglo-Indian complexity like a piece of wire through cheese.

This line of argument suggests that the partition of India lay in the logic of *British* history; a conclusion with which one can hardly expect the generality of Indians to agree, since it suggests that the intelligence shown, and the blood spilt, were largely wasted on a *raj* which, at the end, was removed from the scene of action by the British at home as smartly and perhaps as callously as the Indians were divided; arbitrarily, down the middle, to fulfil a British ideal, a British political ambition. . . .

Like his predecessor, Wavell, Mountbatten cared about Indian unity. He failed to conjure it. A charge often made against him is that, anxious to deal efficiently, he dealt too hastily. . . . [Yet] the speed with which the imperial company was wound up was a mark not only of Mountbatten's energy and grasp of essentials, but of his humane approach to a human problem. The steam was running out of the administration because the administrators

knew their days were numbered. The great adventure was
over. It would have been unkind as well as dangerous to
prolong the agony. It was the decision to quit that dictated
the pace. The decision, made in Whitehall, according to a
mandate, revealed the extent to which 'unity' was a possibility and the extent to which it was illusory. . . .

Perhaps if the *raj* had ever exerted itself to solve and
not use the communal problem, Mountbatten . . . might
have . . . saved the day. But the *raj* had not so exerted
itself. The day was already lost. . . . One does not, in a few
emotional weeks, wipe out a century of cold, self-seeking
appraisal of conditions that could be, and were, manipulated to imperial self-advantage. . . .

The creation of Pakistan surely cannot be seen as a result
of honourable recognition of the rights of a minority? If it
can be, then the Christians, Sikhs, Eurasians, tribesmen
and Princes must be seen as having been thrown to the
wolves. Pakistan – the impression is overwhelming – was
the political price exacted by an encouraged, stubborn and
indigenous minority power from an alien power now intent
on resignation and equally stubborn in pursuit of its ideals
and aims.

It may be argued that the supreme factor in the creation
of Pakistan was the gulf that separated the British at home
from the *raj*-in-exile. Ignorance and indifference at home
had always aggravated the instinct of the men on the spot
to guard, preserve and possess. Increasingly, in the first
four decades of this century, there was a notable lack of
sympathetic correspondence between them. The Englishman at home was demonstrably of the same species as
his counterpart in India, but the emotional and intellectual
climates they enjoyed might have been those of two quite
different planets. The one was natural to the English genius
for social and political thrust, restlessness. The other was
stultifying and encouraged nothing so much as the instinct
to stand by old values, by sitting comfortably on them.

It was the latter type of Englishman with whom the
Indians were used to dealing and from whom they took
their cue. . . . The Britain that was determined to give
independence was not at all the same Britain the Indian
Congress had fought and the Muslim League (by and large)
had cooperated with. Partition was inseparable, one may
argue, from the determination of the now existing Britain
to force independence upon the 'India' that also existed
at that time. Partition, one may therefore continue to

argue, lay in the logic of British domestic history, as a fortuitous creation of a Coronation Street electorate which did not and still does not know a Pakistani from an Indian, and – regrettably – now describes both as immigrants, if entrance into the headquarters of the Commonwealth is sought or effected by either.[28]

The article is Scott's most complete statement on the roots of independence and partition, a formulation essential to his completion of the *Quartet*. The 'melancholy exiles' and 'triumph of principles' of *Towers* and *Division* are illuminated by it.

5

In a long review of Wavell's Indian *Journal* in mid-1973 Scott clarifies the penultimate Viceroy's inability to solve the Congress–League dispute. The *Journal*

shatters the illusion that given more luck, more time, more friends, fewer enemies and wiser advice, Wavell might have handed India over in one piece; and supports an opinion that fundamentally Partition was a result neither of Hindu–Muslim intransigence nor of Wavell's failure to find an answer to it, but lay in the logic of British domestic history, of a parliamentary tradition of indifference to and ignorance of Indian affairs (mitigated by patches of localized expertise), and the reigning government's determination never to let those affairs divert it from the task of satisfying an equally indifferent and ignorant British electorate.

The first well-known drawback to Wavell as a proconsul was his dislike and distrust of politicians and his inability to deal with them effectively. . . . The second disability [was that] he sympathised with Indians in the mass, admired the soldierly qualities of the martial classes, had a liberal belief in their right to control their own destiny; but when it came to individual Indians he could not really bring himself to like them. His view of how a man should conduct himself was killingly rigid, insular, Edwardian, English upper-middle-class. In his heart he favoured Muslims and his mind was never open for a moment to the reality of Congress's national and non-communal claims. For him, Congress meant Hindus; caste-Hindus at that.

This book ought, I think, to settle forever the question

whether Wavell was unduly influenced by senior members
of the ICS. He did not need to be. He shared all their most
liberal hopes and many of their most reactionary but under-
standable reservations but what neither they nor he ever
accommodated themselves to was the unpalatable truth
that politically the *raj* was utterly irrelevant to India. . . .

There reposed in him many of the limitations of the *raj*;
but he embodied all its virtues.[29]

Scott had Governor Malcolm deliver much the same verdict in
Division:

the English manner has never been much of a medium for
communicating feeling. Sometimes I think that's at the
bottom of half our troubles. Wavell's a good example.
One of the sincerest and best disposed men who's ever
held that wretched post. But also one of the most silent
and unbending and outwardly austere. It's the English
manner come to perfection. It won't do. And the irony is,
Nigel, that at home it's been going out of fashion for years.
Rather like one of those strains of indigenous plants that
turns out to flower more profusely abroad and withers away
in its home soil.[30]

In 1976 Scott did sound a more tentative note in correspondence with Freya Stark, which marked his respect and admiration for the soldier–scholar–gentleman of the Raj:

I wish it had fallen to him to be the man who negotiated the
withdrawal (which had, historically, to be) because that
would have been a fitting end to an intensely honourable
career. Given more time, by Attlee, I fancy he might have
just pulled it out of the hat, because Nehru and Jinnah were
possibly just beginning to sink their suspicions of him and
recognise his sincerity in regard to his wish to see India
remain united, not in regard to his relationship with them,
though that reads as though it were blunt enough. When you
read his Journal of the Viceroyalty you see how much he
disliked Nehru, and Gandhi, and Patel (Patel less than the
others, I recall). And of course, blunt soldier that he was,
he let it show. Disastrous for a statesman.[31]

Freya Stark had known the Wavells well. Scott's summation of

Wavell was that he was a 'great man, in his bone a bigger man than Mountbatten', but 'inarticulate', and 'there was something in him that put the Indians off'.[32]

6

Scott's last long review on Indian history was of Sir Conrad Corfield's *The Princely India I Knew* (1976).[33] Corfield, the last head of the Political Department and Political Adviser to the Crown Representative, was a sort of prototype for Conway. Scott took some pains to obtain a review copy. The book

> fills what has been a conspicuous gap in the record of the negotiations for withdrawal and partition, because the absence of an account by the man qualified to explain his own and his department's attitude, to the princes' rights and the Crown's obligations, has left largely unchecked the hints and allusions about intransigence and reactionary plots to thwart Congress ambitions. . . .
> It has to be remembered that Corfield was head of the Political Department only for the last two years of the Raj's life, a situation like that of a general taking command of forces already ordered to retreat; so he was the natural target for Congress's final attacks on men whose duty it had been to preserve the sovereignty and dignity of personal rule. . . .
> That the Crown could no longer fulfil its obligations to Princely India once it had transferred power in British India exposes the supreme illogicality of its dual presence in India: on the one hand committed by declarations to advance British India to democratic self-government, on the other to uphold personal autocratic rule in over 500 states that could not survive independently and whose existence was unlikely to be tolerated (and indeed was not) by Congress. The princes' overwhelming fear was that in transferring power the Crown would also transfer paramountcy and they found it difficult to see beyond that.

Mountbatten and Corfield collided on the issue of the Viceroy's role in the accession of the princes to India or Pakistan before independence. Mountbatten's diplomacy was called 'the apogee of persuasion' by V.P. Menon. For Corfield it amounted to unconstitutional pressure by the paramount power to ensure

the transfer of the states to Congress India; the states should
be allowed to negotiate their own futures from a position of
independence. Scott, though entirely sympathetic to Congress,
admired Corfield as a man 'of firm opinion and adherence to
principle'.

7

Scott sends Perron to view the end of the Raj from Mirat, for it
was in the states that British ignorance and indifference were
most evident. Like Tradura in *Birds*, Mirat's relations with the
Political Department were the responsibility of the Resident of
Gopalakand, Sir Robert Conway. Anticipating the state's complete absorption by the Dominion of India in due course Conway
attacked the Mountbatten plan for states to hand over to India or
Pakistan at once the three portfolios of foreign affairs, defence
and communications. In *Division* he is talked around by Rowan,
who, with Bronowsky's help, secures Mirat's accession to India.
Muslim opposition to the accession sparks the slaughter of the
Muslim travellers, including Ahmed, in Scott's 'last train from
Mirat' finale, the event that stands for the massacre of hundreds
of thousands of Indians and Pakistanis at partition.

The historical realism of Mirat is remarkable. Mirat was a
tiny state, a left-over remnant of the Mughal Empire, with
which the British came to terms in the late-eighteenth century. Its dynasty was of Turkish ancestry, Shias ruling over
a 20 per cent Muslim populace (including some Sunnis) and
including a Hindu majority. It was remote from other states
and was confirmed as an ally of the Raj by the Mutiny. Its
ruler from c.1920 was H.H. Sir Ahmed Ali Gaffur Kasim Bahadur, whose relations with his father were not cordial, and who
was an extravagant prince redeemed by Bronowsky from an
embarrassing liaison with a European woman (Madame X) on
the Côte d'Azur. He became a reformed character, entreating
Bronowsky to become his Diwan and 'make me modern'. Under
Bronowsky's guidance the arbitrariness of the Nawabi darbar
was replaced by a nominated Council of State, the judiciary
and the civil and criminal codes were reformed, and a chief
justice from outside was appointed. Hindus were admitted to
the Council and a Hindu Boys' College, with a fine library,
established with the help of funds from Hindu businessmen,

notably Kiran Shankar Chakravarti, who supported both Muslim and Hindu political parties. The extravagant prince became a ruler–statesman. The palace had courtyards of Mughal style but its interior reflected French tastes of the *fin de siècle* period, ritzy Edwardian or Côte d'Azur grand hotel, with lincrusta on the walls and furniture of plush and gilt. As the communalism of 1946 infected the populace, the state secured help from the British-controlled States' Police.

In many respects the state of Mirat corresponds to Rampur, the only Muslim-ruled state in the UP. Rampur was a relic of the decay of the Mughal Empire, a jagir granted to Faizullah Khan by the Nawab of Oudh with the blessing of the British, who confirmed the arrangement in 1800 and rewarded the state's loyalty in 1857 liberally.[34] The Nawab of Rampur, a Shia, ruled a population of Sunni Rohillas (originally Pathan adventurers) and Hindus. In 1931 the population was 465,000. The Muslims were in the minority, 46.7 per cent, and the Hindus the majority, 52.5 per cent, but the administration was Muslim-dominated. The twenty-four-year-old Nawab, H.H. Sir Sayed Raza Ali Khan Bahadur, who succeeded in 1930, had not enjoyed good relations with his father and had been a spendthrift. However, under British pressure he became a reforming, modernising ruler. He reorganised the judiciary and appointed new ministers and High Court judges of integrity from outside, including an Englishman. The Hindu magnate, Sir Jwala Prasad Srivastava, built sugar and textile mills, bestowed philanthropy and supported both the Muslim League and the Hindu Mahasabha. The palace was described by Mrs April Swayne-Thomas when she stayed there as a guest in December 1946.[35] It had lovely architecture of tall columns and arches looking on to smooth lawns and marble fountains, reflecting European landscape gardening. It was furnished from Europe, with cut-glass and plush upholstered sofas and chairs and cut-glass and silver chandeliers and lamps. Gold, pink and magenta abounded in the textiles used, with French influence apparent in pictures and bronzes and 'huge nudes from the Paris schools'. The author, John Lord, writes of the survival of the aesthetics of Islam at the Rampur court in its library, one of the finest in the East, but the rest of the palace was made 'sombre by teak panelling and vulgar by recent copies of European masterpieces'.[36]

But there was a major contrast between Mirat and Rampur. In the latter modernisation of the administration and the economy, without concomitant political reform, offended the Rohilla influence. Without a Bronowsky at the helm, internal and external pressures oppressed the state. British intervention to restore order was required. The overhaul of the State's Police and political reform began as early as the mid-1930s in Rampur. The state was also more enmeshed than Mirat in the politics of the surrounding province, perhaps because the kinship between the Nawab of Mirat and the Congress Chief Minister of Ranpur made for harmony.

Scott's attention was drawn to the small state of Rampur by Gerald Hanley in March 1961. His notes for *Birds of Paradise* record from Menon's *Integration* that the Political Agent there was murdered in 1937. Menon noted other details of Rampur that Scott might find of use: 'It was well known for its enlightened administration', and its Nawab was the first Muslim ruler of importance to accede to India.[37] For information about Rampur in July–August 1947 Scott might have turned to Sir Francis Tuker's *While Memory Serves* (1950), a book of which he certainly knew. Tuker records that Muslim Rohilla insurgents caused disruption towards the end of July, in protest at the Nawab's accession to India.[38] They wanted Rampur to join Pakistan. At the Nawab's request the Government of India sent in troops to support the State's police and troops. The 6th Jats went into action on 5 August. Some Muslims were killed and a curfew was imposed. By 10 August peace had been restored.[39] Further details became available in the 1971–4 period through the publication of much of the correspondence of the States' Minister, Vallabhbhai Patel.[40] The Nawab appealed to Patel for troops on 4 August because of serious rioting by Muslims. Crowds were setting fire to government property. Four hundred Jat troops arrived next morning. On 12 August the Nawab reported that law and order were being restored. He requested the loan of 'a smart, experienced and reliable officer' to establish 'a proper Intelligence Department'.[41]

Elements resembling the end of the Rampur story appear in Scott's novel. Merrick was transferred to Mirat from Rajputana, where he was temporarily attached to the States' Police, in December 1946. He overhauled the Mirat Police. He was killed

at the end of July 1947. There was communal unrest when Perron
arrived on 4 August. Next day the Nawab acceded to India. The
accession was arranged on the 6th and Perron's diary recorded
'the reflection of fires in the night sky above the city' that
night.[42]

8

Scott uses Perron as the mouthpiece for three main explana-
tions of the end of the Raj. The first was that of the academic
economist, Leonard Purvis, and it resembles Clark's denuncia-
tion of the Raj in *Scorpion*. The Raj had neither developed nor
unified India:

> It's taken me no more than three months to write it off as a
> wasted asset, a place irrevocably ruined by the interaction
> of a conservative and tradition-bound population and an
> indolent, bone-headed and utterly uneducated administra-
> tion, an elitist bureaucracy so out of touch with the social
> and economic thinking of even just the past hundred years
> that you honestly wonder where they've come from. Not
> England, surely? . . .
> The fact is places like this have always been a magnet for
> our throw-backs. Reactionary, unco-operative bloody well
> expendable buggers from the upper and middle classes
> who can't and won't pull their weight at home but prefer
> to throw it about in countries like this which they've always
> made sure would remain fit places for them to live in.
> They've succeeded only too well. The most sensible thing
> for us to do is get rid of it fast to the first bidder before it
> becomes an intolerable burden. . . .
> Don't sell me that divide and rule stuff. The bloody
> place was divided when the sahibs first came and will be
> divided when the stupid sods go because they've always
> been content to sit on their bums in their bloody clubs
> and interfere only when the revenues were slow coming
> in. The place is still *feudal*. . . .[43]

Perron's Aunt Charlotte spoke for the British electorate, accepting the simple necessity of withdrawal and denying responsibility:

> as a result of the war, the policy of Indianisation, the run-
> ning down of the machinery of British recruitment to the

civil service and police, and as a result of the infiltration of
political, communal and nationalistic modes of thought into
the Indian armed services (the Naval Mutiny in Bombay in
1946 was always cited as an example) it would have been
difficult, even impossible, to maintain in India any form of
stable government with a responsibility to Parliament at
home and for law and order and national defence in India,
except at a cost which even if the will and the means were
available would have been excessive and just not on from
the British taxpayer's point of view. . . .

It would never have occurred to her to examine her
conscience in regard to those one-quarter million deaths,
although she had, in fact, as I had done – voted for them.
It would not have occurred to her because she held single-
mindedly to the Purvis principle, the view that a British
presence in India was an economic and administrative
burden whose quick offloading was an essential feature
of post-war policy in the welfare state. I'll give her this,
though: in adhering to this principle she never once introduced the ethical argument that colonialism was immoral
– an argument that supported so many of us. I don't think
the ethical argument ever entered her head. She was essentially a pragmatist.[44]

Perron himself reflected on British ignorance and indifference,
realising 'how little any of us knew or cared about a country
whose history had been that of our own for more than three
hundred years and which had contributed more than any other
to our wealth, our well-being'.[45] It was he who spoke of the end
of the Raj's mission and it's survival as within a time-warp:

For at least a hundred years India has formed part of
England's idea about herself and for the same period India
has been forced into a position of being a reflection of that
idea. Up to say 1900 the part India played in our idea about
ourselves was the part played by anything we possessed
which we believed it was right to possess (like a special
relationship with God). Since 1900, certainly since 1918, the
reverse has obtained. The part played since then by India in
the English idea of Englishness has been that of something
we feel it does us no credit to have. Our idea about ourselves
will now not accommodate any idea about India except the
idea of returning it to the Indians in order to prove that
we are English and have demonstrably English ideas. All

this is quite simply proven and amply demonstrated. But on either side of that arbitrary date (1900) India itself, as itself, that is to say India as not part of our idea of ourselves, has played no part whatsoever in the lives of Englishmen in general (no part that we are conscious of) and those who came out (those for whom India had to play a real part) became detached both from English life and from the English idea of life. Getting rid of India will cause us at home no qualm of conscience because it will be like getting rid of what is no longer reflected in our mirror of ourselves. The sad thing is that whereas in the English mirror there is now no Indian reflection . . . in the Indian mirror the English reflection may be very hard to get rid of, because in the Indian mind English possession has not been an idea but a reality; often a harsh one. The other sad thing is that people like the Laytons may now see nothing at all when looking in their mirror. Not even themselves? Not even a mirror? I know that getting rid of India, dismantling all this old imperial machinery (which Purvis sees as hopelessly antiquated, a brake on economic viability – his word) has become an article of faith with the intellectual minority of the party we have just voted into power. But we haven't voted them into power to get rid of the machinery, we've voted them into power to set up new machinery of our own for our own benefit, and for the majority who voted India does not even begin to exist. . . . Terrific insularity. Paradox! The most insular people in the world managed to establish the largest empire the world has ever seen. No, not paradox. Insularity, like empire-building, requires superb self-confidence, a conviction of one's moral superiority.[46]

9

Scott's account of the Kasim family conveys clearly the divisive aspects of British rule. Mirat under the Nawab was subject to British paramountcy through the Political Department of the Government of India. Ranpur, which surrounded it, was temporarily (1937–9) governed by a Congress ministry headed by the Nawab's kinsman, MAK, who was installed by the Governor of the province. When Congress resigned after war broke out the Governor ruled the province direct. In 1942 the Governor tries to detach Kasim from the essentially Hindu Congress. There never was an historical case of a Muslim chief minister in a Congress province with a Hindu majority population. But the situation of the Kasims is plausible. It emphasises nicely the nature of the 'two Indias' ('British' and 'princely') and the element of expediency in keeping them, as well as the Congress and the Muslims, apart.

Britain's major constitutional experiment between the wars, the 1935 India Act's scheme for an all-India federation, accorded separate blocs of seats to princes, Muslims and others. When the Act failed for want of the princes' support for it, the Raj continued to rule India divided. Scott correctly sees the Cripps Mission as the first British sanction of separate nationhood for Congress India and Muslim India. The Mission's failure to bring Congress and the Muslim League together in a reformed Government of India, and the consequent Quit India movement, exacerbated the Hindu–Muslim divide. In some provinces the League now governed while Congress leaders spent the war in gaol.

The post-war Labour Government inherited deep-rooted divisions and was soon resigned to transferring power to either a united or a bifurcated India. Scott explains the tragic sequence of events in 1947 in terms of the long history of British attitudes towards India and Anglo-India, and of the Anglo-Indian attitude to Indians that it generated. He is not recriminatory towards the Labour Government but sees its policy as in the line of longstanding British deficiencies: ignorance, indifference, insularity.

The history of Labour policy in the crucial year, 1946, is more complex than Scott allows. If Perron had still been extant at the end of the 1970s, with time for research in a straitened British university, he could have probed deeply into Labour policy. Where Beloff praised the novelist's imagination for opening up interpretative options denied historians by the inaccessibility of archives, from 1978 scholars could consult the official files left by the policy-makers.[47]

The documents reveal that when the Cabinet Mission failed to achieve agreement between Congress and League on terms for a transfer of power and the defence of the subcontinent, the British Government at first resolved that the Raj must remain, supplemented by troop transfers from other locations. That was in mid-1946. However, the failure of the Indian parties to agree produced massive communal disorder. The extreme case was Calcutta, which fell out of control for several days in August, as some 5000 people were killed and 15,000 injured. Wavell warned of a progressive erosion of the Raj's capacity to administer. 'Pressures from below', economic as well as communal, were, as an Indian historian has shown, 'catalysts' of policy changes.[48] In late 1946 it was officially estimated that volunteer private armies had grown to a total strength of 400,000.

By the end of the year, in a bitter winter of discontent at home, economic and international realities plagued the Government. As the Cold War intensified and the USA hesitated to make global commitments, British forces remained huge and over-extended, in Europe and the Middle East as well as in South and South-East Asia. The troops were needed back in the civilian workforce. The labour shortage amounted to some 600,000 and that winter factories and mines closed because of it. Industrial growth was essential to service the massive debts that had accrued during the war. It was a time for load-shedding, for escaping from burdens of Empire.

That winter Cabinet decided to quit India. Attlee conveyed the essential reasons to doubters. On 2 January 1947 he explained the position to his own Foreign Secretary, Ernest Bevin. Neither the army, nor Indian collaborators, nor the regeneration of the civil administration, would enable the Raj to continue:

> The Indian Army has so far stood up well and has not exhibited communal leanings, but I do not think that any-one doubts that in the event of communal strife breaking out on a large scale, the Army would be split. . . .
>
> We have always governed India through the Indians. Without the tens of thousands of lesser functionaries we could not carry on. In a typical district of one or two million population it is quite common for there to be only one or two white officials. Under the regime of constitutional governments, which have now been in existence with some intervals for a number of years, the loyalty of Indian officials is increasingly directed towards the Indian Governments and not to the British Raj. With the knowledge that the termination of British rule in India is not far off, how can you expect them not to look to the future?
>
> It would be quite impossible even if you could find the men for a few hundred British to administer against the

active opposition of the whole of the politically minded
of the population. I presume when you suggest getting
administrators from the Indian Army you mean the British units in India. How could Army officers with only
a slight knowledge of the language and no knowledge of
administration deal with such a matter as the collection of
land revenue, the backbone of Indian Finance, if they had
not even got Indian clerical assistance? If you proposed to
govern by main force, you would be driven into shootings
and the like for which you would find very little support in
this country.

   You suggest that we are knuckling under at the first blow,
but this entirely ignores the history of the past twenty-five
years. I must ask you if you are prepared to take the strong
hand in India, to announce that we intend to stay there and
to put in enough troops to enforce our rule? This is to go
back on the pledges that have been given by Governments
of every political colour.

   We are seeking to fulfil the pledges of this country with
dignity and to avoid an ignominious scuttle. But a scuttle
it will be if things are allowed to drift.[49]

He wrote to Smuts:

   We are advised by the Viceroy that to re-establish British authorities in the face of opposition of Congress and
possibly also of Muslim League would require four or five
divisions of British troops, which are not available, and a
declaration that we should continue to rule India for 10 or
15 years at least, and that sternest measures of repression
would be necessary. We do not think that the public here
would support such a policy apart from our inability to find
the necessary forces.[50]

No more than the novelist does the historian wish to render
the past through myths of inevitability. But in the light of the
documents it is difficult to suggest alternatives to independence
and partition in the circumstances that Labour faced. Would a
Churchill Government have held on? Possibly, but by quitting
the provinces that Congress could govern while staying on as
suzerain to sustain a multiplicity of quasi-nations in Muslim and
princely India.

10

At the level of the Labour Cabinet's policy-makers Scott's allegation of ignorance and indifference is unfair. Scott does rather
parody the ignorance of Labour politicians, failing to appreciate
that Attlee had been a member of the Statutory Commission of
Inquiry that visited India in 1929 and 1930. He chaired the India
Committee of Cabinet throughout its existence, from 1942 to 1947.
Cripps, whom Scott disliked, visited India at his own expense in
1939 to study the political problem and made himself an expert on
it. He volunteered for his hazardous Mission in 1942.[51] They were
exceptional but they guided Labour's policy from an informed
standpoint. It is absurd to suggest, as Scott does in one of Halki's
cartoons, that as a member of the Cabinet Mission in 1946 Cripps
was ignorant of the extent of the princes' territories.[52]

Scott is on surer ground when he criticises the ignorance and
indifference of the electorate and Parliament at large. When
Attlee farewelled the Cabinet Mission at Westminster there were
only thirty-five members present in the House of Commons. In
the early 1930s, when Churchill entered his wilderness years by
resisting Baldwin's support for a modest advance towards Dominion Status, members did pack the Commons to hear the great
orator's speeches (much as they would do later to hear Powell's
performances). But in general when Indian business was brought
before the House its members fled to the bars and dining rooms.
A survey of leading British journals reveals that in 1935, when the
India Act was passed, 173 articles were published on India. The
'momentous events of 1947 passed comparatively unnoticed', and
only fifty articles on India appeared in the journals.[53]

It was indeed the case that few in Britain identified with the
Congress freedom movement. In a recent analysis of British perceptions of Congress Professor W.H. Morris-Jones concludes:

Nothing can be more astonishing to the eyes of the present
day than the total absence in the sixty-two years prior to
Independence of any serious study focussed on the Empire's
largest political organization. This is a nice measure both
of the privacy of Empire and the late development of scholarly exploration in this type of field. Congress came under
scrutiny only by those who were (or had been) engaged in

the business of governance and a few others who noticed Congress in the course of reporting more generally to the (British) public on the Indian scene.[54]

In general, India was the province of British experts rather than the educated public or the electorate.

In large measure, it had always been policy to keep Indian affairs out of party contention and thus in the hands of experts out of sight. For twenty-five years after it lost its Indian trade, 1833 to 1858, the East India Company was left to govern the Indian Empire. It was discredited by the Mutiny but for over fifty years the Secretary of State for India continued to be advised and checked by a Council of old India hands. The complexities of, for example, Indian land tenures and taxation systems – where the Raj touched the masses of India – were considered inaccessible to the understanding of parliamentarians. The same would be said of the social organisation and the electoral system that were based upon it. At times of political reform, 1907–9, 1917–19, 1929–35 and 1942, there were real attempts to achieve inter-party agreement in Britain.

Within broad policy limits set in London, the administration of India was indeed left to the experts of the Raj. It was largely a family affair, infrequently exposed to comment by British tabloids. The Raj was screened from the gaze of the great British public. When its servants returned home in retirement they had spent a full career in exile and were marginal to British public life. Until enlisted and conscripted soldiers were drafted to India as a vital support to the war in the Middle East and South-East Asia there were few Britons who knew much about the largest imperial possession. Perhaps that indicates a national insularity. More particularly it reflected a longstanding assumption by British authorities that it was not in the national interest, or India's interest, to open the Raj to public scrutiny. A recent survey of 'peripatetic MPs' who visited India between 1870 and 1940 casts doubt upon their capacity 'to comprehend pressing social and political problems'. Anglo-Indian caricatures of the species had flesh-and-blood counterparts.[55]

The renowned author of *On Liberty* himself, John Stuart Mill, applauded the consignment of the government of India to agents independent of the constant intervention of Parliament. He explained the 'true theory' of 'double government' in his *Representative Government* (1861):

[The] government of one people by another, does not and cannot exist. One people may keep another as a warren or preserve for its own use, a place to make money in, a human cattle farm to be worked for the profit of its own inhabitants. But if the good of the governed is the proper business of a government, it is utterly impossible that a people should directly attend to it. The utmost they can do is to give some of their best men a commission to look after it; to whom the opinion of their own country can neither be much of a guide in the performance of their duty, nor a competent judge of the mode in which it has been performed. . . .[56]

Mill spent thirty-five years in the service of the East India Company in London. His conclusion on the government of India was that 'it required far wider political conceptions than merely English or European practice can supply . . . a much more profound study of Indian experience . . . than either English politicians, or those who supply the English public with opinions, have hitherto shown any willingness to undertake'.[57] The Raj of Scott's fiction was direct heir to this *principled* detachment of Anglo-India from the mainstream of public life at home. Ignorance and indifference at home were severely exacerbated by the calculated consignment of India to a segment of the British middle classes.

It is ironical that Mill took pride in 'the most honourable characteristic of the government of India by England, that it has acknowledged no such distinction as that of a dominant and a subject race'.[58] For the Raj depended heavily on the prestige, the myth of invincibility, of the ruling race. In India the finest British specimens were on display; the presence of others was not encouraged. Neither, of course, was the probing or criticism of the Raj by outsiders. As Scott shows from Sayed's comments to his father, the imperial ramparts crumbled when British officers were cowed by Japanese gaolers: 'So much for the *raj*. They too can be made to act like peons. I shall never forget.'[59]

11

Scott's essential achievement as the historian's novelist is to have exposed the mechanics of the Raj.[60] Empire depended on maintaining racial distance, manipulating divisions between communities, preserving inconsistencies in governing structures, practising paternalism and enlisting collaborators, holding physical force in reserve but being prepared to use it ruthlessly. Such activities were to the subject empire what fighting is to war. Scott revealed them and thereby enlarged his readers' moral sensibilities. The human costs to rulers as to ruled emerge. Historical understanding is finally extended by showing how the mechanics of the Raj contributed to the denouement of summer 1947.

After The Raj Quartet

1

About a year before Scott finished *Division* he looked ahead in a letter to David Higham to show that he was 'not creatively destitute'. His next book was 'tentatively entitled Sahib's Face: Or a Slight Case of Cultural Shock because I'm now pretty sure that this is what I want to do as a final departure from India – quite a short affair, using a lot of the background I've picked up during my recent trips – short, rather comic, slightly sinister. An entertainment, to coin a phrase. After that, or after that and a non-fiction, then I think we have the big one I've often thought of doing about business life since the war and which for many years I have thought of as *The Careerists*.'[1] With *Division* completed, instead of 'Sahib's Face', the title 'Mango Rain', discarded a decade earlier, reappears.

It is attached to an idea for a comic novella about an Englishman visiting an Indian village and attracted to the sixteen-year-old daughter of his host's house. Here was another return to Timmapuram. Scott wrote to John Willey:

> At the moment my problem about leaving India . . . is that in doing so I seem to be threatened with leaving what has been what you might call my own literary dimension. . . . At its most banal level, that dimension could be called exotic. Abandoning it is rather like throwing out one's colour TV set and reverting to black and white. . . . I look out of my window and see the buses and lorries going past and feel that I haven't seen things under my nose this past twenty years.[2]

But five months later he confessed that he was 'suffering the most monumental and seemingly impenetrable writer's block'.[3] In January 1975 he still had no first paragraph for 'Mango Rain' and doubted it could work. He kept his appointment with the muse most mornings but she didn't turn up. He stared at the blank page and often picked up a book waiting to be reviewed, a task he usually reserved for afternoons. The *Quartet* had drained him out for the moment. Dorothy Olding thought 'Mango Rain' sounded a bit depressing and Scott tried to assure her that he was seeking the tone of Perron at the Maharanee's rather than that of Hari at Mayapore.[4] But his attempts to draft produced 'creative excisions', not words that stayed on the page.

In February 1975 Scott set 'Mango Rain' aside temporarily and began *Staying On* as 'therapy'.[5] He described the project to Dipali Nag in June, when he wrote his first letter to her in three years, as 'a comic novel which I think of as an Indian version of *The Bender*. . . . I call it *Staying On* and set it in 1972, in a place where the last of the stayers-on from the old raj are fading rapidly away. It may not work. There's so much I need to find out about the minutiae of their lives.'[6] Next month he was still 'dickering with a sort of comedy called *Staying On*, about English people who did', and appealed to Dorothy Ganapathy, 'Tell me anything funny about that and I'll be as ever grateful.'[7] At that time he confided to Francine Weinbaum: 'Unfortunately the man I knew best, who did [stay on], and whom I was relying on to tell me this and that dropped dead in Belgaum.'[8] The man was Peter Goodbody, of whose death in the water closet from a ruptured aneurism he heard in December 1974. The life of Peter and Maisie Goodbody, in the annexe to Green's Hotel in Belgaum, had given Scott the germ of *Staying On*. Peter was the eponym for Tusker Smalley, and though his wife was Eurasian her situation was substantially Lucy Smalley's. Maisie was left without funds. Green's Hotel, like Smith's at Pankot, was sold and altered out of recognition – according to Malgonkar painted red, and offering disco music to swingers – to compete with a new hotel that had taken away its overnight-businessman custom.[9] Maisie was unable to remain in the annexe. In August Scott sought Sir Conrad Corfield's advice on the level of Tusker's pension. In November he was seeking 'anecdotes about all the marginally legal, or illegal, things stayers-on got up to' but he presumably found none as none appears in *Staying On*.[10]

In December he sent the first hundred pages to Dorothy Olding. If she or Willey liked them he would continue. He explained that he had picked the Smalleys up from the *Quartet*,

where he had left them intending to stay on.[11] He joked that they
had always hung about to cadge a lift and had failed to get one
home. By 1947 Tusker had become a lieutenant-colonel, which
made him eligible for an offer of contract by the new Indian
dominion. It was a disappointing experience and he had then
worked unsuccessfully on the administrative side of commerce,
perhaps in an agency like Bird and Co.[12] He was also writing a
history of Pankot.

By February 1976 *Staying On* had taken shape. That month
Lady Butterfield, the wife of a former Regius Professor of
Modern History and Master of Peterhouse College, Cambridge,
congratulated Scott on the creation of Perron, whom she thought
was a Peterhouse man and perhaps a pupil of her husband's.
Scott confided to her some details that would appear in *Staying
On*, 'a little coda to the whole'.[13] Perron had married Sarah and
held a History chair at a new English university. Also, the train
from Ranpur to Pankot still went daily. The book was finished
in April and had been 'comparatively fun to do, after the ten
year stint keeping (more or less) a straight face'.[14] The wonder
is that Scott could for so long have suppressed the comic genius
in himself.

2

Staying On was not published until 1977, but with the manuscript
completed in April 1976, Scott reopened his notebook for 'Mango
Rain'. He soon abandoned his earlier scheme for an Indian novel
of that title, which he now attached to a book about family
and professional life in London and Sussex, set in the drought
of 1976:

> For some years now I have been thinking about doing
> some novels mapping what has happened in England since
> 1945/47, the post-war, post-imperial age. Such a thing
> would be the logical movement away from India, back
> home. It might produce one novel or several. The quartet
> was never a grand design, but sort of worked that way. This
> is not a grand design either but the bracket for thinking
> about what I'm up to. Occasionally it has had a sort of study
> title, The Careerists. Which may or may not evolve. . . . The
> title is now *out*, and this other one, which has also worried
> me for years (since 1964) Mango Rain, has suddenly fallen

into place, although it sounds like a title for yet another
Indian novel.[15]

The work did not prosper. Neither did his ideas for non-fictional
studies. He had thought of writing a book on the daily working
life of the Raj.[16] He had collected together some of his reviews,
lectures and occasional pieces for publication as a volume, 'A
Small Hard Rectangular Object', one section of which would be
titled 'Imperial Issues'.[17] He had looked forward to an eventual autobiography, 'The Studio', an account of his childhood
and youth in north London.[18] None of these projects came to
fruition.

In July 1975, when Dorothy Ganapathy asked Scott whether he
had finished his 'long tryst of love with India', he had replied: 'I
shall never finish thinking about India, even if presently I shall
have to stop writing about it.'[19] In December he wrote a three-
page illustrated article for *Country Life*, 'Dreaming of a White
Man's Christmas: Home Thoughts from Abroad (1778–1921)'.[20]
It was mostly about Anglo-India. That the obsession remained
after the novels were finished is shown by his notes on a volume of documents in the weeks that followed his completion of
Staying On. It was the sixth in the twelve-volume series, *The
Transfer of Power in India, 1942–7*, and the only one he ever
saw.[21] It contained over 500 documents and 1200 pages on the
eight-month period between the accession of the Attlee Labour
Government to power and its dispatch of a Cabinet Mission to
India, August 1945 – March 1946. Scott received it from *The
Times* for possible review, but eventually the editor agreed that
he should simply keep it. His notes reveal his concern to assimilate minute details to his own established view of the subject. He
makes cross-references to Wavell's *Journal*. He lists the main
issues facing Attlee's Government, including the INA problem,
elections in India, pressure for an inquiry into official excesses
during the Quit India movement, and the Indianisation of the
Viceroy's Council. He found vindication for his own conclusions
on the importance of the INA trials, the persistent prospect
of recruiting young Britons to the Indian services, Cripps as
a nagger, British racial contempt, and Wavell's stature. The
modesty of his literary acclaim was drawing out an assertive
historian *manqué*.

3

The writing of *Staying On* in 1975 and early 1976 gave Scott respite from the large personal financial and domestic problems
that confronted him. Since 1960 he had lived a hermit's life in
Hampstead Garden Suburb. He had existed through his fiction,
reviews, lectures, occasional writings and 6000-odd letters. In
some sixteen years as a full-time author he spent a total of only
a few months abroad: some four months on three visits to India;
about a month on two visits to the USA, and a few weeks in the
early 1960s on family summer holidays at Tamaris on the Costa
Brava. His travels within Britain did not go much beyond brief
holidays in a relative's cottage in Sussex, and visits, often as
lecturer, to Writers' Summer School at Swanwick. From the way
he wrote of visits into London one would think he was travelling
from the Outer Hebrides. They were indeed few and mostly for
lunch, *cuisine flambé* at his favoured L'Épicure (where he is
fondly remembered), or as a guest at a club or a restaurant.
The unnatural confinement of a house-bound life often placed
intolerable strains on his relations with his wife, whilst from
1968 the illness of his younger daughter was a constant anxiety.
The artist surmounted these problems but the man was severely
depleted. He drank heavily. 'My own capacity and liking for
alcohol is pretty big,' he wrote in 1965.[22] The world of authors
and publishers is not notably abstemious but one literary friend
recalls that Scott's appetite for alcohol was the largest he ever
encountered. A friend who had not seen him since 1962 met
him in the USA in 1975 and noticed a serious deterioration
in his appearance. At least one of his lectures on that tour
was incoherent and he was upset that another was hopelessly
misreported in the press.

Overhanging almost his entire life as a full-time writer was
financial anxiety. From 1960 he lived on publishers' advances
on books yet to be written. Even in 1975–6 his total pre-tax
income was a mere £3324. Of that sum £1164 was earned by
reviewing and £360 by lecturing in the USA. The pre-tax income
from his twelve novels, all in print, was an unbelievable £1800.
In the 1965–75 period his highest taxable income was £3032, his
lowest £1999. As early as 1963 he thought he might have to return
to his career in publishing. In 1966 he reflected that he must have

been crazy to have retired. From 1972 he undertook regular reviewing for *Country Life* as a kind of safety net. At thirty guineas a fortnight, that raised the total of his reviewing fees from £200–£300 a year to some £800. The sale of manuscripts to the University of Texas helped to keep him afloat. He hoped that the proceeds would seem silly to his official biographer but he welcomed them: £750 in 1964–5 for all the pre-*Quartet* material that he possessed; and from £450 to £700 for manuscripts and notes relating to each of the *Quartet* novels. In 1969–70 he received a British Arts Council grant of £1000. Until about 1969 the publishers' advances on which he lived were more or less covered by credits on sales. Thereafter, as each novel took him longer to write, he became a 'red figure' author. From mid-1970 he began approaching publishers – John Murray, Faber and Faber, Hodder and Stoughton – for part-time editorial work, but without success. In February 1975 he was chagrined by his failure to get a £3000 p.a. job for two or three days' work a week as chief editor of a book club, the New Fiction Society, run jointly by the National Book League and the Arts Council. Early in 1976 he applied for support from the Royal Literary Fund, expecting that the last advances due for *Staying On* would be largely required to meet his taxes. Scott was certainly not destitute and had paid off his house (worth some £25,000 at that time). But he was at a loss to know how he could afford to live in it. The future was 'rather worrying': 'I am much aware that on paper I'm neither in want nor distress. I am, I think, about to be extended beyond the point that sorts well with the business of concentrating on what I want to do.'[23]

These were the circumstances in which Scott accepted an invitation to spend Fall semester, 1976, as a lecturer and writer-in-residence at the University of Tulsa, Oklahoma. He did so without enthusiasm, though in a bleak year it would be something to look forward to. 'It is not a place I would choose for preference,' he wrote to Freya Stark.[24] He confided to Dorothy Ganapathy: 'One would not do it if it weren't for the financial reward. . . . Feel I'm being driven out of my own country just to keep my head above water. . . .'[25] The fee for his four-months' residence at Tulsa would be $12,000, which would yield him a pre-tax profit of £3885. In mid-July, a month before his departure, his wife, to whom he had been faithful for the thirty-six

years of their marriage, but whom he did not plan to take to
the USA, left him. He pleaded with his daughters to beg her to
return: 'I do not *want* to go to Tulsa. I *have* to go to Tulsa, to
try to earn some real money or what passes for real money in
my sort of profession.'[26] The offer had come from his meeting
and staying with Professor Bernard Benstock and his wife in
Illinois during his 1975 lecture tour. Benstock recommended
him to Professor Thomas F. Staley, Dean of Graduate Studies at Tulsa, who was seeking a writer-in-residence. He would
teach a creative writing workshop and a British literature
course. Benstock assured Scott that Tulsa was 'a rather unique
corner of America, a magnificent composite of affluence and
vulgarity'.[27]

4

At Tulsa Scott taught a course on 'Rhetoric and Writing' and
another on 'Literature of the Empire', a 'very public' task, as
Staley realised, for 'a very private man'.[28] He had enjoyed
lecturing to American students during his 1975 tour, finding
them courteous and responsive. He was so warmly appreciated
at Tulsa in 1976 that he was invited and agreed to return for
the Fall semester the following year. He was so affectionately
remembered that in 1988 eleven students and colleagues who
knew him during those Fall visits gathered in the meeting room
of the splendid Philbrook Museum to read tributes to him, published as *After Paul: Paul Scott's Tulsa Years*.

At his first lecture, in the serviceable but institutional Oliphant
Hall, he moved the Writing class to his small apartment, dark,
smoky, grubby, sparsely furnished, with an ancient threadbare
brown carpet. Most of the students and Scott himself sat on
the floor. He wrote to his elder daughter: 'They seem to like
my unacademic, unorthodox attitude. The number of people in
class seems to grow a bit as word gets round that I'm an amusing
sort of bloke!'[29] However, he struggled with his Fiction class and
students felt that he didn't care for 'the "lit crit" game'.[30] On 15
December he held a farewell party for both classes, played a
tape he had made for the occasion, bringing together excerpts
from Gounod's *Faust*, Shirley Bassey, John Betjeman, Eliot's
'East Coker' and Conrad's *Youth*, and bade them farewell Hindi
style, 'Chalo'.

Scott left Tulsa on 17 December 1976, spent a few days in New York, meeting Dorothy Olding and John Willey, and reached home on Wednesday 22 December. The following week he lunched at L'Épicure with David Higham and no doubt looked forward to resuming 'Mango Rain' in the New Year. But 1977 was not to be a productive year. His continuing interest in India appears in reviews of R.K. Narayan's *The Painter of Signs* and Kamala Markandaya's *The Golden Honeycomb*. The latter was the story of a princely family, set mainly in the years preceding the First World War. There was tension between the Anglicised prince and his non-Anglophile lover. Scott hoped that Markandaya would carry the Prince's story up to 1947 and welcomed the prospect that an Indian might write of the country's long experience of living with and under the British.[31] His last review was of V.S. Naipaul's *India: A Wounded Civilization* for the *Washington Post* in June.

5

In mid-1977, when he gave a party at his house to launch *Staying On*, Roland Gant half suspected that Scott was a sick man. Before he left for America at the end of July Scott said to Mrs Gant: 'I am so tired, so tired. I don't know if I'll ever get there or, if I do, I'll ever get back here again.'[32] He flew to New York and went on to see Francine Weinbaum in Michigan. As the Weinbaums watched him leave by taxi they felt they would not see him again. He returned to New York for the publication of *Staying On* in early August, stayed with John Willey in Connecticut and saw Burjorjee in Washington.

He arrived at Tulsa on Sunday evening 28 August and was met by Professor Donald Hayden, from the Faculty of Graduate Studies, and some former students. They went off to Scott's apartment – a different one – for a welcome-home party. 'He was in excellent spirits,' Hayden recalled, 'though he was indeed thinner and a bit wan looking.'[33] One of the students noticed a great change: 'Paul was too thin. He was walking too slowly.'[34] Another wrote that he was 'used up', 'grown slight with age and illness'.[35] He was relieved that he would not have to teach a British Fiction course again but would have a Writing Workshop and a Directed Writing Group. Hayden recalled that he showed magnificent spirit that semester, and 'All of us who knew him cherished the man greatly.' Though he remained in Tulsa for the semester he was admitted to St Francis' Hospital in October with cancer and underwent surgery. He returned home for Christmas and expected to undergo chemo- or radio-therapy. His wife had returned and on New Year's Eve he wrote bravely to his tax accountant: 'Actually I feel pretty well.'[36]

When he was awarded the Booker Prize for *Staying On* in November 1977 his elder daughter, Carol, collected it for him while he celebrated, drinking sparkling catawba juice with the Reviews Editor of the *Tulsa World* in his apartment. In summer he had told M.M. Kaye that he had 'nothing left to say' about India.[37] Now he was quoted as saying, 'I have finished with India for ever. It just needed some little valedictory thing.'[38] A reviewer called it the *nunc dimittis* that crowned his achievement.[39] Frank Giles urged Scott to stick with India: 'For the sake of your admiring, and now surely increasing, public, think again, Mr Scott, think again.'[40] As nice an appreciation of *Staying On* as any was Auberon Waugh's:

> Of all the novels I have reviewed in the past ten years, only one – Paul Scott's Staying On, about a couple left behind in India after the British have left – haunts me as the authentic, sad, slightly absurd accent of our time, the true voice of a country whose past dignity and vigour survive only in the fuddled memory of a few kindly old buffers, long past playing any active role.[41]

It is fitting that Scott's last publication in his lifetime – three weeks before his death in Middlesex Hospital on 1 March 1978 – was an article on holidays in India for *The Times*: 'India always extends me by subtly undermining the structure of my normal Western responses and replacing them with attitudes that promise to lead to an ever fuller sense of identity with the place and its people. I have been too long away.'[42]

6

Had Scott lived, might he not – given the unaccustomed rewards of the £5000 Booker Prize and the enhanced sales of the *Quartet* that it (and its TV adaptation) brought – have written Parvati's story? His characters did live on.[43] After independence Hari got a post teaching at a government college or an Indian public school run on English lines. In 1964 the Stranger had seen Parvati at MacGregor House. Lady Chatterjee had adopted her and she was known as Parvati Chatterjee. Subsequently Hari had made contact with Lady Chatterjee, keeping tabs on Parvati's career as a singer, a protégé of someone like Ravi Shanker (with whom Dipali Nag had appeared). He attended her first solo recital.

MAK returned to politics in 1950 at independent India's first elections. He became Minister of Agriculture, later Chief Minister of Ranpur, and eventually Governor of the province. Sayed entered the Pakistan Army. Guy Perron (D.Phil.) married Sarah in 1949. They acquired *The Jewel in Her Crown* from Edward Bingham and bought Mr Hapgood's Guler-Basohli-style paintings (two of them bearing faint stains of Purvis's rum) when Mrs Hapgood sold them in 1965.

Epilogue

1

It is remarkable that the huge cinematic potentialities of Scott's fiction were only realised after his death. Over the years he had emphasised that the novelist must start with an image that he saw clearly: the woman in the doorway of *Birds of Paradise*; a couple arriving somewhere in disgrace in *Corrida*; the girl running in *Jewel*. While he was at Tulsa he told an interviewer that 'underneath every novel – though a good novel will not have all the trappings of the stage directions, etc. – still, every page should be in a proscenium arch: well lit, dressed, directed, spoken, filled with action'.[1] In his Writing Workshop he insisted, 'A novel is a series of images. It is connected with cinema. The only difference is that it exists in a prison, a book, a small hard rectangular object.'[2] And 'When you open a novel the curtain must rise.' Through a lifetime the creative habit of beginning with an image, which was formed by his childhood film-making, endured. Until he began the *Quartet* his work was often presented on the BBC in the form of drama. *Johnnie Sahib* was anticipated by a radio play on its theme in 1951. *Alien Sky* was presented on television in 1954, *Mark of the Warrior* on the radio in 1959, and *The Bender* on television in 1964, adapted by Irene Shubik (then Story Editor, Play Parade) and with Paul Rogers in the leading role.

In the 1950s and 1960s Scott saw television as essentially theatre rather than film, relying on sustained, confined performance for want of the full resources of a film unit. In 1956 he set a television play about sahibs and memsahibs, *The Colonel's Lady*, in Smith's Hotel and insisted that it be played there, not taken outside.[3] In 1969 he again insisted upon the essential confinement of a play's setting. More than two years after writing it for *Scorpion*, he was struck with the stage potentialities of 'The Situation', the scene in which Rowan interrogates Hari

while Lady Manners listens unobserved. In the stage setting,
however, Scott has Lady Manners meet and talk with Kumar.
It was a long enclosed setting, not open air but underground. The
Royal Shakespeare Company and the Garrick Theatre thought
the play 'too static'. Margery Vosper, an authors' representative who liked the play, also found it 'enormously static' and felt
that the isolation of the scene from the context of the book made
its mood 'wildly anti the British Raj', despite the late appearance of Lady Manners as the voice of liberalism and humanity.[4]
In June 1970 Scott's agent told him that he was unable to sell the
script to the commercial theatre.[5] Scott was too busy with the
Quartet to make changes, so that the play remained 'a kite that
nearly flew'.[6] This was his sole playwriting venture during the
decade of the *Quartet*. He explained: 'Juxtaposition rather than
chronology of scene produces the effect of historical movement
and overall intention. It is because I now write this kind of novel
that I've stopped attempting to dramatise them for radio and
television. Quite simply it is impossible.'[7]

Yet Scott would have welcomed the filming of the *Quartet*.
Soon after its publication the agent of the maker of *Lawrence of
Arabia*, David Lean, had a copy of *Jewel*.[8] Scott held no hopes
of a film eventuating. A film unit would have to be sent to India
and there would be huge costs and endless complications with
censorship rules and regulations. He wrote wistfully to Dipali
Nag that a film was a pipe dream, but 'what fun' if it happened.[9]
As he approached the completion of the *Quartet*, and in the
very different world of high-budget colour television, he pressed
David Higham to consider the prospect of a BBC series on it.[10] In
August 1974 he acquainted Dorothy Olding of the need to bring
the *Quartet* to the attention of John Freeman, formerly British
High Commissioner in Delhi and now Chairman of London
Weekend Television.[11] At that time Freeman was not aware
of Scott's work. Scott was still pessimistic, for 'the Indian government . . . are extremely sensitive to anything that doesn't
represent India in the most angelic light'. But 'perhaps one day
the TV people might do a dramatised series. Which would . . .
be nice.' In December he again made the point to Higham 'that
the *idea* for a dramatic serial about the last wartime years of
the Raj might be implanted in the TV producers' minds (if it
isn't already there), without regard to chapter and verse, only

in regard to the fact that novels on the subject do exist'.[12] In mid-1975 when John Rush of David Higham Associates was frankly discouraging about the prospects of an eventual television series on the *Quartet*, Scott responded that he would like to be involved in any 'documentary end-of-empire programme' that might be made.[13]

2

In spring 1975, as he waited for *Division* to go through the press, he prepared a speculative outline for a possible television book programme, *Scott's Raj – Or India Returned*.[14] The interviewer is Melvyn Bragg, as they take a leisurely stroll through Scott's life. The curtain rises on a photograph of Scott, with sitar music playing. A shot of the *Quartet* novels follows and the camera settles on Bragg and Scott in the studio. As the dialogue traverses Scott's Indian novels, he is shown with Bragg driving and strolling past the north London scenes of his early life – the house in which he was born, his aunts' house, Southgate, and so on. Back in the studio, a group of panellists discuss Scott's work, the critics Zulfikar Ghose and Francis King, Dr W.G. Archer, ICS Bihar retired, and Keeper of the Indian Section of the Victoria and Albert Museum, and Veronica Bamfield, the colonel's wife who wrote *On the Strength*. Bragg sums up the discussion and the *tête-à-tête* resumes, with Scott relating his wartime experience of India. Shots of India – the countryside, Calcutta, street crowds, courts, bungalows, government houses, New Delhi, a princely occasion, Mrs Gandhi – are interposed with shots of England – Palmers Green, Southgate, the City, derelict Lancashire cotton mills, English shopping centres, English politicians, young Indians in English streets. The intention is to emphasise by the overlay of images the interconnection of British and Indian history, the shared experience. As the last shots revert to Scott and Bragg walking and driving in north London, Bragg's voice-over is heard:

you start to wonder again how a man born and bred here, still affectionately attached, even to its ugliness, could write books about places so far away. But there is a passage in the recent book, the one that ends the sequence, which, driving through here, seems to me to make the

connection. There is a sergeant called Perron who has
been benighted in a military office in Bombay. The time
is August 1945, the night before the atom bomb was dropped on Hiroshima. The only other man awake is a British
corporal of the Guard. The corporal asks the sergeant how
long he has been out in India. ' "Two years", Perron said.
The corporal studied him respectfully, but looking for signs
of deterioration. "I reckon I'd be round the twist if they kept
me here that long". . . . Perron glanced at the sleeping men.
Only one of them had his face turned towards the light.
He looked about 19; so, come to that, did the corporal.
The faces were those of urban Londoners and belonged to
streets of terraced houses that ended in one man shops:
newsagent–tobacconist, fish and chip shop, family grocer,
and a pub at the corner where the high road was. What
could such a face know of India? And yet India was there,
in the skull, and the bones of the body. Its possession had
helped nourish the flesh, warm the blood of every man in
the room, sleeping and waking.'

Sitar music comes in, speeds up, and fades away. Scott sent
the outline to Gant at his home but dismissed it as 'much too
long' and 'the roughest of blue-prints', and with a comment
that really explains why no attempt was made to use it: '. . . I
wouldn't want people in the office to see this sort of confessional
thing.'[15]

3

Scott was delighted at Gant's instant response to the typescript
of *Staying On* in April 1976:

He thought it would make a splendid play for Ralph
Richardson and Celia Johnson – and he's xeroxing the
ts and showing it to a friendly impresario to whom he's
already spoken. What fun that would be if anything could
come of it. I've been near to theatre production several
times in the past thirty years, and still hanker for it, rather
than TV. But of course I know the road there is strewn with
a lot of buoyant chat and no action.[16]

Shortly before his death Scott learned from Gant of plans to film
Staying On for television. The rights to the book were bought by
Anglia Television, who hoped to present it as a drama starring

Wendy Hiller but shrank from the expense of filming the whole in India. Now at Granada, Irene Shubik realised the television potentialities of the rich characterisation in the book and secured Sir Denis Forman's interest. He reached an agreement that enabled Granada to proceed. Across a gap of twenty-five years since their joint triumph in Noel Coward's *Brief Encounter*, Celia Johnson and Trevor Howard were brought together again in Irene Shubik's production. In March 1980 the British stars and a team of thirty-six technicians set off to make the £400,000 budget film at Simla.

Sir Denis Forman, Chairman of Granada Television, recognised *Staying On* as 'a natural for television'. It led him on to the *Quartet* and, he writes,

immediately I was back in the India that I had known in the years before Independence. . . .

On second reading I wondered if the Quartet might be susceptible to television. The rights were free. It could be the chance of a lifetime.

Could it be done on television? The narrative was told in a form so complex as to make all the flash-backery of Conrad and Ford Madox Ford look like a children's game. The book was heavy with references to a political scene that was never familiar and today almost wholly forgotten by the Western world. At least four months shooting in India would be needed, and no unit from the United Kingdom or America had at that time attempted anything on such a scale (Richard Attenborough's *Gandhi* was not shot until 1981).

It seemed sensible, indeed necessary, to do two things before committing Granada to such a major operation. First, we would make *Staying On* in Simla as a single play and so gain some experience to help us decide whether the logistics and cost of a lengthy shoot in a distant subcontinent were within our reach. Also, before recruiting a production team, we must be satisfied that it was possible to do justice to the Quartet if it were translated into the form of a television series.

Staying On was made in 1980. Although there were problems in plenty, the finished film, with Trevor Howard and Celia Johnson as Tusker and Lucy, was much liked. Meanwhile, I had set about an exercise on the Quartet. The first step was to arrange all the events in the story into chronological order, starting from the riots of 1942 and continuing until Guy Perron flew towards Delhi in the week of Independence in July 1947. It was not a simple task. Some incidents were told and retold a second and third time. There were no less than thirteen separate references to the rape, each one throwing some new emphasis or a different interpretation upon it. There were excursions off the main track (notably the opening tragic story of Miss Crane). There were a great number of direct references to the political scene. There were seven main geographical locations, and, worst of all, we lost our first hero and heroine, Hari Kumar and Daphne Manners, just as they had aroused our interest and engaged our sympathy.

The next move was to see how the chronological narrative would break down into sequences each of which would form a one hour episode for the television screen. This was done by chopping a roll of wallpaper into thirteen segments about one yard square, pinning them round the walls of a room and writing down on each the outline of scenes for each episode. After walking some miles around this gallery, touching, retouching, shifting and deliberating, it did, at last, seem feasible that Paul Scott's great book could be made into a television series that would not betray the quality of the original work.[17]

Granada has published its own full and illustrated account of *The Making of The Jewel in the Crown*, of the assembling of the production team and cast and the filming in India and Britain. It is complete with an outline of episodes, a personal and often distorted view of the Raj by James Cameron, and memoirs by Roland Gant and M.M. Kaye.

4

It was intrinsic to the linearisation or chronological ordering of the serial that the repetitions of the text would be reduced. In the *Quartet* the characters define themselves largely by the varying accounts they render of events at Mayapore in August 1942. The historian Natalie Davis observed the consequences of reducing her research on the celebrated case of Martin Guerre into a screenplay. The story concerns a rich peasant of sixteenth-century Languedoc who leaves his home for some years. He apparently returns but after a time his wife realises that an imposter has taken his place. Natalie Davis suffered misgivings as important historical details were sacrificed as filming proceeded:

> These changes may have helped to give the film the power-ful simplicity that had enabled the Martin Guerre story to become a legend in the first place. . . . [But] where was there room in this beautiful and compelling cinematographic recreation of a village for the uncertainties, the 'perhapses', the 'may-have-beens', to which the historian has recourse when the evidence is inadequate or perplexing?[18]

In the television *Jewel* the texture of testimony, its intimation of character, the doubts about the truth and reality of observa-tions, are largely lost in the process of adaptation.

Important aspects of the British–Indian relationship are also lost. Sir Denis Forman believed that Scott showed the Raj as it was, not as it was recorded in books, for like Scott he viewed the record as seriously deficient, but as those who knew it might confide it to have been. In governing an empire there was necessarily the same ultimate ruthlessness that fighting a war required. Yet in the serial the Indian Army is largely silent, its main spokesman, Brigadier Reid, reduced to a walk-on. As an agent of continuity, Merrick assumes a more central role in the serial and his methods assume greater emphasis. Robin White's voice, that of the liberal member of the ICS, is muted, though Mabel Layton and Lady Manners do express his view-point. Perhaps the most serious loss is the reduction of Kasim's role, as symbolic of nationalist aspirations for a united India. The opening scene of *Scorpion*, when he opposes the nationalist's outlook to Governor Malcolm's play to enlist his collaboration, is wholly absent.

Inevitably, the serial focuses on characters, the tensions between them and their developing situations. The historical context is brilliantly conveyed by newsreel clips so patently pro-British that they serve as a parodic commentary, though too much reliance is placed on them to emphasise that during the war India was an armed camp. Moreover, the Congress–Raj political arena, in which Scott's main 'blocks of interest', Bri-tish traditionalism and Indian nationalism, subtly confront each other, is little more than suggested. For many of Scott's loyal readers the politics doubtless seem inessential. To such a one

Scott wrote: 'I suppose the politics are things to take or leave, but they are essential to the framework and the overall structure. However, they emerge best when connected with a major character, such as Mohammed Ahmed Kasim in the second and fourth books.'[19]

Yet the losses in transmutation scarcely diminish Granada's achievement. The makers of *Jewel* grappled with the inner meaning of Scott's text, and reached conclusions that Scott would have endorsed. Sir Denis Forman reflected that the British did not relax and become part of India as the Spanish might have done, nor remain tyrants like the French or Dutch as colonial masters. They 'tried to find a way into a country through its fabric; it was a noble ideal but it was pathetic, because it could never succeed'.[20] For Christopher Morahan (producer and co-director), 'The tension between those who thought they knew best and those who didn't want to be told what was best for them brought about the end of the Indian Empire.'[21] He sees Barbie as symbolic of the failure of the Christian mission in India. She is played by Dame Peggy Ashcroft in what an American critic called 'the best acting I have seen on TV'.[22] The emotional heart of the *Quartet* is thus revealed. Jim O'Brien (co-director) saw Scott's concern as 'flies caught in amber. The struggle of his characters in their inability to cope with a changing world; that's the real drama. Scott didn't attempt to come to a conclusion; he realized how complex it was.'[23] Ken Taylor (scriptwriter), rather than trying to reconstruct the novels, concentrated on character and story: 'The two things that appeal to me are character and narrative. Scott's a marvellous storyteller. You read the characters and you live with them. . . . During the war I met such girls in India and they were awfully boring – ghastly little memsahibs. In Scott, each one is an individual, they're all interesting.'[24] The use of flashbacks and voice-over preserved much of Scott's technique and complex time planes, so that the Manners case does reverberate and echo through the serial. A British television critic applauded the choice of locations in the series for encapsulating Scott's view of the Raj: 'There was a handful of beautiful landscape shots, but almost none of the usual screen clichés: few teeming bazaars, horsemen thundering across empty plains, temples in the moonlight. Instead, the action takes place in dingy offices, cells, claustrophobic sitting rooms. It is about a society turned in on itself, obsessed with itself, fearful as its old certainties give way to doubt.'[25]

John Bayley, Warton Professor of English Literature at the University of Oxford, has argued that the *Quartet required* the television screen to bring it to life:

> Paul Scott's India is entirely believable. The reader is speedily convinced that everything happened exactly as he says it happened: that India in the last days of the Raj really was like this. . . . All the strangeness of India so artfully concocted by other writers, all its imputed paradoxes and enchantments, all the stories made up about it, must be scrupulously forgone. . . .
>
> Scott's story is at once meagre and over-documented, laboured but obscure, and it dwindles away just as unsatisfactorily as such things do in life. . . .
>
> Scott was a theorist. He pondered, and pondered very intelligently, the problem of how he could write a novel, present his material in fictional form. He asked himself questions like 'In what does reality consist?' – and when the novelist asks himself that things begin to look bad.
>
> He decided that where the novel was concerned reality consisted for him in 'a sequence of images': when arranged in sequence, such images 'tell a story'. . . .
>
> Scott was probably quite unconscious of the fact that he had developed a technique of novel-writing which could only realise itself fully by being translated into another medium. . . . When 'images' are converted into actors and actresses the whole thing falls into place: the distance from the reader of the novel's cast of characters is exactly matched by the distance dictated by the screen. No viewer who has read the book is likely to say: 'but that's not my idea of Daphne, or of Barbie, or Tusker Smalley.' Novel and picture, dialogue and script, glide effortlessly into one another. . . . Television is in one sense an almost slavishly faithful and literal medium, at home with any story which does not exist by virtue of having created a world of its own.[26]

It is the ultimate paradox that praise for the serial should deride the literary sequence on which it is based.

John Leonard, an American television critic of thirty-five years' experience, praises the achievement in both genres:

'Until now, no great novel has gotten a movie or a television program worthy of it.'[27] He applauds Scott's posthumous partners in the production and the performance. 'These people love him. So, obviously, do I,' he wrote.

Professor W.H. Morris-Jones has reviewed the serial at length. As an authority on the government and politics of India, a former Director of the Institute of Commonwealth Studies at the University of London, his conclusions demand attention:

> It is an advantage of age that one can sometimes say 'I was there at the time.' My own years in the Indian Army coincided closely enough with the *Jewel* period, and my recollections confirm the authenticity of the book and film. Scott got it brilliantly right as to atmosphere and mood, and the film has been faithful. Additionally the film has got the scenes amazingly right – helped no doubt by Scott's quite meticulous descriptions – so that the length and cut of the khaki shorts, the sounds at a railway station, the clubs of the sahibs as well as the approach to the house of Kumar's aunt, the inside of the newspaper office as well as the hospital, the tone of the racially mixed soirées as well as the looks received by Hari and Daphne from both whites and browns – none can be faulted. A strange past world has been recaptured. . . . A doom is closing in on the transposed *tranche* whose authority is draining away. . . . [*Jewel*] takes us in towards the core of each participant – yes, even Merrick – before inviting us to see the scene whole. That whole is not glorious – not at all the stuff for patriotic nostalgia. Rather it is bleak, desperately sad, with little shafts of brightness, above all movingly true.[28]

Morris-Jones is Guy Perron's direct contemporary. Both were born in 1918, both were at Cambridge in 1939, both joined the Indian Army in 1941. Perron was in India from 1943 to 1945 and returned in August 1947 to observe the lapse of paramountcy. Morris-Jones was in India from 1941 to 1946 and returned in June 1947 as a member of Mountbatten's staff and was much concerned with the lapse of paramountcy. His conclusions fix authenticating seals of personal experience and scholarship on book and film.

Note on Sources and References

There are two large deposits of Paul Scott's papers. The core of the collection at the Harry Ransom Humanities Research Center, University of Texas at Austin, consists of working papers, holograph drafts and typescripts that Scott accrued whilst writing his novels and sold in a series of transactions. It also includes Scott's working library on India (some 160 volumes) and notes for reviews, which were purchased from his estate. The collection at the McFarlin Library, University of Tulsa, contains the bulk of Scott's correspondence as a full-time author (some 12,000 items), and holograph and typescript drafts and working papers for lectures, plays, articles, reviews, reader's reports and some novels (notably *Staying On*). It was acquired from Scott's estate.

The following notes provide brief references to items used in the preparation of the text. The main sources used are the letters in the Tulsa collection. They are referenced in the simple form 'S. to addressee' or 'addressee to S.' and may be located readily in the Hollinger boxes and files at the McFarlin Library, which are arranged by addressee and date. In cases where letters are filed by institutions rather than addressees, the institutional name is provided, that is 'S. to addressee (institution)', except for Scott's two most frequent correspondents in New York. Scott's correspondence with his American editor, John Willey, appears in the William Morrow files, and that with his American agent, Dorothy Olding, appears in the Harold Ober Associates files. Scott's correspondence with his London agent appears in the David Higham Associates (DHA) files. Where anomalies arise, or sources may not be found readily, Hollinger box and file numbers are provided in the form '00:00'. For all references to the Texas collection the acronym 'HRC' is used.

It has been a convenience to have Shelley C. Reece's edition of Scott's lectures, *My Appointment with the Muse: Essays, 1961–75* (Heinemann, 1986), published in the USA as *On Writing and the Novel: Essays* (Morrow, 1987). References to Scott's lectures are, except where otherwise indicated, to the text of *Muse*.

The abbreviation 'TP' refers to Nicholas Mansergh, E.W.R. Lumby and Sir Penderel Moon (eds), *The Transfer of Power*, 12 vols (HMSO, 1970–83).

References

Prologue

1. 13 February 1984.
2. Unpublished, 14 February 1984. Collection of Mr Andrew Robinson.
3. 22 March 1984.
4. *Listener*, 29 March 1984.
5. *Private Eye*, 6 April 1984.
6. 5 April 1984.
7. 'Outside the Whale', *Granta*, April 1984. A shorter version appeared in the *Observer*, 1 April 1984.
8. *Time Out*, 5–11 April 1984.

Chapter 1: An Obsession with India

1. S. to Willey, 13 December 1960.
2. S. to Willey, 22 September 1960.
3. S. to Gerald Hanley [August 1961].
4. S. to Spark, 9 November 1961.
5. S. to Green, 25 April 1963.
6. S. to Clive Sansom, 11 July 1963, 32:27.
7. S. to Hugh Corbett, n.d., 22:30.
8. S. to Sujit Mukherjee, 8 May 1974, 38:34.
9. S. to K.B. Rao, 3 October 1975, 43:33.
10. S. to Alan Jenkins, 4 October 1974.
11. 'Scott's Raj, an outline for a possible TV book programme', May 1975, 1:49.
12. S. to Storm Jameson, 18 February 1975.
13. Autobiographical fragment, 1960, 9:1.
14. 'A Writer Takes Stock', lecture by S. as president of

London Writers' Circle, 22 October 1973, in Shelley C. Reece (ed.), *My Appointment with the Muse: Essays, 1961–75, Paul Scott* (Heinemann, London, 1986), 151–64, 153–4.

15. S. to Peter Scott, 31 August 1974.
16. *Muse*, 153.
17. Ibid., 154.
18. The following account of OTS Belgaum draws on Scott's *The Mark of the Warrior* (Eyre & Spottiswoode, London, 1958), Part One. Scott acknowledged that Belgaum was 'really the scene for' the novel (S. to Peter Green, 31 December 1974).
19. *Warrior*, Granada 1979 edn., 11.
20. Scott's introduction to W.H. Saumarez Smith, *A Young Man's Country* (Michael Russell, London, 1977), xi; S. to M.M. Kaye, 30 August 1965.
21. *Warrior*, 11–12.
22. Leasor's recollection, mostly quoted in Roland Gant, 'Paul Scott Remembered', in Granada Television's *The Making of The Jewel in the Crown* (Granada Publishing, London, 1983), 119–20.
23. Interview with Francine Ringold, 'A Conversation with Paul Scott', *Nimrod*, 21.1 (Fall/Winter 1976), 16–32, 28.
24. 'Scott's Raj'.
25. Ibid.
26. L.F. Rushbrook-Williams (ed.), *A Handbook for Travellers in India, Pakistan, Burma and Ceylon*, 21st edn (John Murray, London, 1968), 500.
27. *Johnnie Sahib* (1952), Granada 1979 edn, 10.
28. Reader, 'Memories of an Improbable Soldier', *Indo-British Review*, XVI.1 (March 1989), 89–101, 98.
29. Harrison, 'A Temporary Officer in a Temporary Battalion', ibid., 103–20, 106.
30. Purkayastha to S., 10 August 1946.
31. Dass to S., 28 October 1946.
32. Palit, 'Indianization: A Personal Experience', *Indo-British Review*, loc. cit., 59–64, 60.
33. *Johnnie Sahib*, 28.
34. Ibid., 16.
35. Loc. cit., 96.

36. 'Reflections on the Indian Army over Forty Years', *Indo-British Review*, loc. cit., 35–8, 37, note on 'The Mai-Bap tradition'.
37. Ringold, loc. cit., 29.
38. 'Scott's Raj'.
39. Loc. cit., 105.
40. S. to Dame Freya Stark, 14 February 1976; review of W.G. Archer, *The Hill of Flutes, Country Life*, 7 November 1974; report on Mary H. Moore, 'Palaces and Pujas', 8 December 1962, Box 18; review of Geoffrey Moorhouse, *Calcutta, Guardian*, 21 October 1971.
41. S. to Stark, loc. cit.
42. Introduction to Saumarez Smith's *Young Man's Country*, xi.
43. Ibid.
44. 'Scott's Raj'.
45. 'After Marabar: Britain and India, A Post-Forsterian View', *Muse*, 112–29, 120.
46. 'India: A Post-Forsterian View', lecture delivered to Royal Society of Literature, 5 December 1968, Mary Stocks (ed.), *Essays by Divers Hands* (OUP, 1970), 113–32, 115–16.
47. *British Soldier in India: The Letters of Clive Branson* (The Communist Party, London, 1944). The quotations in the following paragraph are drawn from this pamphlet, published by the Communist Party and introduced by Harry Pollitt.
48. 'Scott's Raj'.
49. Review of John Morris, *Hired to Kill*, *Times Literary Supplement*, 2 December 1960.
50. Palit, 'Indianization of the Army's Officer Cadre, 1920–47', *Indo-British Review*, loc. cit., 55–8, 55.
51. Loc. cit., 94.
52. Memorandum on the future efficiency of the Indian forces, c. 1944–5, cited in Hugh Tinker, 'From British Army to Indian Army', *Indo-British Review*, loc. cit., 1–17, 6.
53. Palit, loc. cit., 55–8.
54. Tinker, 'The Diary of a Military and Civil Nobody', *Indo-British Review*, XIII.2 (July–December 1987), 12–25, 13.
55. Loc. cit., 120.

56. 'Scott's Raj'.
57. Introduction to Saumarez Smith's *Young Man's Country*, xii.
58. Review of Moorhouse, *Calcutta*.
59. *The Day of the Scorpion* (Heinemann, London, 1968), 405.
60. Review of Moorhouse, *Calcutta*.
61. Kaye's memoir in Granada's *The Making of The Jewel in the Crown* (1983), 127.
62. S. to Ralph Arnold, 2 November 1968.
63. Radcliffe, *Not in Feather Beds: Some Collected Papers* (Hamish Hamilton, London, 1968).
64. *Muse*, 1962.
65. S. to Purkayastha, 29 April 1951.
66. S. to Dass, 14 January 1964.
67. 'India: A Post-Forsterian View', loc. cit., 115–16.
68. Ibid., 120.
69. S. to John Mellors, 16 May 1975.
70. 'After Marabar', *Muse*, 120.
71. 'Aspects of Writing', lecture to Writers' Summer School, Swanwick, August 1961, *Muse*, 23–38, 29.
72. Ibid., 34.
73. Ibid., 36.
74. S. to W.H. Holden (Heinemann), 18 March 1966, concerning a photograph of 1960, 27:1.

Chapter 2: Return to India

1. Granada 1969 edn, 174.
2. Lecture to National Book League, 22 November 1961, *Muse*, 13–21, 13.
3. Ibid., 15.
4. Ibid., 17–18.
5. Ibid., 19.
6. *Birds*, 161.
7. Ibid., 163.
8. Ibid., 177–8.
9. Ibid., 179.
10. Ibid., 180.
11. Ibid., 187–8.

12. Notes for the lecture in 7:1.
13. *Birds*, 234–5.
14. *Muse*, 21; *Birds*, 223.
15. Author's Note in *Birds*.
16. Letter of 1 August 1961; *Birds*, 114.
17. D.C. Potter, *India's Political Administrators, 1919–1983* (OUP, Delhi, 1986), 99.
18. Hanley to S., 3 March 1961.
19. S. to Gillespie, 20 April 1962.
20. 'India: A Post-Forsterian View', 120.
21. S. to David Bolt (DHA), 5 December 1961, 28:4.
22. *Daily Telegraph*, 19 April 1962.
23. Willey to S., 29 November 1961.
24. S. to Bolt, loc. cit.
25. Ibid.
26. S. to Willey, 27 May and 5 December 1961.
27. S. to Bolt, loc. cit.
28. S. to Stark, 14 February 1976.
29. Meridian edn 1960, 327.
30. *TLS.*, 10 March 1961.
31. Ibid., 18 August 1961.
32. Ibid., 29 December 1961.
33. Ibid., 26 October 1962.
34. Ibid., 12 December 1963.
35. Report on Lt.-Col. Denis Russell-Roberts, 'Malayan Tragedy', 18 June 1960, 18:38.
36. Report on Col. H.L. Mostyn-Owen, 'Before We Forget', 7 December 1962, 18:12.
37. Report on Mary Hanson Moore, 'Palaces and Pujas', 8 December 1962, 18:11.
38. S. to Gant (Secker and Warburg), 27 April 1963, 40:36.
39. S. to Francine Weinbaum, 14 February 1976.
40. S. to G. Smith, 1 February 1964, 41:32.
41. *The Times*, 8 February 1978.
42. 'Experiences in India', 25 February 1964, 9:48.
43. 'India', n.d., 9:10.
44. Ibid.
45. 'Enoch Sahib: A Slight Case of Cultural Shock', lecture to Commonwealth Countries' League, 11 November 1969, *Muse*, 91–104, 98.

46. Ibid.
47. 'Experiences in India', loc. cit.
48. Ibid.; and 'India', loc. cit.
49. 'Enoch Sahib', *Muse*, 98.
50. 'Experiences in India', 6 March.
51. 'Enoch Sahib', *Muse*, 98–9.
52. Ibid., 100.
53. S. to Kaye, 15 January 1964.
54. Dass to S., 28 January and 3 October 1963.
55. 'Method: The Mystery and the Mechanics', lecture to Writers' Summer School, 1967, *Muse*, 51–69, 58–9.
56. 'Enoch Sahib', *Muse*, 102.
57. Ibid.
58. Kaye to S., 26 April 1964.
59. Ghosh to S., 4 September 1964, 20:22.
60. S. to Rosaleen Whately, 30 October 1964.
61. S. to Hugh Corbett (-Palmer), 21 December 1975, 39:1.
62. 6:1.
63. S. to D. Olding, 28 November 1964.
64. S. to Olding, 7 April 1966.
65. S. to Olding, loc. cit.
66. 'Abstracts and Brief Chronicles', 6:1.
67. 'Experiences in India', 1 March 1964, loc. cit.
68. S. to Willey, 14 April 1964.
69. S. to Allen Drury, 18 July 1969, 23:43.
70. *Muse*, 99.

Chapter 3: The Daphne Manners Case

1. *Muse*, 60.
2. S. to Wally Olins, 1 August 1975.
3. Only the first sentence of this quotation appears in the lecture as delivered and printed in *Muse* (p. 60). The remainder has been restored from the text in 7:4.
4. *Muse*, 63, except for the restoration of the first two sentences from 7:4.
5. *Muse*, 64.
6. Ibid. 68.
7. 'Abstracts and Brief Chronicles', 6:1.
8. In blue notebook in 'Jewel in the Crown' box, HRC.

9. *Muse*, 65.
10. Blue notebook.
11. Ibid.
12. S. to Gant (Heinemann), 22 July 1965.
13. S. to Olding, 19 July 1965.
14. S. to Willey, 22 July 1965.
15. S. to Gant, loc. cit.
16. S. to Willey, 19 June 1965.
17. Sally Dennison's 'Course Notes', Alice L. Price (ed.), *After Paul: Paul Scott's Tulsa Years* (HCE Publications/Riverrun Arts, Tulsa, 1988), 31.
18. 'Abstracts and Brief Chronicles', 6:1.
19. *A Division of the Spoils* (Heinemann, 1975), 503.
20. *Jewel* (Heinemann, 1966), 269.
21. Ibid. 323–4.
22. *Muse*, 66.
23. S. to Weinbaum, 26 October 1975.
24. Ibid.
25. Notebook, 7:10.
26. 'The Jewel in the Crown Working Notes', HRC.
27. S. to Monteith, 16 August 1964, 24:26.
28. S. to Kaye, 16 August 1964.
29. Letter of 15 August 1964, 44:23.
30. Memoir in *The Making of The Jewel in the Crown*, 127–8.
31. Hamilton to S., 1 September 1964, HRC.
32. S. to D. Higham, 29 March 1965.
33. S. to T. Newman, 18 April 1965, 45:2.
34. Francis G. Hutchins, *Spontaneous Revolution* (Manohar, Delhi, 1971), 292–3.
35. S. to Roy, 20 March 1965.
36. S. to Roy, 12 June 1965.
37. Blue notebook, 28 June 1964, HRC.
38. S. to Mrs Frederick Kroll, 4 December 1968.
39. Lady Manners to Lady Chatterjee, June 1948, *Jewel*, 447–8.
40. S. to Willey, 22 July 1965.
41. *Muse*, 23–38, 31. The penultimate sentence in the quotation was not in the lecture as delivered and printed but has been restored from a draft in 7:3.
42. S. to D. Ganapathy, 23 October 1964.
43. Ibid.

44. S. to Jean Leroy (DHA), 9 April 1966.
45. S. to Olding, 7 April 1966.
46. *Jewel*, 352.
47. Ibid. 450.

Chapter 4: Ruling Divided India

1. Blue notebook, 28–30 June 1964.
2. S. to Olding, 19 July 1965.
3. *Jewel*, 444.
4. S. to Olding, 7 September 1965.
5. 1:39.
6. Scott's copy of 1903 edn, 8.
7. S. to Ganapathy, 18 September 1965.
8. Ibid.
9. S. to Ganapathy, 30 September 1965.
10. 1:39.
11. Review in *TLS* of Patrick Macrory, *Signal Catastrophe*, 7 April 1966.
12. Ibid., and reviews of Noel Barber, *The Black Hole* (1965), *TLS*, 14 October 1965; and M. Edwardes, *Bound to Exile* (1969), *The Times*, 8 November 1969.
13. Review of P.C. Gupta, *Nana Sahib and the Rising at Cawnpore, TLS*, 12 April 1963.
14. Entry, n.d., after 28 September 1965, 1:39.
15. 1:39.
16. Ibid.
17. Red notebook, with *The Quartet* Notebooks, HRC.
18. *Scorpion* (Heinemann, 1968), 1.
19. Blue notebook, HRC; Strachey, 5–6.
20. S. to Ganapathy, 7 May 1967.
21. S. to Ganapathy, 30 July 1967.
22. S. to Willey, 14 February 1968.
23. *Scorpion*, 3.
24. *Discovery of India*, 443. See Scott's note in 'The Original Notebook', HRC.
25. Ibid.; Mason, *Guardians*, 290.
26. S. to M. Felton, 18 November 1965.
27. S. to Felton, 6 November 1965.

28. Felton to S., 11 November 1965.
29. S. to Felton, 3 March 1966.
30. *Scorpion*, 17.
31. Ibid., 18.
32. 'Original Notebook', HRC.
33. S. to Weinbaum, 31 December 1975.
34. S. to D.M. Burjorjee, 7 June 1976.
35. See S.'s draft obituary of Nabokov (9.41), submitted to C. Watson of *The Times* on 24 January 1968 (42:11).
36. 'Original Notebook', HRC.
37. S. to Felton, 17 March 1966.
38. *Scorpion*, 475.
39. S. to Felton, 17 March 1966.
40. S. to Burjorjee, 25 January 1976.
41. S. to Willey, 26 March 1971.
42. S. to Diane Lloyd, 14 January 1972, 31:38.
43. *Scorpion*, 393.
44. Ibid., 397.
45. Ibid., 298–9.
46. Ibid., 425–8.
47. S. to Martin Pick, 15 July 1968, 39:14.
48. S. to Jameson, 2 September 1968.
49. S. to Drury, 18 July 1969, 23:43.
50. S. to Weinbaum, 26 October 1975.
51. S. to Weinbaum, 5 November 1975.

Chapter 5: Melancholy Exiles

1. S. to Willey, 14 February 1968.
2. Encl. with S. to Gant (Heinemann), 15 December 1968.
3. S. to Richard Price, 11 September 1971.
4. S. to Gant (Heinemann), 23 August 1970.
5. S. to Willey, 22 August 1970.
6. S. to Willey, 26 March 1971.
7. *Scorpion*, 426.
8. 18 May 1967.
9. For the lecture as delivered, see *Muse*, 39–49. For Scott's excisions see the text in 7:6–7.
10. Stocks, *Essays by Divers Hands*, loc. cit.
11. *Scorpion*, 236.

12. Martin Gilbert, *Winston S. Churchill*, VII (Heinemann, London, 1986), 1166.
13. *Country Life*, 4 July 1974.
14. Ibid, 20 July 1967.
15. *Towers* (Heinemann, 1971), 13.
16. Ibid., 69.
17. Ibid., 68.
18. Ibid., 82.
19. Ibid., 195.
20. Ibid., 200.
21. Ibid., 269.
22. Ibid., 381.
23. Ibid., 359.
24. Ibid., 230.
25. Ibid., 378.
26. Ibid., 379.
27. Ibid., 387.
28. Ibid., 256.
29. Ibid., 252.
30. Ibid., 255.
31. Ibid., 236.
32. *Scorpion*, 426.
33. 'After Marabar: Britain and India, a Post-Forsterian View', lecture delivered in India in 1972, *Muse*, 112–29, 122.
34. *Towers*, 271.
35. Ibid., 272.
36. Ibid., 52–4.
37. Ibid., 43.
38. Ibid., 392.
39. S. to Willey, 26 March 1971.

Chapter 6: A Triumph of Principles

1. Blue exercise book, 'Volume 4 Raj Sequence, A Division of the Spoils', in *Division* box, HRC.
2. Ibid.
3. Gilbert, *Churchill*, VII, 1166.
4. S. to Burjorjee, 25 January 1976.
5. The denial is in S. to Sir Herbert Thompson, 26 June 1975. Quotation from S. to Jameson, 2 June 1975.

6. Report, 36:17 and 17:17–19; *TLS*, 31 December 1971.
7. S. to Burjorjee, 7 June 1976.
8. S. to Willey, 9 August 1971.
9. S. to J.A.E. Heard, 8 October 1975.
10. Churamani to S., 16 March 1967, 19:5.
11. S. to Gupta, 21 April 1967.
12. Gupta to S., 26 April 1967.
13. S. to Drucker, 17 February 1969.
14. S. to Ganapathy, 14 October 1968.
15. S. to Ganapathy, 12 November 1968.
16. Cited by Gant in 'Paul Scott Remembered', *The Making of The Jewel in the Crown*, 121.
17. S. to Heard, 8 October 1975.
18. S. to Willey, 16 February 1969.
19. Biographical details, encl. to S. to Weinbaum, 19 July 1975.
20. S. to Hanley, 28 March 1972.
21. S. to Willey, 22 January 1972.
22. S. to West, 15 August 1975.
23. *Division* (Heinemann, 1975), 479.
24. Ibid., 100.
25. S. to Gant (Heinemann), 9 May 1973.
26. Blue exercise book, loc. cit.
27. P.S. Gupta, 'Imperial Strategy and the Transfer of Power, 1939–51', in Amit K. Gupta (ed.), *Myth and Reality: The Struggle for Freedom in India, 1945–47* (Manohar, New Delhi, 1987), 1–53, 9. See also Sucheta Mahajan, 'British Policy, Nationalist Strategy and Popular National Upsurge, 1945–46', ibid., 54–98, esp. 70–5.
28. S. to Gant (Heinemann), 9 May 1973.
29. Ibid.
30. Ibid.
31. S. to Willey, 11 November 1973.
32. Ibid.; *Division*, 498.
33. *Division*, 592.

Chapter 7: The Prose-Poet of the Raj in Decline

1. *Observer*, 2 October 1960.
2. 22 July 1966.

3. 28 July 1966.
4. *Scotsman*, 16 July 1966.
5. 26 July 1966.
6. 17 July 1966.
7. S. to Raymond, 19 July 1966, 41:32.
8. 21 July 1966.
9. 17 July 1966.
10. 28 July 1966.
11. *New York Times*, 29 July 1966.
12. 19 July 1966; S. to Ganapathy, 20 July 1966.
13. S. to Ganapathy, 15 November 1969.
14. 6 September 1968.
15. 6 September 1968; S. to M.M. Kaye, 17 September 1968; 'After Marabar', *Muse*, 115.
16. *Sunday Times*, 1 September 1968; S. to Jameson, 2 September 1968.
17. *Daily Telegraph*, 12 September 1968.
18. 8 May 1975.
19. S. to Keating, 1 May 1975.
20. 4 May 1975.
21. S. to Dipali Nag, 9 June 1975.
22. 8 May 1975.
23. 8 May 1975.
24. 4 May 1975.
25. S. to Jameson, 2 June 1975.
26. Ibid.
27. 23 May 1975.
28. S. to Jameson, 2 June 1975. For Perron's criticism see *Division*, 103 ('The corporal . . .').
29. S. to Cadell, 12 August 1975.
30. S. to Crowcroft, 27 July 1975.
31. S. to Ganapathy, 10 February 1975.
32. S. to Ganapathy, 14 July 1975.
33. S. to Cameron, 9 May 1975.
34. Cameron to S., 13 May 1975.
35. *Guardian*, 10 April 1984.
36. S. to Olding, 4 July 1975.
37. S. to Dipali Nag, 9 June 1975.
38. S. to Ganapathy, 7 October 1975.
39. Ibid.

40. Ibid.
41. S. to Ganapathy, 26 October 1975.
42. S. to Olding, 4 July 1975.
43. S. to Willey, 14 November 1975. Two of the quotations above incorporate Scott's corrections.
44. S. to Willey, 26 September 1975.
45. S. to Pick (Heinemann), 6 July 1975.
46. S. to Beloff, 27 April 1976.
47. S. to Gant (Heinemann), 26 April 1976.
48. S. to Olding, 26 April 1976.
49. Rubin, *After the Raj: British Novels of India Since 1947* (University Press of New England, Hanover and London, 1986), 156.
50. *TV Guide*, 15 December 1984.
51. Malgonkar to S., 13 August 1969.
52. Malgonkar to S., 14 March 1972.
53. Ibid.
54. Kaye's memoir in Granada's *The Making of The Jewel in the Crown*, 127.
55. Stark to S., 7 January 1976.
56. Stark to S., 1 February 1976.
57. *On the Strength: The Story of the British Army Wife* (Charles Knight, London, 1975), 169.
58. Stephen James to S., 9 February 1969, 30:32; J.A.E. Heard to S., 30 September 1975; H.I. Winner to S., 15 June 1969.
59. Burjorjee to S., 2 June 1972.
60. Shiraeff to S., 1 July 1972.
61. S. to Shiraeff, 18 July 1972.
62. Review of *My God Died Young, TLS*, 15 August 1968.
63. S. To Weinbaum, 14 April 1976.
64. Morris's script encl. with Patricia Ellis to S., 23 September 1966, 21:6. Scott reviewed his book, *Hired to Kill*, in the *TLS*, 2 December 1960.
65. *Illustrated Weekly of India*, 4 September 1966.
66. S. to Weinbaum, 9 February 1975.
67. *Hindustan Standard Magazine*, 20 February 1972.
68. E. Standring to S., 24 June 1967; S. to Standring, 29 June 1967. Mrs Standring was a descendant of Sir Arthur Phayre, a proconsul in Victorian Burma.
69. A.St.J. Shuttleworth to S., 29 July 1966.

70. Hugh Corbett (-Palmer) to S., 17 August 1975, 39:1.
71. *Listener*, 7 March 1979.
72. Thompson to S., 21 June 1975.
73. S. to Magnus Lindberg, 19 July 1975.
74. S. to Thompson, 26 June 1975.
75. 'Paul Scott's Raj', *South Asian Review*, July/October 1975, 359–69.
76. S. to Olding, 5 November 1975.
77. S. to Weinbaum, 5 November 1975.
78. Ibid.
79. Esp., 'Paul Scott's India: *The Raj Quartet*', *Critique*, 20.1 (1978), 100–10; 'Psychological Defenses and Thwarted Union in the *The Raj Quartet*', *Literature and Psychology*, 31 (1981), 75–87. The dissertation is available from Xerox University Microfilms, Ann Arbor, Michigan.
80. S. to Violet Wilkinson, 7 May 1962.
81. Allen Boyer, *Modern Language Quarterly*, 46 (1985), 64–80.
82. *Paul Scott* (Twayne Publishers, Boston, 1980), 148.
83. *Paul Scott: Images of India* (Macmillan, London, 1980), x.
84. 'Paul Scott's Guardians', *Journal of English Studies*, 13 (1983), 244–58.
85. P. 103. For a detailed reading of the *Quartet*, see Janis Tedesco and Janet Popham, *Introduction to the Raj Quartet* (University Press of America, Lanham, 1985).
86. S. to Sir Conrad Corfield, 4 August 1975.
87. P. 198.

Chapter 8: Someone with Power who Rules

1. *Division*, 503.
2. *Sunday Telegraph*, 4 May 1975; *The Times*, 8 May 1975.
3. *TLS*, 23 May 1975.
4. Jameson to S., 30 May 1975.
5. *Division*, 573.
6. 'The Original Notebook'.
7. S. to Jameson, 2 June 1975.
8. *New York Post*, 18 October 1975.
9. *The Times*, 20 October 1975.
10. *Scorpion*, 398, 407.
11. S. to Weinbaum, 5 November 1975.

12. S. to Rosalind [surname unknown], 26 May 1975, 41:19.
13. S. to Goodbody, 14 May 1972.
14. S. to Willey, 26 March 1971.
15. S. to Olding, 16 February 1968.
16. *Scorpion*, 398.
17. S. to Thompson, 26 June 1975.
18. S. to Lloyd, 14 January 1972, 31:38.
19. *Division*, 302.
20. Ibid., 208.
21. Ibid., 209.
22. Ibid., 561.
23. Ibid., 547.
24. Ibid., 571.
25. Ibid., 302. See S. to Gant, 25 March 1974 (1:48) for the perspective.
26. *TLS*, 30 July 1971.
27. 'Fiction as History, History as Fiction', *Illustrated Weekly of India*, 8 July 1984.
28. Martin Wynne (ed.), *On Honourable Terms: The Memoirs of Some Indian Police Officers, 1915–1948* (BACSA, London, 1985), 6.
29. Stephen Henningham, 'Quit India in Bihar and the Eastern United Provinces: The Dual Revolt', in Ranajit Guha (ed.), *Subaltern Studies, II, Writings on South Asian History and Society* (OUP, Delhi, 1983), 130–79, 143.
30. P. 6.
31. P. 121.
32. P. 167.
33. Amery to Linlithgow, 1 October 1943, TP, IV, 355.
34. Potter, op. cit., 78.
35. Ibid., 78–9.
36. Ibid., 77–9.
37. Ibid., 89.
38. Ibid., 130.
39. Sumit Sarkar, *Modern India, 1885–1947* (Macmillan, Delhi, 1983), 392.
40. Roland Hunt and John Harrison, *The District Officer in India, 1930–1947* (Scolar Press, London, 1980), 168.
41. *The Journal of Imperial and Commonwealth History*, 14.2 (1986), 34–90.

42. Hyam, 34.
43. Ibid., 35.
44. Cited ibid., 48.
45. Ibid., 53.
46. Cited Christopher Thorne, *Allies of a Kind* (OUP, Oxford, 1978), 356, 643.
47. Linlithgow to Amery, 23–7 January 1942, TP, I, 60; Linlithgow's marginal notes on Amery to Linlithgow, 3 April 1942, TP, I, 632.
48. Cited Hutchins, *Spontaneous Revolution*, 190.
49. Auchinleck to Army Commanders, 12 February 1946, TP, VI, 941.
50. Ibid., 943.
51. Wylie to Wavell, 19 February 1946, ibid., 1019.
52. Penderel Moon (ed.), *Wavell: The Viceroy's Journal* (OUP, London, 1973), 14 February and 22 July 1946, 212, 321.
53. Wynne, op. cit., 189.
54. P.N. Chopra (ed.), *Quit India Movement: British Secret Documents* (Interprint, New Delhi, 1986), 277.
55. Ibid., 188.
56. Op. cit., 300–1.
57. Saksena to Linlithgow, 10 September 1942, TP, II, 939–42.
58. Max Harcourt, 'Kisan Populism and Revolution in Rural India: The 1942 Disturbances in Bihar and East United Provinces', D.A. Low (ed.), *Congress and the Raj* (Heinemann, London, 1977), 315–48, 321.
59. Government of India to Secretary of State, 12 September 1942, TP, II, 953. Sarkar cites higher official statistics, op. cit., 395–6.
60. Op. cit., 79.
61. Ibid., 89.
62. Linlithgow to Churchill, 31 August 1942, TP, II, 853.
63. Powell, 'The Imperfect Dream: A Return Passage to India', *The Times*, 7 May 1983.
64. Willcox to Powell, 26 November 1945, with copy of the report at India Office Library. Philip Mason, whose help Powell acknowledged, writes of Powell's work on the Report in *A Shaft of Sunlight: Memories of a Varied Life* (André Deutsch, London, 1978), 198.

65. Copy in the Brayne Collection, India Office Library, MS Eur. F152/169.
66. Powell to Butler, 3 December 1946, quoting his 'Memorandum on Indian Policy' of 16 May, ibid.
67. Wavell's *Journal*, 388. See below, p. 190
68. Cited Andrew Roth, *Enoch Powell: Tory Tribune* (Macdonald, London, 1970).
69. 'The Imperfect Dream', loc. cit.
70. Private interview with Mr Powell, 4 January 1990.
71. Reader's report on Anita Desai, 'O England's Green and Grisly Land', 19 August 1969, Box 17.
72. *Muse*, 91–104.
73. S. to Mrs G. Hirsch, 17 October 1969, 22:23.
74. 'Patriotism Based on Reality, Not on Dreams', *The Times*, 2 April 1964, cited in Paul Foot, *The Rise of Enoch Powell* (Penguin, Harmondsworth, 1969), 29–30.
75. Cited ibid., 115.
76. 'What Commonwealth?' *The Times*, 26 January 1984.
77. 'Enoch Sahib', 92–3.
78. Ibid., 94.
79. Ibid., 95.
80. Ibid., 103–4.

Chapter 9: The Raj at Work

1. *Muse*, 111–29, 115.
2. Ibid., 117.
3. Ibid., 118.
4. Ibid., 127.
5. Ibid., 118.
6. Ibid., 127.
7. *The Times*, 20 October 1975.
8. *Muse*, 123.
9. 'Outline for a possible TV book programme', May 1975, 1:49.
10. Sally Dennison, 'Course Notes', *After Paul*, 30.
11. Loc. cit. 123.
12. Ibid.
13. *The Times*, 24 November 1975. The book version of this popular BBC radio series was edited by Charles Allen

and subtitled *Images of British India in the Twentieth Century.*

14. *A Young Man's Country* (Michael Russell, London, 1977), xiii.
15. Review of D. Dilks, *Curzon in India*, vol. 1, *Achievement* (1969), *Country Life*, 31 July 1969.
16. *Country Life*, 27 February 1975.
17. 'The Raj', Frank Moraes and Edward Howe (eds), *John Kenneth Galbraith Introduces India* (André Deutsch, London, 1976), 70–88.
18. Potter, op. cit., 132–3.
19. 'The Raj', 81.
20. Tinker, 'The Diary of a Military and Civil Nobody', 24.
21. For an exploration of the concept, see Francis G. Hutchins, *The Illusion of Permanence: British Imperialism in India* (Princeton University Press, Princeton, 1967), of which Scott had a copy.
22. 'The Raj', 82.
23. Ibid., 84–5.
24. Ibid., 86.
25. *Division*, 88.
26. 'The Raj', 73.
27. Note on *The Times* invitation of 1 October 1973 to review James Morris, *Heaven's Command: An Imperial Progress*, HRC. S. was commenting on Morris's observation that 'the emotions of the Mutiny found their echoes all over the British Empire, permanently affecting its attitudes, and leaving scars and superstitions that were never quite healed or exorcised' (246). For S.'s review, see *The Times*, 6 November 1973.
28. 'The Raj', 76–7.
29. Thompson to S., 21 June 1975.
30. 'The Raj', 88.
31. 'Fiction as History', loc. cit.
32. *Scorpion*, 16–19.
33. Loc. cit.
34. Seal, 345.
35. Ibid., 350–1.
36. *Time Out*, 5–11 April 1984.
37. In R. Owen and R. Sutcliffe (eds), *Studies in the Theory of*

Imperialism (Longman, London, 1972), ch. 5. Reprinted in
Wm. Roger Louis (ed.), *Imperialism: The Gallagher and
Robinson Controversy* (New Viewpoints, New York, 1976).
38. 'Anglo-Indian Attitudes', *TLS*, 18 May 1967.
39. Gandhi to Home Dept, 27 May 1943, TP, III, 1040–1; Azad
to Linlithgow, 13 February 1943, ibid., 659–64.
40. 'Quit India Resolution', TP, II, 621–4.
41. Govt of India to Secretary of State, 1 February 1944, TP,
IV, 745–8.
42. *Scorpion*, 468–9.
43. *Division*, 409–34. See Richard M. Johnson, '"Sayed's Trial"
in Paul Scott's "A Division of the Spoils": The Interplay
of History, Theme and Purpose', *The Library Chronicle of
the University of Texas at Austin*, 37 (1986), 77–91.
44. C. Thorne, 'The British Cause and Indian Nationalism
in 1940: An Officer's Rejection of Empire', *Journal
of Imperial and Commonwealth History*, X (1982),
344–59, 350.
45. Ibid., 351.
46. Ibid., 352.
47. Ibid., 357.
48. P. 584.
49. *Division*, 476.
50. Ibid., 500.
51. Linlithgow to Sir W.H. Lewis, 27 November 1947,
Linlithgow Collection, India Office Library, MS. Eur.
F 125/154.

Chapter 10: The Historian's Novelist

1. S. to Weinbaum, 19 November 1974.
2. P.449.
3. P.12.
4. S. to Gant (Heinemann), 9 May 1973.
5. S. to Weinbaum, 5 November 1975.
6. *Scorpion* box, HRC.
7. S. to Weinbaum, 26 October 1975.
8. Reader's report on M.M. Kaye, 'The Wound of Spring',
2 July 1960, 17:61.
9. S. to Weinbaum, 26 October 1975.

10. S. to Jameson, 18 February 1975.
11. S. to Gant (Heinemann), 15 December 1968.
12. S. to Jeremy Lewis (André Deutsch), 9 December 1969, 23:10.
13. S. to Higham, 1 May 1970.
14. S. to Higham, 25 November 1973.
15. *TLS*, 27 April 1962.
16. *New Statesman*, 17 March 1961.
17. S. to Hanley, 17 March 1961.
18. S. to Sujit Mukherjee (Orient Longman), 8 May 1974, 38:34.
19. 'Paul Scott Remembered', loc. cit.
20. *Sunday Times*, 16 November 1975.
21. 'Literature and the Social Conscience: The Novel', lecture delivered in India in 1972, *Muse*, 131–49, 145; *Jewel*, 1.
22. 'After Marabar', *Muse*, 121.
23. Reviews of Patrick Macrory, *Signal Catastrophe, The Times*, 10 March 1966, and *TLS*, 7 April 1966.
24. Review of *Heaven's Command, The Times*, 6 November 1973.
25. Review of Geoffrey Ashe, *Gandhi*, *TLS*, 11 April 1968.
26. Review of William Golant, *The Long Afternoon, The Times*, 23 January 1975.
27. Spirax notebook, 7:10.
28. *TLS*, 30 October 1969. The third paragraph, which did not appear in the review as published, is drawn from S.'s typescript, 14:13.
29. 'Opening Pandora's Box', review of Penderel Moon (ed.), *Wavell: The Viceroy's Journal, The Times*, 14 June 1973.
30. *Division*, 186–7.
31. S. to Stark, 14 February 1976.
32. S. to Sir Herbert Thompson, 26 June 1975.
33. *TLS*, 16 July 1976.
34. The following account of Rampur draws on Lance Brennan, 'A Case of Segmented Modernization: Rampur State, 1930–1939', *Comparative Studies in Society and History*, 23 (1981), 350–81.
35. *Indian Summer: A Memsahib in India and Sind* (New English Library, London, 1981), 55–9.
36. *The Maharajahs* (Hutchinson, London, 1972), 44–5.

37. Menon, loc. cit., 309.
38. Tuker, op. cit., 390.
39. Ibid., 464–5.
40. Durga Das (ed.), *Sardar Patel's Correspondence, 1945–50*, 10 vols (Navajivan Trust, Ahmedabad, 1971–4), V, 496–501.
41. Nawab to Patel, 12 August 1947, ibid., 500.
42. *Division*, 551.
43. Ibid., 31–2.
44. Ibid., 219–20, 222.
45. Ibid., 222–3.
46. Ibid., 105–6.
47. My reading of the documents appears in *Escape from Empire: The Attlee Government and the Indian Problem* (Clarendon Press, Oxford, 1983).
48. Sumit Sarkar, *'Popular' Movements and 'Middle Class' Leadership in Late Colonial India* (K.P. Bagchi & Co., Calcutta, 1983), 61.
49. TP., IX, 445–6.
50. Attlee to Smuts, 19 February 1947, ibid., 761.
51. See my *Churchill, Cripps and India, 1939–45* (Clarendon Press, Oxford, 1979).
52. *Division*, 460.
53. K.K. Aziz, *Britain and Muslim India* (Heinemann, London, 1963), 204.
54. 'If It Be Real, What Does It Mean?: Some British Perceptions of the Indian National Congress', Richard Sisson and Stanley Wolpert (eds), *Congress and Indian Nationalism* (University of California Press, Berkeley, 1988), 90–118, 110.
55. H.V. Brasted and G. Douds, 'Passage to India: Peripatetic M.P.s on the Grand Indian Tour, 1870–1914', *South Asia*, n.s. II (1979), 91–111, 103.
56. Cited in my 'John Mill of John Company', Kenneth Ballhatchet and John Harrison (eds), *East India Company Studies: Papers Presented to Professor Sir Cyril Philips* (Asian Research Service, Hong Kong, 1986), 153–82, 168.
57. Ibid., 173.
58. Ibid., 177.
59. *Division*, 415.
60. For an illuminating essay on the *Quartet* as history, see

Antony Copley, 'The Politics of Illusion: Paul Scott's "The Raj Quartet"', *Indo-British Review*, XI.1 (1984), 58–73.

Chapter 11: After *The Raj Quartet*

1. S. to Higham, 26 February 1973.
2. S. to Willey, 2 August 1974.
3. S. to Willey, 17 January 1975.
4. Olding to S., 23 July 1974; S. to Olding, 2 August and 23 September 1974.
5. S. to Willey, 24 February 1975.
6. S. to Dipali Nag, 9 June 1975.
7. S. to Ganapathy, 14 July 1975.
8. S. to Weinbaum, 19 July 1975.
9. S. to James Leasor, 22 October 1972.
10. S. to Martin Pick, 19 November 1975, 39:14.
11. S. to Olding, 7 December 1975, 2:3.
12. S. to Wally Olins, 1 August 1975.
13. S. to Lady Butterfield, 14 February 1975; Lady Butterfield to S., 7 February 1976; 21:28.
14. S. to T.R. Manderson (Heinemann), 21 June 1976.
15. 'Note re "Mango Rain"', n.d. [1976], 6:6.
16. S. to Sir H. Thompson, 2 December 1975.
17. S. to Gant (Heinemann), 7 May 1974. For the collection, see 8:19.
18. S. to Peter Scott, 31 August 1974.
19. Ganapathy to S., 5 July 1975; S. to Ganapathy, 14 July 1975.
20. 4 December 1975.
21. Scott's notes for reviews, HRC.
22. S. to Ganapathy, 20 February 1965.
23. S. to Victor Bonham-Carter (Secretary of the Royal Literary Fund), 15 February 1976, 40:6. The figures for taxable income are taken from S.'s tax returns as submitted by Maw Ellis Warne (boxes 32–3). When S. died his estate was valued at £48,043 (*The Times*, 3 May 1978).
24. S. to Stark, 9 May 1976.
25. S. to Ganapathy, 4 April 1976.
26. S. to Sally and Carol Scott, 28 July 1976, 40:32.
27. Benstock to S., 12 February 1976, 30:1.

28. Staley, 'The Meeting', *After Paul*, 2.
29. Quoted in 'A Letter from Carol Scott', ibid., 13.
30. Dennison, 'Course Notes', ibid., 26.
31. *The Times*, 28 April 1977.
32. Gant's memoir, loc. cit., 126.
33. Hayden to Staley, 8 October 1980.
34. Faye Schuett, 'Return of the Storyteller', *After Paul*, 34.
35. William Wheeler, 'The Storyteller', ibid., 37–8.
36. S. to A.N. Hunt (Maw Ellis Warne), 31 December 1977.
37. Kaye's memoir, loc. cit., 128.
38. *Granada News*, November 1977.
39. David Williams, *Punch*, 15 October 1980.
40. *Sunday Times*, 4 December 1977.
41. *Evening Standard*, 4 March 1980.
42. 8 February 1978.
43. S. to Elizabeth Cadell, 12 August 1975; Gant's memoir, loc. cit., 122; S. to Gant, 21 November 1974, enclosing a *dramatis personae* for the *Quartet*, 27:15.

Epilogue

1. Francine Ringold, 'A Conversation with Paul Scott', *Nimrod*, 21.1 (1976), 16–32, 22.
2. Dennison, 'Course Notes', loc. cit., 23.
3. S. to Valerie White, 19 March 1956, 43:32.
4. Vosper to S., 5 September 1969.
5. Hilton Ambler (DHA) to S., 2 June 1970.
6. S. to John Rush (DHA), 19 July 1975.
7. S. to John Hallett (Garrick Theatre), 20 August 1969, 25:32.
8. S. to Ganapathy, 9 September 1966.
9. S. to Dipali Nag, 27 July 1966.
10. S. to Higham, 25 November 1973.
11. S. to Olding, 2 August 1974.
12. S. to Higham, 8 December 1974; and 17 June 1975.
13. S. to Rush (DHA), 25 June 1975.
14. 1:49.
15. S. to Gant (Heinemann), 3 March 1975, 27:16.
16. S. to Olding, 26 April 1976.
17. *The Making of The Jewel in the Crown*, 7–8.

18. Natalie Zemon Davis, *The Return of Martin Guerre* (Harvard University Press, 1983), Preface.
19. S. to Rosalind [surname unknown], 26 May 1975, 41:19.
20. Cited in Andrew Robinson, 'The Jewel in the Crown', *Sight and Sound*, 53.1 (1983–4), 47–50.
21. Ibid.
22. John Leonard, *New York*, 17 September 1984.
23. Cited in Robinson, loc. cit.
24. Ibid.
25. Simon Hoggart, *New Society*, 5 April 1984.
26. 'The Matter of India', *London Review of Books*, 19 March 1987.
27. Leonard, loc. cit.
28. 'The Jewel in the Crown', *Pacific Affairs*, 58 (1985), 287–92, 291–2. See also Morris-Jones, 'The Transfer of Power, 1947: A View from the Sidelines', *Modern Asian Studies*, 16 (1982), 1–32.

Index